RECOLLECTIONS
OF A LIFE

ALGER HISS

RECOLLECTIONS OF A LIFE

ARCADE PUBLISHING · NEW YORK

Little, Brown and Company

FIRST PAPERBACK EDITION

Reprinted by arrangement with Seaver Books/Henry Holt and
Company, Inc.

CIP data are available.

ISBN 1-55970-024-6

Published in the United States by Arcade Publishing, Inc.,
New York, a Little, Brown company.

10 9 8 7 6 5 4 3 2 1

Designed by Beth Tondreau Design

BP

Published simultaneously in Canada
by Little, Brown & Company (Canada) Limited

PRINTED IN THE UNITED STATES OF AMERICA

To Isabel

CONTENTS

Sixteen pages of photographs begin on page 101.

ACKNOWLEDGMENTS

This book owes its scope—and indeed its very existence—to my publisher and editor Jeannette Seaver. My failing eyesight placed a heavy burden on her and her staff, way beyond the efforts normally encountered when bringing out a book. I thank Calvert Barksdale, of Seaver Books, for his help in the exacting editorial process. Arthur and Peggy Penn supplied vital insights and suggestions at a crucial preliminary stage. Patricia Crown, James Aronson, Albert and Judy Ruben, Mary Collins, Jane Spinak, Tim Horan, and Corinne Rafferty made many valuable suggestions. I am indebted to Jack Taylor for his editorial assistance in my early drafts; and to Lois Metzger in helping with the proofs. The typists had a particularly difficult task; I thank especially Bernadette Verdicchio and Natalia Schiffrin, who managed to decipher my handwriting and transcribe succeeding drafts. Finally, I thank John Lowenthal, who checked for accuracy throughout.

RECOLLECTIONS
OF A LIFE

1

MY AUNT LILA AND THE PLEASURES OF READING ALOUD

My first teacher was my Aunt Lila. Not that she ever thought of herself in that way. In April 1907 my father committed suicide, and my mother was suddenly left a widow with five children. We ranged in age from a few months to fourteen years. The two eldest were my sisters, Anna and Mary; Mary was two years younger than Anna. My older brother, Bosley, was seven when my father died. I was two; Donald was only a few months old.

Upon my father's death Aunt Lila, my father's unmarried middle sister, came to live with us, mostly to help my mother take care of us children. She stayed until I was fourteen, when she moved to live with one of her sisters in their own house. My mother and Aunt Lila are the two adult figures I remember best from my childhood. Both seemed to me to be primordial. I have no conscious recollection of my father. In these early memories Aunt Lila is even more distinct than my mother, perhaps because I remember my aunt in strong primary colors. When I think of my mother in those early years, the scenes are in white and shades of pale gray. Lila had black hair; all the rest of us had blond or light-brown hair. She wore reds and warm yellows.

1

As with the vivid color differences of my initial recollections, the separate roles of Aunt Lila and my mother were always clear. There was no confusion as to their household functions. My mother was in charge. Lila was her assistant, an assistant whose help was pretty much limited to being a companion for the children.

My father had been an executive of a large wholesale dry-goods firm, a man overwhelmed by financial and family worries. Suicide was a blow that was shameful as well as tragic for any family in those years, and mine reacted to the shame by silence. I did not know that my father had taken his own life until I was about ten years old and I overheard the remark of a neighbor sitting on her front steps talking with another neighbor. As my younger brother and I passed by, we heard her say, "Those are the children of the suicide."

Donald and I had been shielded from the shameful act; there was not even a hint of a family secret. The solicitude of relatives and friends for my immediate family was demonstrated in part by their reticence. The tragedy that had overwhelmed the household had been relegated to the sphere of nonexistence. Consequently, I was angered by the callous remark that I believed to be false and insulting. It remains one of my most painful and indelible memories.

On the whole, however, my childhood memories are of a lively and cheerful household, full of the bustle of constant comings and goings. The shock of learning by accident of my father's suicide was lessened by the warm family spirit I remember so well. Donald and I went immediately to Bosley, as our confidant. We wanted to protect our mother from the ugly remark, for we of course accepted the then prevailing view of suicide. But, to our consternation, Bosley did not share our disbelief and anger. Instead, like the journalist he later became, he went to the offices of the Baltimore *Sun* and examined old copies of the paper. He then solemnly confirmed the report we had so vigorously rejected.

I recognized that my mother and the other adults in my life had known of the suicide, but somehow I did not feel resentment at having been kept in the dark. Once I had learned the adult secret, I joined in the family policy of silence. I must have felt that if my mother wouldn't talk to me about it, neither should I talk about it within the family. It was years before I mentioned my father's suicide to anyone but Donald, and even we spoke of it rarely.

I certainly never broached the subject to Aunt Lila, though in many ways I was closer to her than I was to my mother. This may have been partly due to my mother's being the family magistrate, although her severest punishment was a slap with a ruler on the palm of an extended hand. When I went to my mother for solace of a hurt, I was likely to receive a homily on how best to get on in the world. In contrast, Aunt Lila could be counted on for sympathetic understanding. My mother's fortitude in adversity was magnificent, but she was not cut out for the role of confidante. My father had left her our house and a modest income, which she used to raise and educate us all. One of her duties, she felt, was to prepare us for our role in life. Conventional in her values, she was ambitious for our success in a material sense.

Aunt Lila wanted something different for us, something less worldly. She wanted us to share her love of literature, her respect for learning and morality. But she was not preachy, so that her wishes were never just words of advice. I felt I had an ally in her, if a silent one, when I resisted my mother's favorite admonition: "Put your best foot forward." Long before I read Henry James, I was suspicious of the bitch goddess Success. And in retrospect, I can see that Aunt Lila's persistent commitment to things of the spirit gave a nice balance to my mother's emphasis on the importance of life's practical demands.

My clearest recollections of Aunt Lila are of her reading aloud to us. She began this practice before I was old enough to be an orderly member of her audience. This was a carryover of a familiar nineteenth-century American custom. She read in a clear, conversational tone. Yet her readings were a performance, a festive occasion, and perhaps it was here that my lifelong love of the theater began. Lila's audience often included friends of my older siblings and sometimes adults. When the girls went away to college, we boys continued to receive the rich benefits of Aunt Lila's reading and other literate gifts.

Eliza Millemon Hiss, Aunt Lila's full and proper name, was a distinctive individual, strikingly energetic; but it was her tiny size that most set her apart. I always knew she was small, even when I was so much smaller. Yet her size in no way diminished her authority: she was merely a small adult, as there were thin adults and fat ones.

Aunt Lila was most truly our teacher in her choice of the works she read to us. Reading aloud is slow. It is, however, astonishing how much can be covered if regular periods are set aside for that purpose. She pitched the choice of text to suit the most advanced of her listeners. This meant that on some occasions small fry had to swim as best they could in the swirling waters of adult fare. I may misremember how young I was when I listened to Dickens and Scott, but I distinctly recall sitting at Aunt Lila's feet, amid an assemblage of older children and adults, while over my head rolled, like lovely music, the glorious sounds of grown-up words. And there is no doubt that at an early age I was enjoying Dickens and Scott. Shakespeare, it is true, we met only through Lamb's *Tales*, but the two novelists we took neat.

Lila had a minor gift for writing humorous rhymes for birthdays or to accompany the simple objects that help to fill children's Christmas stockings. Part of her unconscious pedagogy was to encourage us to try our hand at jingles of this kind. This is how we learned that words could be used for pleasure if we worked at it. Her love of humor meant that we heard *Alice* and Lear's *Nonsense* verse. And there was her favorite poetry: Gray's "Elegy," "Kubla Khan," the "Ancient Mariner," and the shorter poems of Keats and Wordsworth. In addition, I'm sure it was Aunt Lila who introduced us boys to the world of King Arthur, Roland and Oliver, Bulfinch, the Brothers Grimm, and the Arabian Nights. But this was only to start us on our own. Visiting in such books the world where perils are surmounted by courage, honesty, and quickness of wit soon became my favorite pastime.

Other than that she did not go to college, I know nothing about her education. Perhaps as a child she had been read to and was now passing on to us her literacy in the same way.

Ours was a religious household though not a pietistic one. We children attended Sunday school, and the whole family went faithfully to the neighborhood Episcopal church. We said grace before dinner (apparently food did not need to be blessed if eaten at breakfast or lunch). We also had family prayers on occasion, although I cannot remember what those occasions were. It seems to me that when Aunt

Lila devoted a fair amount of time to read to us from the King James version of the Bible, she selected the more dramatic tales. The stories of David and Goliath, Saul and Jonathan, Samson and Delilah, and Judith and Holofernes are fixed in my memory alongside those of Oliver Twist, Nicholas Nickleby, and Ivanhoe.

Aunt Lila's readings had their own theater, the "Library," so called because it housed our towering glass-front bookcase, which contained sets of the American and British novelists and Shakespeare, along with miscellaneous books. Webster's dictionary, mounted on an iron stand, was prominent, as was a greatly enlarged photograph of my father in his dress uniform as an officer of the Fifth Regiment, Baltimore's prized National Guard unit.

The hour, itself almost as fixed as that of a theatrical performance, was always late afternoon after school. Aunt Lila sat in a straight-backed chair that seemed too large for her. We did not have electricity until after she had moved away, and as the light faded the gas was lighted—a shaded Welsbach burner that gave a splendid glow for reading. Lighting the gas itself added a touch of drama. A Welsbach burner did not go on at the flick of a switch. A match was held beneath it, and the slowly spreading incandescence of the delicate mantle always held our eyes. We children sat on the floor at Aunt Lila's feet, and when the gaslight was fully on, we moved closer to be within the cone of brightness.

Aunt Lila not only read to us; she taught us to read to her. Patiently, passage by passage, she schooled us in modulation of tone and rhythm and encouraged naturalness of pitch and volume. She insisted that her charges give as well as receive the pleasure of reading as an act of sharing.

The readings took place only on weekdays. Saturday was taken up with music lessons and by trips to Mr. Wallace, the neighborhood grocer, to pick up orders telephoned too late to be delivered by Walter Gibson, the delivery man. Saturday was also a day to do chores and errands for my grandmother Hughes, who had a floor-through in an imposing remodeled house at the far corner of the block. And Sunday was devoted to Sunday school (where Aunt Lila taught), church, midday dinner, and visits from friends and relatives.

When I was about ten, the readings became less frequent. Donald and I wanted to be outdoors. We roller-skated on the macadam that had recently replaced the cobblestones of our neighborhood, or we went to nearby Druid Hill Park with school friends or neighbors. Aunt Lila's readings took place only on rainy or snowy afternoons, or when the early dark and cold of winter brought us indoors.

Our house was a small, three-story brick building with a cellar and a wooden front porch, set in a middle-class residential neighborhood in the northwest part of Baltimore. It was separated from the sidewalk by a grass plot surrounded by a low wire fence. The grass suffered from neglect and from frequent wrestling matches that Donald and I had with our friends. Like ours, most of the houses at our end of the block were semidetached, each pair of houses sharing a common wall. Within three or four blocks of us were a couple of grand houses of an earlier day.

Our neighbors included a doctor and his wife and minor officials of local banks. One neighbor had a tiny observatory on his roof and on occasion invited me to look through his telescope.

We had no furnace until I was in my mid-teens; heat was supplied by the kitchen range (which also heated the hot water) and, in the dining room and the parlor, by Latrobe stoves with isinglass windows. We boys tended the Latrobes with coal we carried up from the cellar bin in buckets. With these same buckets we took the ashes to large cans in the backyard.

Quiet neighborhoods need their romantic legends. Mine, unchanging in its habits, developed such a legend. After I had left it, the residents of my block believed that the future Duchess of Windsor, Wallis Warfield, had spent part of her childhood there. She had indeed been a Baltimorean as a youngster. But I know of no basis for the belief that any part of her childhood was spent in my neighborhood. The Wallis Warfield legend replaced a still more romantic one that I grew up with. It was whispered that one of our next-door neighbors, a woman then in her early forties, was a sleepwalker and paraded up and down the sidewalk in her nightgown in the middle of the night. I am in no position to confirm this belief, either.

Relations with our neighbors were cordial, but family mattered much more; we lived our engrossing family life within our little house, where I was born in 1904. Indoor entertainment was largely of our own devising—charades, guessing games, spelling bees—supplemented by Parcheesi, checkers, jackstraws, and dominoes. Dinner in the evening was noisy, full of animated talk and much laughter. It took little to make us laugh: daily incidents, a slip of the tongue by my mother, the recounting of an anachronistic or small-town remark by my grandmother. I still remember a few, illustrative of the limitations of childhood humor.

Grandmother, while being escorted on an errand, passed by the Pennsylvania Railroad station and noticed the crowds entering and leaving, then a normal scene throughout the day. But Grandmother, thinking of the infrequent trains of her youth, remarked, "My goodness, must be train time."

On a similar expedition, she had been annoyed by the shrill cries of a passing newsboy and had admonished him: "Hush, boy! Stop hollering so loud." We greeted these items with gales of laughter.

My mother had trouble with the names of prominent tradespeople. Mano Swartz was a local furrier whom she constantly referred to as Mr. Mano. We thought this and similar slips hilarious.

Mary once told of an incident at the Bryn Mawr School, then frequently visited by the redoubtable M. Carey Thomas, who was president of Bryn Mawr College. During a noon recess a group of girls had locked themselves into a classroom and were passing around a lighted cigarette. Suddenly there was a sharp knock on the door, followed by a scurrying within and a hesitant, "Who is it?" The sharp reply was "It's me—Miss Thomas. Open up!" Quick-witted Mary, as she told the tale, said pertly, "Oh, no, it's not. She would say, 'It's I.'" There followed silence, broken by the sound of tiptoeing footsteps hurrying down the hall.

Unwittingly, I brought on what I recall as the longest and loudest burst of laughter ever. I was definitely the least musical of the tribe, and what I contributed one evening was the proud boast that I had that day sung at a concert. I was then nine, I believe, and pleased with myself for getting full attention from my gay and witty older siblings. The attention was accompanied by skepticism. "Where was this?" asked Bosley, the doubter, already a pretty good violinist and a collector of Red Seal records. "At the Peabody Conservatory," I said, with the firmness of the truthteller. Bosley was not satisfied. He insisted on details, which I was only too pleased to give, enjoying my unaccustomed position as the center of dinner-table attention. I said that I had been chosen from my grammar school by our music teacher to go to a citywide concert. Yes, I had been led right out onto the stage and had sung. Bosley persisted, wanting to know just what my music teacher had said in introducing me. I repeated the introduction perfectly, so important was it to me, though I had no idea of its meaning: "This is what can be done with a monotone."

We all took music lessons. As a small boy I took German conversational lessons and during my teens went to an art class every Saturday afternoon. But the true measure of the sophistication of my family surroundings comes from two large etchings I recall vividly. They hung, because of their size, almost oppressively in the small dining room and were replicated in many other households. One was a reproduction of Rosa Bonheur's *The Horse Fair*. The other, surrounded by a heavy, encrusted metal frame, was Landseer's familiar, disconsolate hunting dog. The large creature is prone, with his muzzle resting on a man's glove. The sentimental scene is entitled *O for the Touch of a Vanished Hand*.

Our favorite diversion remained Aunt Lila's reading aloud. For us children she differed from all other adults to such a degree that it was almost like having a fairy godmother of our own. In our imaginations, we identified her with the realms of wonder and magic of some of the stories she read to us. But it was her own qualities—and a wondrous ailment—that were mainly responsible for her aura. Aunt Lila had wens. The unfamiliar word had an air of mystery. No one else we knew had wens, which are small, hard lumps that appear on the scalp and can be removed only by minor surgery—at least that is what I believed then.

The fascination was greatest when the doctor came to remove a wen. He was installed in the Library, whose door was closed to ensure privacy between doctor and patient. Towels and basins of hot water were carried in and out of the room. Whenever the door opened, my brothers and I caught glimpses of the medical rites within. Aunt Lila was perched on a child's high chair, her long dark hair hanging down, covering her face. We thought she looked like the witch of Endor about whom she had read to us; the rest of her was swathed in towels. Beside her was a small table holding more towels and a tray of instruments. I can still see the scene as if it were an Eakins.

A little more than ten years after Aunt Lila moved to her own house, when I became private secretary to Supreme Court Justice Oliver Wendell Holmes (the post would today be called law clerk), I had a special opportunity to put to use the reading skills she had taught me. Aunt Lila's teaching enabled me to give the Justice many hours of relaxed enjoyment. It also brought me the great reward of an enhanced relationship with that most charming and many-sided sage.

Holmes was demanding as to the quality of spoken discourse—whether by a reader, an attorney, or a friend in conversation. So I think I do not flatter myself that had I been less adept—had I not had the benefit of Aunt Lila's tutelage—I could not have gotten the great Justice to accept so unreservedly my reading to him day after day the books of his choice and occasionally of mine. And only by those readings was I able to get his penetrating views about the books we read.

Now, once more, I am the one read to, as in Aunt Lila's day. My sight has failed so that I can no longer read to myself, much less to others. Friends come in to read to me, a boon I cannot repay in kind. Some of the voices are lilting, some more gravelly; some friends employ an emphasis that clarifies, while the misplaced emphasis of others is distracting; some diction is impeccable, some imperfect. I find the variety stimulating and refreshing, for I have reached the age where perfect cadence can prompt me to doze off—the one gaffe the listener hates to make. I have no hesitation in asking that an unclear sentence be repeated, for that assures the gentle reader that I am alert.

2

FELIX FRANKFURTER
AT BRATTLE STREET—
AND AFTER

When I was a student at the Harvard Law School, from September 1926 until June 1929, Felix Frankfurter was far and away the most colorful and controversial member of the faculty. Brilliant and irrepressible, he was much more than a campus figure. His innumerable close friendships with leaders all over the country and abroad had already made him a man of national prominence by the time I was his student.

He was always conspicuous, despite his small stature, as he moved about the campus. This was because as he bounced along—short, dynamic, articulate—he was invariably surrounded by a cluster of students. Frankfurter was always teaching, in class and out. His didactic style was challenging, even confrontational. He invited discussion and he reveled in sharp exchanges. These continued after class had ended.

But Frankfurter was not popular with the majority of his students or his fellow faculty members. In both cases the reasons, I believe, were the same.

Frankfurter was cocky, abrasive, and outspoken. His style was simply not theirs. In addition, Frankfurter was the leader of the liberal wing of the faculty. Most of his older colleagues were politically conservative, as were most of the students.

The great legal scholar Dean John H. Wigmore of Northwestern University was among Frankfurter's opponents in the dispute over the Sacco and Vanzetti case, calling Frankfurter with distaste a "plausible pundit"—fighting words in the mannerly decorum of academia in those days. A stout civil libertarian, Frankfurter was a vigorous champion of the innocence of Sacco and Vanzetti, right up to their execution in the summer of 1927 and afterward. He participated actively in groups formed to aid them, and he spoke and wrote tirelessly on their behalf. Frankfurter and those who shared his views were shocked at what they considered glaring errors in the conduct of the trial by the prosecutor— errors uncorrected, and indeed compounded, by the judge. Prejudice had run high against the defendants as Italians and as anarchists, and Frankfurter was outraged by instances where prejudice affected the conduct of the case. It raised questions about the fairness of Massachusetts justice, polarized opinions in that state, and aroused strong feeling throughout the nation and the western world.

Frankfurter's prominence in the Sacco-Vanzetti case made him a marked man in Boston, an object of bitter hostility on the part of the conservatives. It brought him into sharp conflict with the president of his own university, A. Lawrence Lowell, who served on the Massachusetts commission that recommended against clemency. The executions did not put a stop to Frankfurter's charges of a gross miscarriage of justice, or to the rancor aroused by the case. Wherever Frankfurter went, he attracted attention. During intermissions at Symphony Hall, where Boston's prominent citizens gathered, he was both glared at and beamed upon as he bounced and bobbed through the crowded lobbies. He seemed to enjoy the notoriety.

At the same time that Frankfurter's fearless championing of Sacco and Vanzetti made him a target of conservatives, it won him national acclaim from liberals as a defender of civil liberties. His stand was thoroughly consistent with his political views in general. He tended to speak with almost ribald disapproval of those he considered the reactionaries in our society, including Judge Webster Thayer, who had presided at the trial of Sacco and Vanzetti and had expressed his prejudices against them to a golfing companion. Such people, Frank-furter would say impishly, regarded themselves as men of importance but were really closer to being "the scum of society." He would utter such comments only at home with friends, but he never attempted to disguise his views in class, either.

Harvard Law School's traditional method of teaching involves sharp, incisive, even sarcastic questioning. While the technique often causes embarrassment or humiliation for the students, the practice, at least in my day, was generally accepted as a helpful means of sharp-ening their wits, teaching them to think and speak precisely when challenged. Frankfurter's obvious enjoyment of this form of verbal fencing made many of his students feel that he was displaying personal hostility, engaging in unfair ridicule. I didn't take any of his large lecture courses, so I can't personally assess those complaints. But I can well imagine Frankfurter being carried away by his showman's gifts and a large audience.

Frankfurter was a dedicated teacher, generous with his time, sym-pathetic to the aspirations of youth. I think his unpopularity with many students was based less on his teaching style than on his political views.

We students in his small seminars had full opportunity to benefit from his remarkable personality. His energy, his vitality electrified the room from the moment he came in. Yet his manner with us was gentle. Usually in high good spirits, he would from time to time explode into laughter or into an outburst of friendly remonstrance if one of us said something he found ludicrously or perversely incorrect. He was as demanding of us for accuracy as he was reputed to be of the men in his large classes, but with us there was no hint of ridicule.

In the two seminars I took with him, our subjects were the federal courts and administrative tribunals. They were fields he had made his special domain. In another's hands, the material might have been dustily technical. Felix, as we students spoke of him to one another, had the love of his subject, and the ability to impart it, that marks the true teacher. He venerated "the rule of law" and passionately strove for its evenhanded administration. He knew personally, or knew all about, the judges and commissioners whose rulings we examined. He was understanding of the pressures they faced, but when they failed to exemplify the high standards he set, he was stern in disapproval.

His emphasis on practical realities, including the human factors, made the courses seem like internships.

Frankfurter's enthusiasm for high-principled federal service was infectious. Many of us who were his students at Harvard later responded to the New Deal's need for lawyers, and he presided proudly over our recruitment into federal service.

I had come to Cambridge with a letter of introduction to Frankfurter from William Marbury, a Baltimore lawyer who was a mutual friend. As a result, I got invited to the Sunday teas. It was there, in his rambling, comfortable Cambridge house on Brattle Street, a brisk walk from the law school, that Frankfurter was at his most winning.

The house itself was undistinguished, made of dark-stained wood. One entered almost directly into a large, high-ceilinged, awkwardly shaped living room. There were overstuffed chairs and sofas, tables piled with magazines, newspapers, and books. Along the wall were shoulder-high bookcases.

That room was the soul of the house. Its scholarly clutter and disarray were inviting. One felt immediately that it was designed for reading and talk. Frankfurter, a restless man, moved quickly about the room while carrying on a rapid-fire conversation. He flew from book to book, magazine to magazine, like an adult Peter Pan. Those books and journals were the props of his great performance as a conversationalist.

Sprightly intellectual discourse was an art form in those days. Many of Frankfurter's close friends—men like Judge Learned Hand, Walter Lippmann, Harold J. Laski, Dr. Alfred E. Cohn of the Rockefeller Institute, and Thomas Reed Powell, the law school's flamboyant, witty professor of constitutional law—had mastered the skill. Frankfurter's idols, Supreme Court Justices Holmes and Brandeis, were renowned conversationalists and welcomed Frankfurter for the brilliant, spontaneous flow of his ideas. He, in turn, was the idol of those few lucky students who were invited to Sunday teas at the Brattle Street house.

There would be ten or a dozen in the room. Frankfurter was a generous host and frequently had weekend guests. Some of his special faculty friends—Powell, James Landis, Roger Foster, Calvert Magruder—would be there. His wife, Marion, intelligent and beautiful, was always a gracious presence, and she too spoke well and readily.

Frankfurter himself was at once the impresario and the catalyst. He directed the flow of talk, calling on this one or that as if conducting an orchestra. The topics ranged from politics and law to literature and history, but practically nothing was barred, and the inspiration could come from anywhere. For example, Frankfurter traveled widely, and if he was just back from a trip to Washington or Albany, he would be full of his meetings with the great and near-great, recounted with wit and brio. These tales could take the discussion far beyond the confines of Cambridge.

The spirit of informality at Felix's house was a special treat for us favored students. Here we were in the presence of a revered, nationally prominent professor and his august friends, free to express our personal views and join in the discussion. One of the risks of participating, of course, was that if we spoke without adequate logic or supporting detail, Felix would expose our shortcomings.

After our host and his illustrious guests had expressed their views on whatever topic was under discussion, Frankfurter often would turn to one of us students and say, "And what do you think?" The query always left me momentarily speechless. One time he asked for my comments on Lord Acton's famous dictum that all power tends to corrupt, and absolute power to corrupt absolutely. I had never heard the dictum before and could only come up with a lame observation, something to the effect that great ends call for great power. But there was, on this occasion as on all others I remember from the Brattle Street teas, a saving grace in the friendly manner with which Frankfurter put his question and challenged the answer.

Felix was extraordinarily well informed in many fields and gifted at extracting personal experience, knowledge, or opinion as he moved from guest to guest. It was, however, his own scintillating talk that made these gatherings most memorable.

Organizing his thoughts cogently, possessed of an astounding memory, fluent and brimming with energy, Frankfurter was an arresting speaker on any occasion. At home on Brattle Street, making use of the books and articles that lay at hand, his discourse became a great performance. Citing a passage from a book or a legal opinion, he would dart from his chair to a bookcase or a crowded table and seize a volume or a journal. Quickly and unerringly, he would turn to the page he wanted and read the supporting passage. He was credited with reading a page at a glance, with a photographic memory that enabled him to recall the exact page whose contents he was citing. Analytical, quick-witted, and eloquent, he possessed a histrionic ability that made his conversational powers unique.

Yet the performance was but his way of conveying the content. We students were meant to, and did, enjoy the afternoon, but what we came away with was what we had learned—what Brandeis had said about a recent Supreme Court decision, what Holmes had said about some point of philosophy, what Governor Franklin Roosevelt had done for conservation in New York. Frankfurter's zest and skill as a performer were at the service of his interest in ideas.

Frankfurter maintained friendships with many of his students during and long after their law school years. He cared about the personal life and intellectual opinions of each of us as though this large group were a small circle of his intimates. I always felt that Felix was available, and a note from him or an invitation to see him never seemed to me unusual. I recall being asked to join him and Dr. Cohn for dinner at the Ritz in Boston while I was in law practice there. Instead of regarding this as a special gesture in my direction by an incredibly busy man, I took it as a normal friendly meal with FF (as his friends spoke of him), not really out of the ordinary at all.

I continued to see Frankfurter often after I graduated from the law school, particularly during the years 1930 and 1931, when I was practicing in Boston. During that period, he became an adviser to Franklin D. Roosevelt, then governor of New York, a relationship that led to Frankfurter's important offstage participation in the New Deal and eventually to his appointment as a Supreme Court justice.

Our friendship was such that when I became the defendant in a sensational trial for perjury, he did not hesitate in responding affirmatively to my lawyer's wish to call him as a witness to testify to my good character. This he did even though it was predictable that he would be attacked for thus supposedly impairing the dignity of his office. Indeed he was attacked, and it is a measure of how controversial his reputation still was that, so far as I am aware, his more conservative colleague, Justice Stanley Reed, who also appeared as one of my character witnesses, was not so attacked.

These attacks on Felix led me to spare him, and also Justice Reed, the risk of embarrassment by appearing in my second trial. And on my release from prison, I avoided direct contact with Felix in order to spare him further hostile criticism. I kept in touch indirectly through friends and through my brother Donald, who, while a student at the law school, had become as close to Felix as I was—indeed, Frankfurter had chosen Donald as one of Holmes's secretaries as he had earlier selected me. Donald maintained constant warm relations with Frankfurter and was the executor of his estate. But, after my first trial, I never saw Felix again. There was no change in my regard for him, and I knew from Donald that there was no change in his regard for me. His coming to my aid was in keeping with his earlier acts of moral courage, and I am happy to express here my gratitude for his testimony in my behalf.

Having written about Felix Frankfurter the professor and friend, I would like to comment on Felix Frankfurter the Supreme Court justice. There is a seeming paradox in the contrast between Frankfurter's increasingly conservative judicial opinions and his earlier liberal attitudes.

That there is a contrast is beyond doubt, and that contrast has been perplexing to many. President Eisenhower is said to have been among those who believed that the contrast represented a change of basic convictions and to have remarked to Edward R. Murrow that there was never any telling about how a Supreme Court appointment would turn out. One would have expected Chief Justice Earl Warren to be a stout conservative, said Eisenhower, and Frankfurter to be a liberal. Instead, he went on, they both turned out to be just the opposite of what had been expected.

Eisenhower's opinion is, I believe, simplistic as to Frankfurter. Both as professor and as judge, he advocated judicial restraint. His devotion to representative government was expressed in his distaste for judges overturning legislative enactments. In truth, Frankfurter's legal doctrine is not only intellectually robust; it squares with his faith in democracy. The legislature, as the representative of the electorate, is the governmental institution closest to the public. In theory it is the voice of the people.

During most of the years when Frankfurter was a professor, a conservative Supreme Court regularly invalidated innovative and liberal programs enacted by legislatures. His legal mentors during that period, Justices Holmes and Brandeis, dissented, enunciating the right of the legislature to experiment. They became identified in the public mind with the liberal causes they futilely voted to uphold. Frankfurter, more liberal than they in many of his own personal views, basked in the congenial doctrine. Then, under the New Deal, changes in the Court's membership (including Frankfurter's accession in 1939) created a liberal Court that sustained liberal legislation. In this brief span of years Frankfurter's personal progressive views were in accord with those of the Court and of the nation's legislatures.

But his service on the Court extended beyond the liberal national mood of the New Deal. The doctrine of judicial restraint, however, protects conservative and reactionary legislative and executive acts as well as liberal ones. The activist-liberal Warren did not adhere so rigidly to that doctrine, and thus Frankfurter found himself often voting against the liberal faction of the Warren Court. Many of Frankfurter's admirers, I among them, felt that his rigidity caused him to take positions at odds with his basic liberal sympathies in such cases.

It is my own belief that the Supreme Court should be politically accountable. I and some other New Dealers had agreed with President Roosevelt's plan to increase the number of justices to ensure a majority with liberal views. Privately, Frankfurter had himself been New Dealer enough to approve of the plan.

I wonder if Frankfurter, when expounding his somewhat inflexible doctrine of judicial restraint, recalled a luncheon with his hero Justice Holmes in the summer of 1930. That was the summer I spent with Justice Holmes as his secretary, in Beverly Farms, Massachusetts. Among my "perks" was attendance at luncheons the Justice provided for occasional guests who drove out from Boston to see him. That particular luncheon was memorable, first, for its guests: Judge Learned Hand, Frankfurter, and Walter Lippmann. But more important was the insight we got into the compassionate side of Holmes the jurist.

Holmes prized the common law for its practicality, realism, lack of sentimentality. He was noted for believing that the law sets forth rules of conduct to be applied regardless of hardship. At the luncheon, however, the great jurist disclosed his vulnerability to the appeal of simple decency and fairness.

The moment the guests arrived, two of them announced that throughout the trip from Boston they had vigorously disagreed about a recent decision by the New York Court of Appeals.* The case, as presented to Holmes by the two disputants, involved two prominent real-estate investors long known to each other. One was the mortgagor, the other the mortgagee, of a valuable piece of property in New York City. The mortgagor, about to leave the country for a vacation, notified the mortgagee of his (the mortgagor's) upcoming absence. He noted that the mortgage payment would fall due while he was away but that his trusted secretary had been directed to make payment on the due date. In fact, as events turned out, the trusted secretary forgot. The mortgagee immediately foreclosed, though he had every reason to believe that a telephone call would have resulted in prompt payment. The mortgage bond had been clear in its terms; foreclosure was technically justified. The case had gone all the way to the highest New York court, where the seven judges were divided four to three. The majority was led by Judge John F. O'Brien, the minority by Chief Judge Benjamin Cardozo—the latter espousing the hapless cause of the absent mortgagor.

During the drive to Beverly Farms, Judge Hand had sided with the O'Brien faction; Frankfurter, with that led by Cardozo. Lippmann had apparently remained discreetly silent in the presence of sharp disagreement between those learned in the law. Hand and Frankfurter had each contended that his view would be supported by Holmes.

Holmes was obviously nettled to have a contentious issue thrust upon what he had expected to be a relaxed luncheon visit. He was also annoyed at being called upon to decide between two friends. He protested that he did not like to give offhand judgments. As a further excuse, he added that the case might come before him. Assured that this was not possible, he took refuge in the assertion that he did not

---

*The case was *Graff* v. *Hope Building Corp.*, 254 N.Y. 1. In presenting the case to Holmes, Hand and Frankfurter had simplified the facts but left fully intact the legal and moral principles involved.

wish to express an opinion without a chance to examine the record. The two contenders insisted that this was not necessary, that they had given him the pertinent facts. Holmes avoided committing himself, and we went to the dining room with his view of the matter still unstated. He never did declare himself forthrightly, but, as he lifted a spoonful of consommé to his lips, he muttered, really to himself, "I sure would have tried to help the fellow."

3

GIVERNY, SUMMER OF 1929

My younger brother, Donald, and I spent the summer of 1929 in Giverny. Monet had died three years before, and the little French village had then largely reverted to its ancient ways of the time before the famous artist had come to live there. It was not only that there was an end to the visits of people of the outside world and of Monet's own circle of friends who had come to see him. A small, largely British colony of artists and would-be artists that had established itself in Giverny had quickly departed. There was not even the occasional tourist who once had come in hopes of a glimpse of Monet or to view the rural world of haystacks and gardens and ponds he had painted.

The reversion to the village's earlier state was not complete; some changes that had come about as a result of Monet's presence had continued. But to my brother and me these seemed few, and in fact they only added pleasure to what was for us an idyllic summer sojourn.

The changes that continued after Monet's death were of two kinds: architectural and demographic—to borrow from the lexicon of guidebooks. The architectural changes included the skylights that had been

added to some of the peasant houses, and a tennis court built some
years earlier by a well-to-do American no longer in residence—a man
forgotten except for his house, a tastefully converted water mill, and
the tennis court, which he had given to the town. The court was across
the through road from the one hotel, a prim little brick building named,
simply, L'Hôtel—a quaint indication of the size of the village and the
simplicity of its ways. That the road was the village's only real street
is a further indication of the hamletlike nature of Giverny in 1929.

A guidebook of the period—which, of course, was not so up-to-
date as to record the changes I have noted—refers to Giverny as being
"sur la confluence de l'Epte et de la Seine"; the village is at the
southeastern corner of Normandy. The nearest town of any size is
Vernon, five miles farther down the Seine, where there was a bridge
across the river. Within its riverine boundaries, the little town was
thus rather inaccessible. This no doubt had helped to keep it small
and isolated from the great world until Monet came, and even his
presence added no new buildings. So, despite the occasional incongruous skylight and the uncared-for tennis court, the tiny village in
1929 looked much as it must have throughout its uneventful history.

The demographic changes that persisted after Monet's death were
also minimal. Indeed, they had for the most part already been absorbed
into the life of Giverny during Monet's period of residence. Monet's
son-in-law, an American artist named Theodore Butler, had long since
become a member of the community. Bearded, brusquely aloof, always
dressed in a turtleneck sweater, he lived in a peasant cottage with his
son, Jimmy. Butler *père* was seldom seen. Jimmy had grown up in
Giverny except for a few years of school in the States. By 1929 he was
as much a part of the village life as any of the peasants themselves.

One other remnant of the Monet changes melted less into the placid
ways of the distant past. Hilaire Hiler, an American artist, had been
drawn by the lure of Monet and had remained after the small foreign
colony had left. But an expatriate American artist (or writer) was a
familiar feature of French life of the 1920s. Consequently, Hiler, like
the other variants in ancient folk patterns, did not mar what seemed
to us the timeless spirit of the Norman countryside.

Donald and I accepted as a boon the intrusive tennis court and also the minimal cost of lodging. We were the only guests at the one other hostelry in town, an unpretentious inn, Au Bon Maréchal, indistinguishable from other village houses. It stood on the through road where a lane with two or three houses led to the fields and to a footpath to the Epte. We occupied a corner room into whose tiled roof a skylight had been inserted. M. and Mme. Jégou were overjoyed to have two unexpected student lodgers. On the ground floor was an unadorned dining room of five or six tables where in the late afternoon a few men of the village would gather for their *café cognac* and perhaps a game of dominoes. The rest of the ground floor was used as the Jégous' quarters, including a large and airy kitchen. Mme. Jégou was not a villager; she came from Rouen, and her good cooking showed it. There was a simple courtyard equipped with a *pissoir*. No other overnight guests appeared at any time; we had the inn to ourselves all summer long. More important, we had a near-monopoly of Mme. Jégou's considerable talent as a cook—our own French cook for a whole summer.

The weather that season was splendid. We ate most of our meals in the courtyard, where we sat after dinner through the long summer evenings, almost always joined by Jimmy Butler, who seemed to welcome our company as much as we certainly welcomed his. He was then unmarried and in his early or mid-thirties. We understood that his mother was Monet's stepdaughter and that after her death Jimmy's father had married Monet's daughter. Thus Jimmy was twice Monet's stepgrandson without being his grandson at all. Double yet nonexistent, this piquant relationship to a great figure seemed to us to symbolize Jimmy's personality. (Only recently have I learned that the village account of Jimmy's relationship to Monet did not precisely reflect Theodore's marriage into the complicated Monet family.)

An artist himself, Jimmy's work was derivative of Japanese art. A gifted conversationalist, to our surprise he never spoke of Monet the artist or Monet the man. Moreover, Jimmy's only reference to his father was to say that because of Butler *père*'s difficult and distant personality Jimmy could not invite us to his house. I don't think he took his own work seriously. He appeared frequently for talk or a stroll. He had no fixed schedule or work habits. He did take a few of his paintings to Paris to display on the Boulevard Raspail during the days when little-known artists placed their work in the annual outdoor show.

Many years later, well after World War II, I saw Jimmy once on my own initiative. He was living in New York with his wife and working as an editor for an encyclopedia. He said that this work was burdensome and indicated that he was struggling to make ends meet. He was otherwise reticent, made no mention of his painting, and indicated no interest in picking up the long-ago summer relationship. The ready flow of lively talk was gone. He seemed dispirited. I respected his reserve and made no attempt to see him again, not wishing to presume on a brief summer's acquaintance of a quarter of a century earlier.

That disappointing last meeting with Jimmy was actually in tune with his somewhat elusive companionship of that magical summer of 1929. Not quite Monet's grandson, not quite a serious painter, Jimmy would appear suddenly and unexpectedly, picking up the diaphanous relationship where he had left it. It was a relationship without demands or commitments, yet it added much charm and gave a distinctive quality to our stay in Giverny. His conversation was usually bookish; his literary tastes, idiosyncratic. He introduced me to Jarry's *Le Roi Ubu*, and he admired Rimbaud. But his true love was Rabelais, of whom he spoke with both enthusiasm and discernment. How congenial such talk was for a summer evening in the French countryside! The Gallic flavor was increased by Jimmy's own resemblance to a late-medieval or early-Renaissance storyteller in the lack of regularity in his comings and goings and in the casualness of his manner of life and dress.

There was yet another thing about Jimmy Butler that set him apart from those about him. His fluent and sophisticated English had a marked French accent. But our Giverny friends emphasized that his French was marked by a strong American accent. In speech, in heritage, in the manner in which he pursued his profession, and in his life-style, Jimmy eluded categories. He was not to be taken for granted. One took him on his terms, and we were happy to do so, recognizing our good fortune in happening upon such extraordinary company.

True to his unpredictable ways, Jimmy once took us without warning into his cottage, explaining that his father was away. It was a narrow peasant house with few windows. One room led to another without a hallway, as in a New York City railroad flat. Paintings were stored in the darkness of the rafters. Some, Jimmy said, were Monets, but we could distinguish only canvases on stretchers. In World War II the Germans crossed the Seine at nearby Vernon, and I wondered then what had become of the Monets in the Butler house. At our last meeting, after the war, Jimmy assured me that the paintings had not fallen into the invaders' hands. But he did not tell me whether they had been removed before the spring of 1940 or had been successfully hidden when the Germans came. Our easy relationship of 1929 was another casualty of the intervening years, and our final conversation was of trivial topics and a bit forced. That we might be for Jimmy Butler as ephemeral as a year's batch of students are for a teacher did not occur to Donald and me during that summer, any more than one wonders whether a stimulating professor will remember one a quarter of a century later. Jimmy was an important source of pleasure but by no means the only one in our unplanned sojourn in Giverny.

I had just graduated from Harvard Law School. My brother was about to enter his senior year at Johns Hopkins. We had set out in early June of 1929 for our version of a European Grand Tour—France, the Low Countries, Germany, Italy. We had a delightful crossing on the *Flandre* with a congenial group of friends who had European plans of their own. Then, without warning, after a week or so in Paris, Donald had a major attack of stomach ulcers. He was very ill indeed. The American Hospital in Paris recommended not only cancellation of travel plans but an immediate return home for possible surgery. He had had no prior symptoms, so we had no medical history to go by. But when I tried to get reservations back, usually an easy matter at that time of year, none was available. The liner *Paris* had burned not long before, with the result that space on all other immediate sailings had been snapped up. This was years before transatlantic plane travel. We would have had to wait a week or two at best.

There was a heat wave in Paris, and I concluded that a stifling city was no place for a seriously ill man. My family had always spent summers on the farm of cousins on the eastern shore of Maryland. For Donald and me the sensible spot to wait for the next sailing was the countryside, where it would be cool and where we assumed one could get plenty of fresh milk. The only thing we knew about ulcers was that milk was a soothing if not curative prescription. Friends in Paris suggested Giverny as both near and likely to have readily available and cheap quarters. And so, of course, Giverny proved—an unfrequented picturesque village.

Installed at Au Bon Maréchal, I first of all sought a dairy. There turned out to be only one cow in the almost deserted village, and few milk consumers, given the French distaste for fresh milk as a beverage. So we were assured of a full supply of our medicinal potion. The cow's barnyard was tiny and filthy, not at all like a proper American dairy. I gave no thought to possible impurities. A cow was a cow in any country, and rich, foamy milk was what we wanted. Whether the unpasteurized, unhygienic milk was the cure or that Donald simply had had a less-severe initial attack than was diagnosed, he quickly improved. When bookings became available, he had become so much better that we decided to wait another week or two. At the end of that time he seemed so much himself again that we stayed on. The fatigue of further European travel seemed unwise, as did getting too far away from French ports. And so we stayed on for a long, untroubled summer. It was indeed, as it turned out, a healthy vacation, perfect for a convalescent. We played tennis, swam in the clear cool waters of the Epte, and ate famously, and Donald was soon able to supplement curative milk with wine. No proper Norman convalescent could dispense with wine. Even our mother had regularly quoted Scripture: "Have a little wine for thy stomach's sake." And besides, conversation with Jimmy Butler through a long summer evening called for wine to give the talk wings.

Giverny's fresh air, its cow, Mme. Jégou's cuisine, and Jimmy Butler's erudition were not the only aids to my brother's return to health and to our idyllic summer. Our wheel of fortune provided us with the companionship of two young Frenchwomen of about our own age. Nitou Salerou and her friend Aniute were both students at the Sorbonne. Nitou's parents had a house in the village for weekend and summer use, and the girls were spending the summer there. The parents' presence, and family chores, kept the girls occupied in the evenings, leaving us and Jimmy Butler free for our memorable after-dinner talk. I don't believe we even knew just where Nitou's house was; that was of no consequence to our relationship. French custom doesn't usually include entertaining at home—or didn't at that time, anyway. Ours was a friendship *en plein air*—and included tennis, swimming, and picnics. It was somewhat like friendships one has at the local country club in an American town. Our daytime companionship was constant. After all, we were the only young people of our tastes and habits, the only vacationers in the village. We therefore saw one another day after day.

We spent several hours a day on the tennis court, of which we were the sole users. Donald and I learned to play tennis in French. The interchange of French and English tennis terms led to some sportive linguistics and etymology. Four young people at the outset of such an experience would naturally ponder how the English word "love" came to be used as a term for a zero score. We were intrigued that despite the reputed French interest in the erotic, there is no counterpart in French tennis usage for the English "love." With true Gallic absence of sentimentality, a zero score is called *zéro*. With such books as the girls and Jimmy Butler could muster, our modest joint Franco-American research efforts absolved the English also of sentimentality when they adopted "love" in tennis usage. We learned that, surprisingly, the English term was of French origin; and our game was derived from an old French court game. It delighted our French friends that typical Anglo-American inability to pronounce French words correctly had produced the incongruous word for *zéro*. Donald and I were able to add our quantum of data to give the Renaissance court usage a current counterpart. The French originators of the precursor of the game of tennis were, we pointed out, in no sense exotic in calling zero score *l'oeuf* (American slang has long dubbed such a score a "goose egg"). But this bit of lore did not distract our friends from the crucial point that "love" is but an English mispronunciation of *l'oeuf*, as London's Rotten Row is of Route du Roi.

Donald and I improved our French vocabulary along with our tennis. But tennis reminded us that borrowing words is reciprocal and continuous. That was the summer of a notable Davis Cup match in Paris. French and American athletes then dominated world tennis.

On a day's excursion from Giverny, Donald and I watched Bill Tilden and "Little Bill" Johnston eke out a victory over René Lacoste, Henri Cochet, and Jean Robert Borotra at the Stade Roland Garros. Our French tennis partners were as knowledgeable as we about Tilden's prowess. An ace of ours was rewarded by Nitou and Aniute with the compliment, "un service à Tilden."

Donald and I picked up more generally used idioms during our swims in the Epte and during picnics on its banks. Many must now be archaic, such as *tomber sur un bec de gaz* to describe a misadventure. That phrase must be as rare today in France as the familiar phrase of my childhood when speed was wanted—"Don't spare the horses"— is rare today here. And we learned once again the lesson that one must beware of direct translation of an idiom of ours or of seemingly logical derivations from known French. Thus *remplie* is not, as we thought, a way of saying one has eaten one's fill, but is French slang for *enceinte* (pregnant). And while *pêcheur* is indeed a fisherman, *pêche* is not a synonym for *poisson*. And so when we unintentionally spoke of peaches in the little river and also said we were pregnant, Donald and I sent our friendly teachers into spasms of laughter that fixed the lessons forevermore.

As Aniute was a strong swimmer and a member of Le Racing Club de France, and Donald was captain of his college swimming team, we frequented the Epte as often as we did the tennis court—perhaps more, for its banks not only afforded a site for picnics but shade for taking our ease of a warm sunny afternoon. Desultory, relaxed chatting is a capital spur to learning a language. Our interests were similar yet varied. Nitou's hobby was bookbinding. She presented me with a handsome Morocco-bound copy of Paul Morand's *Magie Noire*, which I lent to Justice Oliver Wendell Holmes a few months later—exemplifying how much the experiences of the Giverny summer shaped my tastes and my openness to the patterns of French life. This was not my first, or my last, visit to France. Romance languages and history were my college majors, but this extended stay gave me a lasting love for France that no amount of study could supply. The visit was placid, but for that very reason I was open to subtler and more pervasive influences than extensive travel could have provided.

From our own country I knew well the wall between year-round residents and summer folk. I was favored by the unusual moment in Giverny's recent history. In Giverny, not being encapsulated in the foreign enclave of a summer colony, I was neither a tourist nor separated from village life. When the resident foreigners had left, the village was once again made its own master. My brother's youth and my own, and our quiet demeanor, made us no threat. We felt we were guests, around whom village life went on as usual. As the weeks passed, we were greeted on the streets and on paths in the fields without shyness or reserve, with the simple good manners that often characterize villagers.

It was like looking at genre painting. The Parisian grandmother staying at L'Hôtel with her redhaired, eight-year-old grandson admonished him in our presence without taking the slightest notice of us, and added to our limited knowledge of the niceties of French usage. The boy had been summoned from a group of village playmates by his watchful grandmother: "François, François, veux-tu venir." Reluctantly he separated himself from his companions. Looking intently at him as he stood before her, the old lady, mindful of her duty to ensure her grandson's correct use of their noble language, said sharply, "Pas 'les haricots verts,' " carrying over the "s" so as to say "layzariko." She then gave the correct pronunciation of this phrase, one of the few exceptions to the usual sounding of a terminal "s" when followed by a vowel sound. To aid François's memory—and, as it turned out, mine as well—the instructress then cuffed the boy lightly on one ear. We felt we were an integral part of Norman village life.

Generous allowances were made for our lack of fluency. The domino players of an evening in the café, our dining room, would invite us to join a game, treating our poor French as an indication of our general backwardness. We would be given elaborate explanations of the rules. This display of good manners and hospitality was more an initiation into one aspect of village life than a way of signifying how alien we were.

Similarly, M. Jégou's patient slowing of his rapid speech for our benefit was a gesture of thoughtfulness, for he acted as if he regarded us as members of the community. He implied that our halting French was as respectable a category of the spoken language as was his wife's deliberate manner of speech. When we paused, searching for a word or inwardly translating, he would smile and, as if it applied to us as well as to Mme. Jégou, remark with the air of a sage, "Les Rouennais parlent lentement et doucement." The final word seemed added to remove any trace of criticism. His benign manner made us feel that we had been granted a dispensation—or been made honorary citizens of some French region. This was the same *politesse* I had been charmed by when, five years earlier, I had bicycled with two college friends through this same ancient province. As we sat in a café in Lisieux or Bayeux, my accent had been tolerantly assumed to be Alsatian.

Giverny's return to its traditional slumbrous ways after Monet's death was brief indeed, measured in historical terms. After only a decade came the disruption of history's most destructive war, and then, not much later, the resurgence of the artist's influence. The restoration and renovation of Monet's cottage and the famous ponds and gardens— the gift of Mrs. DeWitt Wallace, copublisher of the *Reader's Digest*— have brought tourism and commercialism. These intrusive concomitants of American cultural largesse are likely to be longer-lived than the small, decorous colony of British artists and admirers of the 1920s. One can only assume that henceforth Giverny will be home for a quite different sort of villager. It will no longer beckon invitingly to a major artist on the lookout for picturesque tranquillity and solid village comfort. Nor will it again be the magical setting of a summer vacation for two young foreigners in need of restorative repose and thirsty for direct contact with the ancient daily rounds of the French countryside.

Seeming ill-luck had instead brought my brother and me the greatest of blessings. Two Maryland Yankees had been warmly welcomed into a tiny part of Europe's richly textured past. And we had gone Mark Twain's traveler-in-time one better. Unlike the Connecticut Yankee, we had shared for a brief period the modern European heritage of unbroken continuity with that timeless past. Our visit to Giverny helped us to attain some of the sense of history that Europeans so often possess. Living even briefly as accepted participants in a cohesive social life whose traditions stretched back through history to legend permitted us to recognize a continuity in man's slow fashioning of civilization over the centuries. And from that recognition came a feeling of awe for the grandness of the accomplishments in all the realms of our world.

The tranquil Giverny of 1929 exists now only in the memories of a few of us. But the sense of history it evoked in me returns today with special force because of the threat to the continuance of all human history.

4

JUSTICE HOLMES, HIS BLACK BOOK, AND THE REWARDS OF READING ALOUD TO ITS AUTHOR

Near the conclusion of my final year at Harvard Law School, I was surprised—indeed, overwhelmed—to receive a handwritten note from Justice Holmes. It informed me that on the recommendation of Felix Frankfurter, my favorite Harvard professor, the Justice had chosen me as his private secretary for the following year. Holmes wrote that if I were to accept I was to report to his house in Washington on the Friday before the first Monday in October (the fall term of the Supreme Court begins on that Monday). He added that because of his age— he was then eighty-eight—he must reserve the right to resign or die. This appointment was to me a much more important certification of my accomplishment as a law student than was the diploma itself. The opportunity to continue my legal education under the supervision of this eminent jurist was by far the greatest prize the law school could offer.

Holmes had had a new secretary annually since his appointment by President Theodore Roosevelt to the Supreme Court in 1902. As Holmes and his wife were childless, the secretaries had played a special role in the Justice's life, in some ways serving as surrogate sons. I was the

31

first of them, however, to be permitted to read aloud to him. That privilege enabled me to have a considerably closer personal relationship with the Justice than the post itself called for and also brought about that special bonus that I would otherwise have missed in my year of service with him: I became privy to the existence of the Justice's Black Book, his most personal record of his legal and general reading and the nearest thing to a diary that he kept. After his death, his executor, John Palfrey, had facsimile copies made of the Black Book and sent one to each of his secretaries, with the appropriate stipulation that none of us permit publication or duplication of it. The original is kept with the Holmes papers at the Harvard Law School Library, where it is available for examination by scholars.

I had had no previous hint of any possibility that I might spend a year with the great Justice. He was the revered and beloved idol of students and faculty. I had not even known how his secretaries were chosen. Frankfurter, who had become my friend as well as my teacher, had with proper delicacy not mentioned his role as the selector of secretaries for both Holmes and Justice Louis D. Brandeis, much less that he had chosen me. No other honor or piece of good fortune has been such a source of delight for me as was that enchanted year I spent with Holmes beginning in October 1929. And no other relationship has had a deeper or more lasting influence.

Later that October, I was attending the performance of some now-forgotten play. At intermission, I witnessed a number of men hurrying up the aisles and to the exits, leaving their companions behind. In the lobby, there was an air of agitation, and a great many men were waiting impatiently in lines that had formed at the few public telephones. Others dashed out to the sidewalk. Only when I saw the next day's newspaper did I realize that I had witnessed the herald of the Great Depression in the stock market crash of October 24. The anxious men must have been trying to reach their brokers in attempts to salvage something from the margin accounts that were a feature of the prosperous late 1920s and their constantly rising bull markets. The news made little impression on me at the time, because I was completely preoccupied with a wholly different world.

On the appointed Friday earlier in the month I had presented myself, filled with awe and admiration, at 1720 I Street, N.W., Justice Holmes's brownstone house in Washington. To enter the house and to share its daily activities with the Justice was to step into an H. G. Wells time machine. Within the first week or two in the course of casual conversation—if any conversation in that house could be called casual—Holmes had referred to his lifelong friends Harry and Will James. I, of course, had never thought of Henry James and William James as Harry and Will, and had never heard anyone use those nicknames easily.

Holmes was born in 1841. When he was a small boy, his grandmother told him of having seen the British troops enter Boston. The British commander, Lord Howe, had commandeered the Holmes house on Beacon Hill for his headquarters. The Justice also spoke frequently of the Civil War, in the course of which he had been wounded three times.

As a youth of twenty, Holmes had volunteered at the start of the war. His four years of service were an immense influence on his life. During my year with him he mentioned on its anniversary each of the major engagements in which he had fought, such as Ball's Bluff, Antietam, and Fredericksburg. We even drove several times to Fort Stevens, the site on the northern outskirts of Washington where Holmes, a seasoned veteran, had impulsively shouted to the incautious Lincoln, "Get down, you fool!" Skirmishers of Jubal Early's raiders had, late in the war, approached that close to a largely undefended capital. Holmes, on leave in the city, had been among those hastily gathered to repel the attack, and Lincoln had thought it his duty to be at the place of peril.

Holmes frequently used martial terms or military metaphors in ordinary speech, in formal addresses, and even in his legal opinions. For example, when President Franklin Roosevelt, during the very first hectic days of his presidency, called on Holmes on the latter's birthday, Holmes's admonition to the President was, "Form your battalions and fight, sir." It was my brother Donald who, as Holmes's secretary at the time, had the good fortune to be present on that stirring occasion. But I recall only the more mundane use of military expressions, such as Holmes's remark about a prominent figure, bested in an argument, that he had "quickly withdrawn his pickets."

Perhaps more lasting in influence on him was the war's demonstration of the courage and capabilities of ordinary men. Holmes had himself come from a privileged elite, but he often said to me that the war had taught him true democracy. He had over and over again witnessed bravery and leadership on the part of simple fellows with little or no education or background.

The I Street house was a hall of history, but Holmes was a far from spectral guide. His gusto, intellectual vigor, and expansive charm were extraordinary. The following summer—he was then eighty-nine—at a formal dinner party, a guest referred to an octogenarian as "feeling her years," and Holmes boomed out, "What's eighty among adults?" Holmes's way with words was such that he could phrase even casual utterances in a form that would cause them to be quoted. I remember that when two of the members of the Harvard Law School faculty, Austin Wakeman Scott and Sayre McNeil, called on him, Holmes sauntered into the room where they waited, fingered their calling cards, and said gaily, "First you shuffle and then you deal. Which is Scott and which McNeil?"

In keeping with the air of times past in the Holmes house, the function of the secretary was rather like that of a nineteenth-century private secretary in upper-class British life. No typing; the Justice permitted no typewriters in the house. All correspondence was in longhand. The manuscripts of Holmes's opinions were accurately described by that word, *manuscripts*, as were the careful notes he took with him to the Saturday conferences of the justices, where cases were decided by vote and majority opinions were assigned to be written.

My legal duties were not onerous. My chief job was the almost daily delivery of oral reports on the numerous petitions for review by the Supreme Court. I also had the routine task of entering in the Justice's bulky docket the names of cases to be argued and assembling the relevant briefs and records that had been sent to him in advance. The docket was used by each justice to jot down observations during oral argument, notes later used in voting on cases and in preparing opinions.

In almost all instances, the Supreme Court has the authority to consider in full only those cases it believes warrant such attention. Each year the Court receives many hundreds of petitions seeking its review (petitions for certiorari) of asserted errors in lower court judgments. The Supreme Court grants somewhat less than five percent of the petitions and then goes on to consider only those cases in full; the rest are denied, letting the lower court judgments stand without Supreme Court review. In reporting on these cases, "bloody certs" in Holmes's pun,* I stood beside the Justice's big desk. While he made notes on an unlined pad for use in voting at the next conference of the Court, I gave the facts of each case, summarized the decision of the lower court and the arguments of counsel, and offered my comments on what I thought was the adequacy or inadequacy of the petition to meet the standards the Court had developed for granting review. Holmes's sense of responsibility was such that, invariably, after my report he leafed through the record to check for himself the accuracy of my summary.

For the cases that the Court did take for full review and in which Holmes wrote an opinion, he seldom called on me for discussion or research. His opinions were uniformly brief. They simply set forth the legal principles he thought to be controlling and the precedent and other authorities he wished to rely upon.

During my service, I managed to bring about a series of changes in the secretary's functions in the Justice's habit-encrusted routine. Chief among these was getting Holmes's permission to let me read aloud to him. In the I Street house, the Justice's study, located on the second floor, was his office, his chambers. (The Court then used to sit in the Old Senate Chamber in the Capitol building, refitted as a courtroom but without separate offices, or chambers, for the members of the Court.) Holmes's study was a large, sunny, book-lined room. The secretary's room, also book-lined, was immediately adjacent and separated from the Justice's office only by sliding doors, which were never closed. His Court work permitting and visitors not preempting his leisure time, it was Holmes's practice at about teatime on most afternoons to relax for an hour or so by reading for pleasure. From my adjoining room I could see him stretched out at those moments in his easy chair, often dozing and letting the book slip to the floor. In

* The pun relates to the alleged "bloody shirts" provocatively waved by lynching parties as supposed evidence of rape in Reconstruction days.

consequence, he would lose his place and, when he woke, show his annoyance at having to locate the proper page and passage. I felt sure that he would find being read to a much more satisfactory way to relax.

His wife, who had died the winter before, had read to him in the evenings. Neither my duties nor my privileges included staying with him at night. Both the Justice and I were at pains to respect the professional nature of my job. The relationship was, however, necessarily informal and close. It had been traditional for the Holmes secretaries to be a part of the household. Each working day, I ate lunch and had tea at the Justice's. This meant that when the Court was not in session and he was therefore at home for lunch, I ate with him. That pattern was rarely broken, even when the Justice had guests for luncheon—except for close women friends, with whom he preferred a tête-à-tête.

After I became familiar with the Justice's daily habits, the informality of the relationship and my belief that I read well led me to volunteer to read aloud in the afternoons whenever he had a period of leisure. My first offer was refused summarily, almost brusquely. He muttered that it wouldn't work, it was too personal. I was wary of pressing to take over a function that had been Mrs. Holmes's, but I also sensed that he considered it incompatible with the professional status of his secretary.

Fortunately for my project, I learned that one of the Justice's favorite visitors, Sir Esme Howard, the British Ambassador, was read to by his secretary. I mentioned this to the Justice in as casual a manner as I could manage. What I did not include was the fact that Sir Esme's secretary was his son. Enlisting Sir Esme's assistance, I urged him to tell the Justice how relaxing and pleasant he found the reading to be. Before long the Justice asked if I was still willing to try reading aloud. Somewhat gruffly, he then added his original comment—that he didn't think it would work. Aunt Lila's early schooling stood me in good stead. It did work.

Thereafter I read to Holmes almost every weekday late afternoon. When the Court was not in session, we would read for two or three hours if work on his opinions was not heavy and we were not interrupted by a privileged visitor. Even on Court days, we often got in an hour or so of reading after his return. That was a measure of his astonishing vigor in his late eighties and of his avidity for the written word. When he was in his usual high spirits a regular greeting on coming back from the Court was, "Shall we have some culture?" or, perhaps, "Will it be murder, or shall we improve our minds?" The reference to "murder" was in recognition of his frequent indulgence in mystery stories.

And so, reading aloud became a normal part of the duties of his secretaries from then on. I was also able to see to it that the reading aloud continued even during the Court's summer recess. Normally, the secretaries had the summer off and the Justice went on to his summer place in Beverly Farms, Massachusetts. Realizing that he would be alone during the summer, I persuaded him to let me continue my duties at Beverly Farms. Since the Justice's workload decreased markedly in the summer, there was time for scenic drives about the North Shore and for visits by friends. There was also much more time for reading aloud.

When Holmes retired, in 1932, the succession of secretaries continued—my brother Donald was among them—and they read to him for hours on end. And when the spring of 1933 brought a group of us former secretaries back to Washington as New Dealers, the hours were still further increased. For such a purpose we found time in our busy schedules to take turns reading to him at night. His Black Book lists of books read became longer than ever.

Once I began reading aloud to him, the Justice made no secret of the existence of the Black Book and of his entry in it of books he was currently reading, but I knew little else about it until after his death. The Black Book is a sturdily made, unlined notebook with stiff black covers. The pages are 8½ × 11 inches. The contents are 162 pages of detailed notations of Holmes's prodigious scholarly research, the earliest dating from 1871 and the latest from 1897, plus annual lists of the titles of books that comprised his general reading from 1881 until his death, in March 1935. With the lists are occasional diarylike personal notes.

Following his youthful valiant service in the Civil War, Holmes had studied at Harvard Law School, from which he graduated in 1866. He then practiced law in Boston (without much liking the practice), edited Kent's *Commentaries*, taught two law courses at Harvard College, wrote five annual articles for the *American Law Review* on the origins of the common law, and used the articles as the basis of the Lowell Lectures that he delivered at Harvard in the fall of 1880. His scholarly research in those years, embodied in elaborate notes in the Black Book, culminated in the spring of 1881 with the publication of his great work, *The Common Law*.

In the course of time, that volume on the history and development of Anglo-American law was to change the way American and British judges, lawyers, and law teachers saw the nature and function of what they call the "common law," that is, judge-made law. Holmes taught them that the common law was the ever-changing product of society—the result of long years of social and political history—rather than a fixed body of principles justified, and somehow created, by logic and the ideals of justice. Today, with so much of our law imposed by legislative acts, the scope of the common law is much restricted. But Holmes's innovative insight is still valid: our law is the product of the society it rules.

Holmes's meticulous and detailed recording of his research notes makes it possible to know just when he read most of the treatises and original source material that are digested in the Black Book. These entries make it plain that the original purpose of the book was to be a compendium of his working research notes for a comprehensive examination of the history and development of the common law. But Holmes continued his scholarly practice of taking full notes of works of legal history well after the publication of *The Common Law*. Indeed, new duties called for their own kind of legal research: Holmes became a professor at the Harvard Law School in January 1882 and a member of the Massachusetts Supreme Court in December of that year. The last two instances of full scholarly annotations in the Black Book, both of volumes dealing with early German civil law, bear the notations "Read May–August 1897" and "Began Aug/97."

Even a cursory examination of the Black Book reveals that it was an extremely personal document. The volume is organized quite formally; in some ways it is reminiscent of a printed book. But the personal, even intimate, stamp of the initial pages makes it clear that it was to be an entirely private book—obviously limited to an edition of a single copy.

The first two inscribed pages are facing. On the left-hand page appears the author's name in large, flowing script, whose broad letters seem to have been formed with a brush. The capital letters are half an inch high; the effect is like that of the display type on a title page. Beneath his name, in smaller script, Holmes had written "Boston" and "July 1876," again suggesting the title page of a printed book. On the second, and facing, page, Holmes recorded the birth and marriage dates of his parents; next, under the heading "Children," he added his own name and birth date and those of his sister and brother. Under his name is the later entry of his wife's, with her birth date and the date of their marriage. For each individual—except for himself—he later added the date of death; in the case of his wife, even the hour.

The volume has a table of contents (labeled "Index") following the two preliminary pages. Each scholarly entry has the topic, or the title of a book, written in large, cursive characters like a chapter heading. The annual lists of books read usually appear in double columns. On the last page is a list of the Justice's Supreme Court secretaries.

Blessed with a beautiful hand, Holmes was led by his sense of order, his neatness, and his taste to make his notebook a calligraphic work of art. The creative effort invested in crafting the notebook seems to have been solely for the gratification of its designer and author. The entire spirit and style of the book make it seem as private as personal correspondence, as a packet of old letters. The gilt initials "O.W.H." stamped on the spine mark the little book as private property. For Holmes there was no incongruity in using the Black Book to record scholarly notes and personal items. The two types of material were equally private in his mind.

Holmes's strong sense of privacy led him to destroy the manuscripts and proofs of his Court opinions. He wanted no collectors or biographers to have early drafts of his work. Under his watchful eye, one of my duties was to burn in the fireplace of his study the evidence of revision and correction. He wanted to be judged by the final product; how he got there was his own affair. Here, pride and the wish for privacy were closely identified, if not identical. He took pleasure in his gift of expression and took pains to perfect his writing. As scholar and judge, he had over a long life been able to have his say on many topics of significance to him. As he once said to me, what he wanted to say was in his *printed* work.

The ritual burning was, however, certainly in part the private person's distaste for being pawed over, for having the shards of a daily life pounced upon as mementos. During my year with Holmes, the student treasurer of the *Harvard Law Review* kept as a souvenir the Justice's check for an annual subscription. Holmes was angered by this presumptuous intrusion into his personal if routine affairs. He was insistent that I retrieve the missing check, which I did despite my sympathy for the student.

Before I came to work for him, Justice Holmes had made it his practice personally to acknowledge all letters—literally all letters—and he had done so by hand. Similarly, he had himself drawn all his own checks and personally clipped the interest coupons from the bonds in his safe-deposit box. At about the same time that I began to read aloud to him, Holmes consented to my answering letters of no particular importance from strangers. I was also permitted to fill out the checks for household bills and keep a running account in his checkbook, plus accompany him on trips to the bank, where, under his watchful Yankee eye, I would clip the coupons.

My adequate fulfillment of these chores that he had previously regarded either as too personal or too menial to be delegated made me eligible for the far more intimate task of taking part in the ritual of his entering authors and titles in the Black Book. One afternoon, as we finished a volume that we had been reading, Holmes asked me to fetch the Black Book for him so that he could record the completed volume. Though I had seen it before, that was the first time I had the book in my hands. Soon thereafter it became routine for me, without being asked, to bring him the Black Book when we finished a volume so the author and title could be recorded. I did the same at the beginning of our day together when he entered the titles of the books he had read to himself the night before. Next, I would hold the volume to be recorded and read out the title and the author's name as Holmes made the entry. Later secretaries made the entries for him.

I was for a time puzzled as to why anyone would keep complete lists of books of every kind as he read them year after year. My personal knowledge of Holmes and my careful study of the Black Book convince me that the answer in his case is a combination of accident and habit. His first list, for 1881, was not complete—Holmes had written at the top "Novels be not noted"—and was evidently a version of his scholarly practice of noting for future reference his serious readings, mostly books on the law. But he also added some purely personal items, such as "My book—The Common Law—published March '81" and that he had read "Memoirs of Casanova, 10 vols." The entries were soon expanded to include novels and all other books, much as some people pile up playbills or concert programs. After a year or two, habit took over.

Whatever the explanation, the lists record the wide sweep of the great Justice's intellectual and cultural interests. They also supply a unique measure of American high culture during the last two decades of the nineteenth century and the first three and a half of this one. Certainly I know of no other full record of the reading habits of an American intellectual of that period. Apart from indecipherable entries, his list for 1929 shows that before I reported for work that October, he had read his friend Francis Hackett's *Henry VIII*, Shakespeare's *Henry VIII*, Stephen Vincent Benét's *John Brown's Body*, Norman Douglas's *South Wind*, Shakespeare's *Richard III* and *King John*, several of Dashiell Hammett's books, a volume of history by Joseph Redlich, a translation of Mallarmé, a book on Spinoza, J. W. N. Sullivan's *The Bases of Modern Science,* a French text called *L'Ombre de la Croix*, a book about Rasputin, Lewis Mumford's *Herman Melville* (which had just been published), *The World's Best Short Stories of 1928*, Logan Pearsall Smith's *The English Language*, a volume by André Maurois, and C. W. Ferguson's *The Confusion of Tongues*.

When I arrived on the scene, the Justice was reading his friend Walter Lippmann's *A Preface to Morals*, which I didn't get around to for a year or more. Then came a book about Erasmus, and Erich

Maria Remarque's *All Quiet on the Western Front*, followed by my suggestions of titles by Saki and Elinor Wylie. These last entries demonstrate Holmes's receptiveness to new paths of reading, and a fair number of the recorded volumes are offerings I made to him of books I then cherished. Saki caught on more than I remember, for Holmes lists "7 vols." I also introduced him to T. S. Eliot, bringing him my volumes of Eliot's poems published to that date and *For Lancelot Andrewes*. Holmes preferred Eliot the critic to Eliot the poet. I also supplied Max Beerbohm's *Zuleika Dobson* and E. M. Forster's *The Celestial Omnibus*. In addition, I lent the Justice my leather-bound copy of Paul Morand's *Magie Noire*, given to me in Giverny during the previous summer. As I did not dare read French to the Justice, he read the Morand to himself. We read Oliver La Farge's *Laughing Boy* together, though I can't remember whether I suggested it. It has long been a favorite of mine, but, as the La Farges were friends of his, it is likely that this was among the treats the Justice presented to *me*.

Most of the Justice's reading, even after I began reading aloud to him, was done on his own during weekends and at night. True to his youthful bent for philosophy, he read Alfred North Whitehead's *Process and Reality*, noting in the 1929 list that he had read only 182 pages of it. Also that year, he read a work by John Dewey, *The Quest for Certainty*. While I was with him, the Justice read *The Nicomachean Ethics* of Aristotle in translation and a book about Voltaire. And in the field of legal history, which was the object of his dedicated scholarship for so many years, he read Sir Henry Maine's *Ancient Laws* in the new edition of 1930. But the same period of 1929 and 1930 also included such diverse works as Julia Peterkin's *Scarlet Sister Mary*, Jane Austen's *Emma*, J. W. Allen's *Political Thought in the Sixteenth Century*, Claude Bowers's *The Tragic Era*, Ernest Hemingway's *A Farewell to Arms*, a book by Roark Bradford and one by H. W. Nevinson, James G. Huneker's volume of art and music criticism *Promenades of an Impressionist*, and Austin H. Clark's *Nature Narratives* (Clark, a noted biologist, was, as I recall, a Holmes relative of whom the Justice always spoke affectionately).

As the weeks wore on, I read aloud two volumes of Horace Walpole's letters from a set on Holmes's shelves. Holmes read or reread to himself

Anna Karenina. I read aloud Edith Hamilton's *The Greek Way*, but also some P. G. Wodehouse, a great favorite of his, and something by Somerset Maugham—I've forgotten the title and can't make it out in Holmes's script in the Black Book. He read two biographies of Theodore Roosevelt and several books by friends—two by Owen Wister, three by Laski. In mock desperation he once wrote to Laski that Laski could write books faster than he, Holmes, could read them.

I remember the Justice's warm praise of a solid but readily accessible study I read to him that was a precursor of later examinations of cultural influences, *The Religious Background of American Culture* by Thomas Cuming Hall. In a lighter vein was A. P. Herbert's *More Misleading Cases*—lighter, that is, for lawyers. In addition, he read Thackeray's *English Humor of the Eighteenth Century* and perhaps reread Laurence Sterne's *A Sentimental Journey* and Lamb's *Essays of Elia*. That winter the Justice went back to Emerson and recorded that he read two volumes of essays. Of the then-current popular authors, he read James Weldon Johnson and James Truslow Adams.

The lists for 1929 and 1930 take up but a single page of the Black Book. In the Justice's final years, when he was no longer on the Court and had more leisure, the lists grow longer. But the 1929 and 1930 lists are representative of his years on the bench.

For some reason, these entries do not record the Justice's reading of Thucydides in the original, which he began while I was with him. This extraordinary intellectual effort is at once a measure of Holmes's mental vigor in his late years and of his self-discipline in matters of the mind. He admitted that he had frequent recourse to the dictionary in coping with the notoriously difficult Greek text and even an occasional look at a translation. When asked by a visitor why he had undertaken this burdensome task, he replied, with typical roguish humor, "When I appear before *le Bon Dieu*, if He should ask, 'Holmes, can you recite on Thucydides?' what a fool I'd feel to have to reply, 'No, Sire, I've never read him.' " Ironically for this lifelong agnostic, the very last item in the great lists of books read is, in 1935, Thornton Wilder's *Heaven's My Destination*.

For quite personal reasons, I must make some special mention of one lovely book. Some perceptive friend sent the Justice Helen Waddell's *The Wandering Scholars*, a delightful account of the medieval poets, troubadors, and other literate wayfarers who traveled about Europe. Both the Justice and I were charmed by the book. He frequently took it from me to see the Vulgate texts of some of the verses quoted, rightly preferring his own examination to my pronunciation. And when he was alone he often read again parts I had read to him. Soon after I had left the Justice to begin the practice of law in Boston, I discovered a sequel—Waddell's *Medieval Latin Lyrics*. I promptly sent a copy to Holmes. The following March 8, his ninetieth birthday, he spoke very briefly on the radio—the only time he ever did so. I heard the talk in Felix Frankfurter's house in Cambridge, where a number of Frankfurter's friends had assembled to celebrate this momentous event. To my surprise and joy, the moving few words concluded with a quotation from my gift: "And so I end with a line from a Latin poet who uttered the message more than fifteen hundred years ago: 'Death plucks my ear and says, "Live—I am coming." ' "

For me, Holmes's never-flagging appetite for belles lettres and the major works of general literature were the chief mark of his great cultivation. I don't recall his ever mentioning music or musicians. On the other hand, he cared a good deal about etchings and had a collection of his own, housed in sliding flat trays. He enjoyed showing them to knowledgeable friends and was pleased to give Justice Harlan F. Stone, a complete novice on the subject of etchings, primerlike instruction on the art and the artists Holmes collected—particularly Nicolaes Maes and Anders Zorn, different though they are. He made fairly frequent trips to discuss prints with the curator of prints at the Library of Congress.

Holmes was, I believe, rather indifferent to paintings and sculpture. He had, to be sure, the knowledge of art of an educated and well-traveled man of his times—and a perceptive eye, as a casual remark of his indicates. Encountering Felix Frankfurter's fiancée at a gathering a few weeks after he had first met her, he failed at first to recognize her as she came up to him. Gallantly, and most aptly, on admitting he had forgotten her name, he added, "But the face is by Luini."

While I was with him, he sat for a portrait bust, which brought out a few rather trite and even belittling remarks about sculptors. I accompanied him on two visits to the Saint-Gaudens memorial tomb of the wife of his friend Henry Adams in Rock Creek Cemetery in George-town. But, though he spoke admiringly and with emotion of the sculpture, the journeys were essentially sentimental rather than aesthetic. We made no visits to museums or the houses of collectors, and he read but one book of art criticism while I was with him. The lists do show that later he read Vasari's *Lives of the Painters*. He was, I believe, telling me what he regarded as a fact about his feeling for art when he recounted a remark he had made to his nephew. Edward Holmes had taken the post of director of the Boston Museum of Fine Arts. The Justice had jollied him about this, asking him why he had taken the position, as "no Holmes ever had any taste."

Neither was theatergoing important to him. I recall no comments on the delights of the stage—though on one occasion I had no trouble in persuading the Justice to let a group of us take him to a matinee performance of a Marx Brothers musical at the National Theater. A law school classmate of mine and two young women friends made up the rest of the party. Holmes's chauffeur drove us to a side entrance, the walk to our box was short, and he obviously enjoyed himself immensely. A delightful companion, he had us all back to the house for tea and was then genuinely astounded to learn that, as one of our party knew someone in the cast, we could have gone backstage after the performance. The theater seemed to him, I believe, a glamorous but distant world. Serious drama may indeed have been a domain of literature, but, like the other performing arts, the theater itself was not part of his cultural life. With what appeared to be a touch of pride in his ability to enjoy the pleasures of the vulgar, he spoke more than once of having gone alone at times to burlesque shows and of having said to a stranger in the same row, "Thank God my tastes are low!"

Neither Boston nor Washington was a great theater town in Holmes's day, and in any case his scholarly dedication as a younger man left little time for the theater as a diversion. I recall his telling me of a Boston saying, presumably of his younger days, to the effect that "the Bard on the boards is a bore." He said this by way of illustrating the poor quality of Shakespearean performances then in comparison to the much-improved presentation of Shakespeare since, of which he was well aware. I do not mean to portray Holmes as having disliked the theater. But surely he was no theater buff, which further emphasizes the importance of books to him and helps to explain why the annual reading lists were so faithfully kept up year after year. And, bookworm though he was, it was the contents that mattered. He was not a collector of first editions, had no rare books in his library, and did not read about the great printers or the art of the book.

While the Black Book leads me to marvel again at the volume and scope of Justice Holmes's general reading, the entries I have been describing by no means fully reflect the part literature played in his life. His normal conversation was filled with literary allusions certainly not limited to the books he was then reading. Browning, Carlyle, and Ruskin had been major influences on his general outlook. It was Ruskin the moralist rather than Ruskin the aesthetician to whom Holmes paid homage: Holmes was much taken with Ruskin's contention that honest workmanship called for full ornamentation even on the sides of a church tower that could be seen only from the spine of the roof. Carlyle was valued for hardheaded realism, embodied in the famous dictum, "By God! She'd better," elicited by Margaret Fuller's announcement that she had accepted the universe. And Browning meant much to Holmes, especially for the poet's mastery of the sensuous richness of medieval court life and the subtle intricacies of Catholic theology. The Justice quoted from and bade me read "The Bishop Orders His Tomb" and "Bishop Blougram's Apology." His literary references and quotations, invariably apt, facilitated rather than impeded the flow of conversation. Once, to emphasize both the probity of the diligent worker and his enjoyment of interesting work, Holmes quoted an entry in Darwin's diary lamenting a plethora of social engagements: "The future is bleak, pleasure every day."

Holmes's use of the Black Book to note purely personal items, beginning with the family records and continuing with the notations of 1881 about the publication of his magnum opus, was long-lasting. In the final decade of his life, at the top of most of the annual listings of books read, appear observations of the emerging signs of spring— the first bloodroot, the blossoming of the cherry trees at the Tidal Basin, the flowering of the dogwood. Those for the spring of 1930 have a particular resonance for me, for I was with this remarkable man when he saw his first bluebird, his first robin, and his first crocus of that year.

I like to think that the changes in secretarial duties that I was able to initiate led, two years later, to the most striking change of all. The lists for 1932 and the remaining few years are in the handwriting of the secretaries. As increasing leisure gave more time for reading— primarily reading aloud—the burden of entering authors and titles also increased. The secretary having once been granted access to the Black Book could be trusted next to write in it also. By then the secretaries were even permitted to enter their own names in the list on the book's final page.

It was this increasingly full access to the Black Book on the part of the secretaries that led John Palfrey, the Justice's executor, as I have mentioned, in June 1936 to send each secretary a facsimile copy for his personal library.

I think I can pull together some of the lessons that I learned during my year with Justice Holmes. They were lessons of character and of culture and, less important, of the law itself.

When I served with the Justice, he was for some weeks acting Chief Justice. William Howard Taft, who was the Chief Justice when I reported to Holmes, suffered a stroke and was completely incapacitated. Holmes, as senior Justice, became the acting Chief Justice. Among his new duties was assigning cases to his fellows for the writing of opinions, and he made a point of assigning to himself the least interesting and most burdensome cases. In particular, I recall his long hours with the bulky record of a case entitled *Chicago Drainage District* v. *Illinois*. The issue was one of conflicting title claims. It came before the Supreme Court as the trial tribunal under the Constitution, for suits involving states or foreign nations are part of the original jurisdiction of the Supreme Court; that is, the Supreme Court is responsible for the very first stages of the controversy and must pass on facts as well as law.

The Chicago Drainage District case, which had been referred to a master (an official appointed by the Court) for the taking of testimony, involved many volumes of the printed record, each as thick as a metropolitan telephone directory. Holmes sat in his easy chair with a couple of piles of these volumes three or more feet high on the floor beside him. The books were heavy, and the dry facts must have seemed interminable: the lesson of Spartan devotion to duty could not be missed. In all respects, this lesson was more important to me than the limited legal issues involved.

I saw the Justice at ease and at work. At Court he belied his age by his attentiveness and the care with which he inscribed in his docket book those aspects of the case being argued that seemed to him important. Often these notes were full enough to be the basis for his opinion when the case was assigned to him. Nonetheless, when later he was writing an opinion or deciding how to vote, he would meticulously reexamine at home the briefs and records case by case.

Justice Holmes's drafting of his opinions followed a long-practiced routine. It took place during the weeks when the Court was in recess, the normal practice being for it to sit for two weeks and then to adjourn for two weeks. Holmes conscientiously devoted each morning of the adjournment period to working on opinions. Seated at his desk, he would review the docket notes he had made at the time of argument and verify from the record points he took to be decisive. He would then consult the briefs, frequently referring to the authority cited in them. My secretarial function here was often limited to carrying volumes of law reports to the Justice's desk from the surrounding shelves.

When preliminary examination of the record and briefs had been completed, the scene frequently changed. Holmes would finish the actual drafting of his opinion at an old-fashioned standing writing desk. This desk, the only one of its kind I've ever seen, is now an honored relic in the office of the dean of the Harvard Law School. The standing desk faced one of the large windows in the Justice's study. Framed against the light coming through the window, the erect, bulky figure of the old man made a striking silhouette. Almost invariably, the writing at this desk was accompanied by the smoking of a Havana cigar. Holmes relished good Cuban cigars, which were sent to him in periodic shipments by S. S. Pierce & Company of Boston. My most striking visual memory of the Justice is of him working at his desk. Above his head the cloud of cigar smoke created an aureole. The play of light and shadow was as in a painting by an Old Master. The contrast, I remember, brought Rembrandt to mind.

My recollections of the Justice contain many such pictorial images. Always known for his good looks, Holmes remained extremely handsome in old age, a figure six feet tall, rosy-pink and white in coloring. His full head of gleaming white hair and his equally white handlebar moustache accented his wholesomely ruddy flesh tones. Unfailingly well turned out, he was never less than good to look at.

Holmes taught by example, only occasionally by precept. His code of conduct was simple: duty was its main ingredient. As I spent day after day in his company, it became clear that his private life was bounded by the performance of duty and by adherence to intellectual rigor. High-mindedness in personal relations went without saying. It was disclosed only by the way he lived his own life and by his comments when others "blotted their copybooks." He had grown up with patrician patterns of conduct, which had become as natural to him as his good manners. To women, his courtliness was a blend of traditional gallantry and a strong championship—not then at all traditional—of their independence. His casual conversation in the privacy of his study never bore the slightest condescension toward women.

As an adherent to a code of conduct that stressed moral and physical courage, fierce independence of spirit, respect for the rights of others, and a lively feeling for community and for country, Justice Holmes had a deep pride and a strong sense of honor. Years after the slight, he still smarted from Theodore Roosevelt's clumsy failure to recognize that Holmes was his own man. In the Northern Securities case, one of the early cases after Holmes had become a member of the Supreme Court, the new Justice disappointed the President who had appointed him. Holmes decided that the antitrust laws did not apply. Subsequently he learned that an angry TR had said he could carve a justice with more backbone out of a banana. Holmes's indignation, still smoldering more than a quarter of a century later, was the product not only of wounded pride but of scorn for the vulgar assumption that appointment to the Supreme Court brought with it political obligations. The President's hostile remark implied a motive for nomination that could not be squared with Holmes's patrician code.

Holmes had a long memory for instances of bad manners that verged on breaches of duty to one's fellow man. A rude remark by Andrew Lang, the nineteenth-century British writer, rankled even longer than TR's jibe. The incident occurred when Holmes as a young man was on his first visit to England. He had been asked to an evening at a great house. There he was introduced to Lang, who was "draped," as Holmes put it, over a mantel. Lang's response on being introduced to the young American lawyer was, "Oh, you're the son of the man who writes those dreadful novels."* Holmes's natural anger at the incivility was in large part kept alive all those years by his annoyance with himself for having failed to come up with an apt riposte. In 1930 he still had not found a satisfactory answer and fumed over the rudeness.

In his daily life Holmes demonstrated that consideration for others was a primary element of his code of conduct. Never moralistic in tone, he lived nonetheless by a personal code that no moralist could rightly disapprove. He was at once informal with and considerate of those who served him—the incomparable Mary Donellan, his waitress and parlor maid; Annie, his longtime cook; Charlie, formerly the driver of his carriage, turned uncertain chauffeur; and Thomas, his Court messenger. The great are not always gracious to their minions. Holmes was unfeignedly so to his small circle of devoted household servants. For him, right conduct was all of a piece. Manners and morals were one.

The Justice told proudly of a reproof administered by Mrs. Holmes to President Wilson, a Virginian who reintroduced Jim Crow segregation into Washington's mores. At one of the annual dinners given by the President for the members of the Supreme Court, a waiter spilled soup on the starched shirt front of one of the justices. The unfortunate black waiter was roundly censured by the President. The

---

*The reference was, of course, to the Justice's father, Dr. Oliver Wendell Holmes, Sr., best known in the medical world for his essay on puerperal fever and to the public at large for his literary work—popular verse like "Old Ironsides," equally accessible essays like "The Autocrat of the Breakfast Table," and the romantic novels like *Elsie Venner* and *The Guardian Angel* that gave rise to Lang's slighting remark.

no less unfortunate diner was Justice William R. Day, notoriously shy. As the host alternated between apologies and beratings, Day became more and more embarrassed. The situation was dramatically resolved by Mrs. Holmes's remarking quietly, "Mr. President, there are some things one doesn't talk about."

The Justice's respect for the feelings of individuals was matched by his sense of community. He said with conviction that the only debt he paid with pleasure was his taxes, for with them he bought civilization. When he made the statement, startling to some of his listeners, he would continue by enumerating police and fire protection, street lighting, road and sewage maintenance—all the services provided by community governance. And in his will, this soldier-patriot and public servant left the bulk of his estate to the United States, saying simply of this provision that most of his income had come from that source, so it was fitting that the residue return there.

No young lawyer who spent a year with this model of the upright man could fail to wish to emulate him in conduct and character. Certainly Holmes was the most profound influence in my life. Noble in spirit but never priggish, devoted to the taxing duties of his high calling yet lusty and playful, enormously cultivated and learned yet readily approachable and informal, he was for me a paragon of virtue and of charm.

5

THE MAKING OF A
NEW DEALER

My participation in the New Deal began one day in the spring of 1933, when I received a telegram from Felix Frankfurter, my former law teacher. "On basis national emergency," as he put it in the telegram, I must accept the position that Jerome Frank had offered me a few days earlier.

Frank had been chosen to be the general counsel of the Agricultural Adjustment Administration, the agency then being set up to plan and carry out the New Deal's farm programs. Just the year before, I had started to work at Cotton, Franklin, Wright & Gordon, a large Wall Street law firm, and I felt qualms at abruptly pulling out of the work assigned to me. I had therefore delayed my reply, wondering whether I should ask Frank if I could put off joining his staff for a few weeks while I tied up the loose ends.

Frankfurter's peremptory call to duty was most welcome, for it disposed of any reason to delay. Words depreciate rapidly. In March 1933, the term "national emergency" was not a limp cliché. Even now, in the context of that telegram, the words stir me and bring back the almost palpable sense of crisis. In simple truth, the Great Depression had brought on a national emergency. A summons in the terms Frankfurter used carried weight in most quarters, including the senior partners of Wall Street law firms. I delayed no longer and departed for Washington a few days later with my wife and six-year-old stepson.

From "Black Thursday" of October 24, 1929, when panic seized traders on the floor of the New York Stock Exchange, until Franklin D. Roosevelt's inauguration on March 4, 1933, there had been an almost uninterrupted downward spiral in the economic life and social cohesion of the country. Americans in general felt helpless and increasingly bitter as the scope of the disaster widened and its pace quickened.

When Roosevelt assumed office, commerce and industry on any national scale had virtually stopped. Five thousand banks had failed, thirty-eight states (there were only forty-eight then) had closed all their banks, United States Steel had laid off its entire full-time work force. The New York Stock Exchange, the Kansas City Board of Trade, and the Chicago Board of Trade were closed.

Unemployment was somewhere between 13 million and 17 million out of a total work force of probably less than 60 million. Additional millions on the farms were destitute, while unsold grain was piled in the open and the cotton carryover reached 13 million bales. State and municipal funds for relief—never adequate—were near exhaustion where they had not already run out months before.

Roosevelt's inauguration followed a campaign that held out high hopes and promised long-overdue reforms. Once in office, by dint of his dynamic personal leadership and an extensive program of governmental intervention, he turned popular hopes into enthusiastic support. The turnabout in morale was unbelievably swift. His inaugural address attacked fear as the only thing to fear, promised immediate action, and called for unity and governmental initiative on a wartime basis. The next day, Sunday, March 5, he summoned Congress into special session and declared a bank "holiday"—a comfortingly light-hearted word—throughout the nation. When Congress assembled, it passed the Emergency Banking Law in a single day. On the second Sunday of his administration, Roosevelt told the people, in his first "Fireside Chat" over nationwide radio, that they could now safely return their savings to the banks. The following day, March 13, the banks began to reopen and from the outset deposits far exceeded withdrawals. Miraculously, all semblance of panic was over. Succeeding weeks and months brought increased public support, as there came from the White House during the "Hundred Days" a stream of messages to Congress recommending far-reaching legislation, proclamations, and pronouncements that dwarf the opening months of all other administrations in our history.

It was, therefore, to a confident and lively capital that I went as a New Deal recruit. I was then twenty-eight years old. A new America was in the making. Walter Lippmann wrote on March 15 that in two weeks Roosevelt had accomplished a recapture of morale comparable to the "second battle of the Marne in the summer of 1916." By achieving this turnabout in morale, Roosevelt made it possible for the nation to undertake on a united basis the vast projects needed to stem the ravages of the Great Depression, whose impact continued to be felt throughout the span of the New Deal.

My becoming a New Dealer had not been a matter of course. Like many of my contemporaries, I had found that my social and political values were tested and altered by the Great Depression. The vast misery resulting from the economic dislocation it caused during its first several years forced my sense of social responsibility to become more concrete, where it had once been abstract. The seriousness of my new social commitment in turn required changed political beliefs. The threat of a breakdown in our democratic social order aroused my sense of patriotism and hastened my readiness for true political commitment. As Roosevelt suggested, the country's inability to provide the bare essentials of a functioning society threatened national survival as surely as would an invading enemy. We were faced with a threat to the continued existence of the world as we had known it.

My views have altered less in the intervening half century than they did during the early Depression years, especially 1931 and 1932. I shall try to describe those early major changes and what caused them.

My moral code before 1931 had been highly personal and quite formalistic. Young men of my generation tended to be self-conscious about matters of belief and principle. If asked, I would have said that my code consisted of honor, loyalty, pride, an aversion to exploitation of others, and independence. Of course, these are still prominent elements in my code of ethics, but I can now say that such generalities mean little in terms of guidance for one's daily conduct and in how one meets people. A not too uncharitable characterization of my life at that period of my youth could well be: The Progress of a Prig.

To be sure, along with these primary personal attitudes I had a secondary and vague sense of sympathy for those less fortunate than I. And I took it for granted that "good works" (not specific) were obligatory for self-respecting people. It was also, I believed, a necessary though relatively minor function of any decent society to make some institutionalized provision for the needy. Though this latter went without saying, it also went without much sense of responsibility on my part to see whether that function was carried out. My sense of social responsibility was complacently restricted. And I think this was pretty much the content of the social gospel of the churchgoing homeowners in the modest Baltimore neighborhood where I grew up. Decent social responsibility was to see that no one starved, that the sick could have access to hospital—at least on a charity basis—and that the homeless had a shelter. This was hardly much improvement over the Poor Laws of the nineteenth century, and was most inadequate for the catastrophic ills that came with the Great Depression.

My political development before 1931 was no more advanced than my progress in practical ethics. During my college years at Johns Hopkins, I had scorned politics as the necessary but demeaning scut work that in a wasteful and corrupt way had kept the essential, minimum machinery of government running since Andrew Jackson's day. That machinery, created by the talented, elitist, and far-seeing Founding Fathers, needed little learning and less dedication to operate. The operation was, I thought smugly, performed by a low, parasitic class of citizen-politicians. From time to time they were pushed aside by an aroused citizenry, such as during a war or a spasm of reform. At such times men of substance consented to assume high office in the public interest—men like Lincoln, Teddy Roosevelt, Woodrow Wilson. I shared these complacent views with my most congenial college classmates.

Our negative attitude toward politics reflected the conventional wisdom of our elders. They, too, thought of politics as dirty business. As Maryland Democrats in a traditionally Democratic state, they voted the party ticket in elections, and at such times they did discuss issues and candidates. Yet, for them even presidential elections were mostly a periodic national pastime or spectacle. My close college friends and I had accurately extracted the cynicism or indifference in the political stance most familiar to us. H. L. Mencken, the eminent literary critic who wrote for the Baltimore *Sun* papers, caught the cynical tone perfectly and was a hero of ours.

Our unthinking acceptance of the political indifference of the adults we had known best as we grew up has recently struck me as oddly passive for young people. But this was because political apathy was also the mood of the university. Naturally, as students our excitement in encountering new ideas and the clash of opinion that is scholarship's fruit came predominantly from the faculty. With only two exceptions that I can be sure of—one of them a perennial Socialist candidate for governor of Maryland—the faculty was indifferent to politics.

A climate of privilege made my college generation smug and apolitical until we were hit by the Depression. The world of the typical Johns Hopkins student was seemingly a permanently prosperous one. There were no apparent social challenges, such as those in the latter part of the nineteenth century that had stirred some important European writers, artists, and their bohemian associates to make common cause with the underprivileged. Such American national traumas as the Haymarket riots and the Palmer "Red Scare," the police raids ordered by Attorney General A. Mitchell Palmer in 1919 against foreign-born leftists, had dropped from public memory. I recall few if any references in Johns Hopkins classes to the Soviet revolution, which in no way excited my interest. Equally scant public attention was paid to current instances of systemic ills. I don't remember knowing of the Sacco-Vanzetti case until I went to Harvard Law School, in the fall of 1926. Then it was Professor Frankfurter, and not one of my cultural gurus, who acted as the Zola of that case.

In the 1920s I learned that artists and intellectuals, on the one hand, and business leaders and politicians, on the other, did at times speak scornfully of one another. But I now think it was mostly the bark of habit. In the absence of political controversy, there was no real bite in the tension that marks the symbiotic relationship between the patrons of the arts and the artists themselves.

A feeling of distaste for the narrow, self-interested credo of the usual businessman I knew was among my earliest prejudices. It is relevant here because it was an attitude that was shared by many of my contemporaries at college and at law school and was to be a badge of ardent New Dealers of all ages. In my case and for many of my friends, it was a point of view that under the impact of the Depression was to ripen into full support for New Deal reforms that challenged long-standing industrial and financial practices.

Popular opposition during the Depression to the way business had dominated government policy was not only congenial to my own bent but must have been widespread throughout the country. For me, raised in Baltimore in a family of Democrats, suspicion of Big Business as a Democratic heritage from the Populists was an outlook I took for granted, even though my father and uncles had been businessmen. My distaste for business as a livelihood was reinforced by the intellectual currents of the 1920s.

The avant-garde of the 1920s, in which I considered myself enlisted, was concerned chiefly with wit and iconoclasm. It ignored, where it did not deprecate, the practical world of business and earning a living. The political quietism of the university made cultural realms our preeminent field of intellectual exploration, and, stimulated by the academic atmosphere of free inquiry, we had no hesitation in looking far afield for cultural gurus. Not surprisingly, we chose those who, like our professors, were politically neuter. Indeed, we had little choice. Apart from Mencken, we had only the sages of New York to look to— figures like Dorothy Parker, Alexander Woollcott, music critic Samuel Chotzinoff, and Franklin P. Adams of "The Conning Tower."

I tried every day to get the *New York World*, to keep abreast of concerts, plays, and exhibitions, and I read the Sunday book review sections of the *New York Herald Tribune* and the *New York Times*. Then, also, there were the new *American Mercury* and the occasional copy of *transition*. Mostly I merely read *about* the books and places and occasions that so fascinated me. But there was time actually to read Havelock Ellis, Ronald Firbank, George Gissing, T. S. Eliot's "Prufrock," and the Scott Moncrief translations of Proust. And Baltimore did have touring plays, operas, symphony orchestras, and recital artists.

Occasionally, I was able to get to New York for a weekend. And, in my sophomore year, I was also able to afford passage on the *Veendam* for a summer of museums and cathedrals in France and England— a truncated version of the Grand Tour on a budget of four dollars a day. This was the first trip via Student Third Class, an innovation that made European travel possible for students of modest means like myself.

The limits of my avant-gardism and of my pocketbook are indicated by my failure to buy a copy of Joyce's *Ulysses* when I was in Paris. I was unwilling to run the risk of its confiscation by U.S. Customs, which had banned it as obscene. I could afford only a very occasional bottle of decent wine: Wine, too, was mostly read about.

Even though a part of me was deeply sympathetic to the antiwar literature of the time, I nonetheless served in the Reserve Officers Training Corps throughout my college years. I spent a grueling summer at Camp Meade, became cadet commanding officer, and ended up with a second lieutenant's reserve commission. My martial urge was mixed with economics: The uniform I wore two days a week saved clothing expenses, and there was a small stipend in the last two years.

My reaching out for "advanced" culture was the chief method by which I sought to achieve independence from my family group and early surroundings. At the same time, I avidly sought information and sophistication for quite a different purpose—that of coping with the larger world I was about to enter. Yet I remained as open to the appeal of the noble and high-minded as I had been as a child. I was not jettisoning my early ethical influences. Of my reading while in college, I was most moved and influenced by Somerset Maugham's *Of Human Bondage*. His protagonist's self-imposed mission of helping a young woman who had none of his advantages made him a role model for me.

An entirely different slant on politics was prevalent at Harvard Law School in the late 1920s. Politics was taken seriously. It affected a lawyer's bread and butter. Political trends affected court decisions, legislation, regulations—the stuff of daily life at the bar. Indeed, the Constitution and the whole structure of Anglo-American law were the products of an evolving and highly political system. And it was all too clear that these legal and political usufructs of that system determined the totality of the environment in which we live. To pay no mind to politics, I learned quickly, is to join in putting in the hands of others control over the major determinants of one's life.

But beyond learning of the practical importance of politics for a lawyer, I encountered at Harvard the doctrine of disinterested, dedicated public service. This tenet, which I had thought absent from our country since the early nineteenth century, was not only taught in class but exemplified by members of the faculty. Professor Frankfurter had served in various governmental posts, especially in Washington during World War I, and Professor Edmund Morgan had been a key adviser to Tom Johnson, the reform city manager of Cleveland. We students came to know of a host of judges, members of Congress, governors, and civil servants who were incorruptible, able, and totally committed to the public interest.

High resolve and moral courage seemed to fill the air. Civic duty also summoned the dutiful to oppose injustice, by political activity where appropriate. Again, example was potent instruction. Frankfurter's courageous efforts to save Sacco and Vanzetti were a part of my legal education. Law school thus brought me abreast of political realities. Yet, though I became interested and concerned, I remained a passive member of the electorate.

As Justice Holmes was wont to say of idealistic ventures beyond his own reach, I admired but I did not emulate. I now respected devoted civil servants and those high-minded citizens prepared for the sacrifice involved in public service. But, certainly, my position as the Justice's secretary involved no feeling of sacrifice for the public good. It was a plum and a sojourn in Elysium. And, as a matter of course, I left that post of delight to take a job with a private law firm. It is true that I did consider an offer of a position in Washington with the Antitrust Division of the Department of Justice, but only as a job, not as entry to a career of public service.

From my post as Justice Holmes's secretary, I had taken the job of associate in the Boston law firm of Choate, Hall & Stewart. I took an apartment in Cambridge and went by subway to their offices on State Street. I felt at home, having so recently lived in Cambridge when a student at Harvard Law School. But the advent of the Depression had already made a difference in the mood and general atmosphere of Boston. Along with others who had been concerned only occasionally, and in a minor way, with social conditions, I became increasingly aware of the growing unemployment and economic malaise. One's responsibility for the worsened conditions of others became a recurring topic.

I recall a talk that Frankfurter gave to an assortment of businessmen and bankers who were among Boston's leading citizens. He pleaded with them to make larger contributions to private charities for the benefit of the unemployed and others in financial difficulty. He intimated that this would be a means of forestalling social unrest with its consequent threats to their persons and properties. I found myself, somewhat presumptuously, believing that Frankfurter should have gone beyond a call for personal generosity. From his teaching and my own observations I had become convinced that only large-scale governmental activities could meet the demands of the Depression. I had begun to see the total inadequacy of private charitable activities, and I became acutely aware of the shallowness of my conventional concern for the welfare of others.

Later, when I moved to New York City, I saw daily the growing breadlines and soup kitchens, the shanty towns in parks and vacant lots, the beggars along with men who masked their appeal for alms by "selling" an apple. My continuous personal encounter with mounting misery gave sharp reality to accounts of similar and even worse conditions throughout the country.

Once Roosevelt's candidacy was announced, I was strongly attracted to his banner, but had no thought that I would do more to advance his cause than urge my friends to vote for him. Nonetheless, I had wanted to do something constructive in a private capacity, something that would help in a small way to set things right. That desire to participate led me to offer my legal skills to a small group of young and similarly motivated New York lawyers who had come together to issue a journal for labor lawyers and those representing hard-pressed farmers. The group had assumed a rather grandiose title: The International Juridical Association—the choice of the word "International" no doubt to make clear the more than American extent of the Depression. As I recollect, though, our efforts were limited to examination of domestic decisions.

We reasoned that most lawyers engaged in helping those severely hurt by the Depression would be hard put to undertake extensive research on their own. Therefore, we could supply a needed service. Like the others in the group, I contributed some of my free time to reading the latest court decisions in order to find current precedents that would be of use to those we wished to serve. By personal choice and because of my boyhood summers on an uncle's farm in Maryland, I became responsible for reading the decisions that dealt with agricultural issues.

The part-time research—my initiation to *pro bono publico* work that is part of a lawyer's social responsibility—was a step in my growing acceptance of political commitment. The cases I read for the journal in 1932, which would not otherwise have come to my attention, made me realize how little access the victims of the Depression had to legal services and how little geared to their needs our legal system was. I learned that social justice also required political reform.

My work on the little journal likewise gave me a sense of identification with members of organized groups like labor unions and farm associations, who by joint efforts and with concrete social and political programs were actively trying to help themselves weather the Depression. Here was a sizable constituency urging reforms and prepared to support political action to gain them. Without realizing it, I was already indirectly in touch with the grass roots of the New Deal.

By the time of Roosevelt's victory that November, I had become totally convinced that he was bound to succeed in the urgent task of relief and reform. I had concluded that the Depression was not a natural disaster; it had been avoidable. It was the result of decrepit social structures, of mismanagement and greed. The old order had for long years blocked needed reforms and by its blunders and corruption had precipitated the crash. Our nation, rich in resources and talent, would under vigorous new leadership undo the damage and enact reforms that would prevent future disasters. My optimism was plainly shared by great numbers of those supporting Roosevelt; that in turn bolstered mine. Here was the emergence of a cohesive political force. This was not the fictive public of cartoonists and editorial writers. I was conscious of a feeling of kinship with a host of like-minded fellow citizens. The feeling was exhilarating and new to me.

My acceptance of a political commitment in response to Roosevelt's assumption of office represented the final major change in my social and political attitude. At the time, I did not sort out the various changes in my thinking. But in retrospect I can see that there was a gradual progression.

My awareness of acute social needs demanded a shifting of perspective in my ethical outlook. I was no longer concerned with what convention expected from me. The focus became the needs of others as I saw them. Before, the essence of my posture was propriety—my living up to what was expected of me. This pharisaical position, possible in the 1920s, was no longer so when misery and suffering were the common lot of millions of Americans.

My desire to follow the directive in Frankfurter's telegram was therefore prompt and wholehearted. I was more ready for it than I had realized. Here again, as with my participation in the International Juridical Association, I found that the views I had so recently reached and my inclination to act on them were shared by others of my age with backgrounds quite like my own. But though I was thus not the only young lawyer who went to Washington that March of 1933, there were not all that many of us. We were entitled to think of ourselves— and we most certainly did—as a select few. I had this time taken a step or two in advance of the ranks of my generation, even of my close associates, though some of them came soon after.

The position offered me by Jerome Frank was to be one of his two assistant general counsels in the Agricultural Adjustment Administration. That agency, created by the Agricultural Adjustment Act of May 12, 1933, was set up as an integral part of the Department of Agriculture. The act was one of the torrential series of major enactments that issued from Congress during the "Hundred Days."

Until the agency's administrative procedures were established, Jerome Frank and I and other AAA recruits worked without salary, preparing drafts of proposed legislation and working on proposed future projects. Our time was fully occupied by these tasks and by consultations with experts from the Department of Agriculture, who educated us about the details of the catastrophic agricultural situation. My boyhood farm experiences and my recent experience with the International Juridical Association made much of this tutoring familiar and all of it congenial.

Agricultural production had been expanded during World War I, often by the sowing of marginal land. Cessation of wartime demand soon led to surpluses of cotton, corn, and wheat—to mention only the basic crops. This in turn had brought low prices, lowered farm values, and made a heavy burden of mortgages taken out before the stock market crashed in October 1929. The protective tariff, the Smoot-Hawley Act, passed in 1930 in an attempt to reduce competition in the domestic market for a variety of industrial products, had made matters worse for farmers. By reducing U.S. imports, it also reduced foreign holdings of dollars for the purchase of American farm exports, thus increasing the glut at home and further driving down prices.

The main thrust of the AAA was to raise farm prices by reducing production. This was to be done by two programs: contracts between the government and farmers to reduce their crops, and agreements among food processors and wholesalers to restrict their output. My job was in the former area. I was in charge of the section, composed of about twenty-five lawyers, that drafted contracts for paying farmers to reduce their production. This meant that my fellow lawyers and I worked with the commodity experts within the Department of Agriculture and the AAA on provisions suitable for controlling the production of the individual crops. In this manner we ourselves became familiar with the details of land tenure and informed about the soil and climate conditions most beneficial for the basic agricultural products.

With the appropriate agricultural experts, we would then hammer out the separate provisions of the various types of contracts. Drafts of the contracts were also taken up with the Farm Extension representatives in the local areas where contracts would be sent for signature.

My responsibilities also included supervision of the Opinion Section, which, as its name suggests, was responsible for giving legal opinions as to the meaning and scope of authority permissible under the act we were administering.

Cotton was already in bloom when the act was passed. For this reason, the cotton contracts called for plowing under a proportion of the plants, while, with respect to most other crops, contracts became effective only for the succeeding year and provided for reduced planting. Because the glut in cotton was extensive and because of the importance of cotton to the entire South, the cotton "plow-up" program was by far the most significant of the AAA's early programs. It was at the same time the most controversial. Destruction of useful products cut across the grain of popular sentiment at a time when those who were out of work found themselves short of necessities.

Some of the criticism of the cotton program relied on humor to make its point. Though a stubborn animal, the southern mule had been trained to walk delicately between the cotton rows at this time of year, pulling the cultivator to turn over the weeds. Soon it was reported that farmers found it difficult to persuade the mules to forget their training: The animals balked at having to trample the cotton plants as they dragged behind them the plows turning up the rows. When Paul Porter, one of my friends in the AAA, told of this item of mulish behavior in a public account of a trip he'd made in the South, it drew the jibe from critics that even a jackass knows better than to plow up cotton.

Those opposed to the AAA's programs also objected to the contract that called for the slaughter of pregnant sows and little pigs in order to raise hog prices. But hog prices did go up, as did cotton prices. So, in terms of the AAA's principal objectives, the result of these and other programs was gratifying. Farm prices in general rose, the morale of farmers improved, and we were on our way to the creation of a farm production control program, which, with increasing drawbacks, has lasted to this day.

For those of us who had come to the New Deal as social reformers, there were, however, some disturbing aspects of the AAA's cotton programs. Wheat, corn, and tobacco crops could be subjected to production controls with beneficial results to all who produced these crops. Cotton, by contrast, was still produced in the main on large plantations, which supported numbers of tenant farmers and sharecroppers. Each contract normally covered a separate farm, and its benefit payment went to the owner. For cotton, it seemed to us liberals in the AAA that, instead of this practice, shares of the compensation payment should go directly to the tenant farmers and sharecroppers whose crops were actually turned under. The contract form we drafted so provided. However, some of the landlord-owners, whose relations with their tenants were highly paternalistic, almost feudal, thought that all payment checks should go first to them and that they should make the disbursements.

The contract provision brought me, a mere bureaucrat, the distinction of a personal call in my office from the formidable dean of conservative southern senators, "Cotton Ed" Smith, Democrat from South Carolina. He wanted to know why he shouldn't be trusted to pay out shares of benefit payments to his own "nigras." I replied that I did not make policy; the Senator would have to address himself to my superiors. They stood firm. And, fortunately, most cotton farmers found the payment provisions acceptable. The sign-up campaign was not adversely affected, and this conflict between long-established traditions and liberal principles was handily solved.

But as we began drafting the contract for the cotton crop that would be harvested in 1934, we were faced by the plight of tenants and croppers who would be idled by the reduction in acreage. The political power of the big plantation owners was too great for us to prevent evictions.

A different conflict of interest was raised for us by the marketing agreements that permitted processors and wholesalers to fix prices and limit output. On one occasion, Senator James Pope of Idaho, a Democrat, a model of propriety and a stalwart supporter of the New Deal, called Secretary of Agriculture Henry A. Wallace to say that some of the finest people in Idaho, large-scale pear growers, had complained to him that young lawyers of the AAA had been insisting on provisions in their marketing agreements that would be injurious to their interests. He told Wallace that he didn't want to bring pressure on the Secretary's independent judgment—he just wanted to pass along the information. On the following day, the Senator called again, now to say that a delegation of small growers had just paid him a visit. They had been delayed in reaching Washington because, for financial reasons, they had come east by car. They complained to him of the undue influence of the big growers and praised the efforts of AAA officials to protect the rights of the small fellow. Pope said he was washing his hands of the situation and leaving it entirely up to Wallace.

My chief colleagues in Jerome Frank's office and I were part of a legion of Young Turks who manned many of the legal jobs of the early New Deal. We were few enough in number and similar enough in backgrounds and beliefs to feel common bonds. We were a band of brothers—members of a citizens' militia in mufti, mustered to fight the ills of the Depression. As a matter of course we consulted one another on our official problems. Our mutual stimulation ensured group efforts that went beyond the sum of our individual talents and energies. Functioning in a novel national predicament, we were creating our own precedents. The latest solution of one legislative or litigative problem was shared as likely to be useful in the daily duties of our fellows. We came together at lunch or dinner or of an evening in informally assembled work teams to deal with common concerns or with assuring coordination or cooperation among our various bureaus. Plans to create a new agency—such as the National Labor Relations Board—quite naturally called forth a gathering of an ad hoc group to formulate a program, to draft legislation or regulations.

That distinctive principle of the American political system, the separation of powers, gave the lawyers among us a special influence and authority. Because the Supreme Court was still a roadblock to innovative legislation, each new program had to be drafted with a wary eye to the Court's obstructionist views. The special need was for those trained in the most sophisticated and advanced analyses of constitutional theory and precedents. And thus it was that a unique prominence was given to the lawyers among us Young Turks.

As recent students or teachers, we were fresh from years of rigorous research and regular exposure to the latest scholarly output of faculties of legal specialists. As Justice Holmes said of the young secretaries who each year came to him directly from law school, we knew more law— in its theoretical sweep and analytical niceties—than we ever would again, and more than most of our seniors in government.

Among the Young Turks, Abe Fortas at first served along with me in the AAA during his summer vacation as a law student in 1933. He went on to become an assistant secretary of the interior. Much later, his New Deal friendship with Lyndon Johnson resulted in his becoming a justice of the Supreme Court.

Fortas was no doubt one of the few who began their working lives as New Dealers, but there were others. My brother Donald joined the Solicitor's staff of the Department of Labor when he finished his year as Justice Holmes's secretary. But most of us had had at least several years of seasoning behind us. In the AAA, these included my colleagues Lee Pressman, Francis Shea, John Abt, Telford Taylor, Nathan Witt, and Margaret Bennett. At all events, throngs of ebullient, cocky, extroverted newcomers were conspicuous in Washington's public places. Our youthful tendency to flock together increased our visibility. George Peek, one of the two original co-Administrators of the AAA, employed a different metaphor. He referred to a "plague of young lawyers" who had descended on his agency.

As conservative opposition to the New Deal developed in later months, we young lawyers became a conspicuous target for Roosevelt's opponents. After Hearst reversed his earlier support for the administration, his press referred to us as the "Happy Hot Dogs," because so many of us had been recommended by Felix Frankfurter. We were well aware that the epithet was a demagogic appeal to anti-Semitism, the printable version of the sally in some businessmen's clubs, "the Jew Deal." We took this and other attacks lightly. Roosevelt was a popular hero on a scale not seen since Jackson's day, and his measures of reform and relief won widespread support no matter who helped in drafting or administering them.

We were the shock troops of the new administration. Hardworking, idealistic, high-spirited, talented, the young recruits did put a stamp on the New Deal that was in keeping with the very name of the regime of which they were so prominent a part.

The stamp was more than superficial. Among the contingent were men like Thomas Corcoran and Benjamin Cohen, who jointly drafted some of the most innovative and significant legislation of the period— notably the law setting up the Securities and Exchange Commission and, as well, the Public Utility Holding Company Act, which provided the needed reforms to prevent recurrences of scandals like the Samuel Insull public utility empire.

Corcoran had come to Washington in the waning days of the Hoover administration to join the fledgling Reconstruction Finance Corporation. He, too, had been a Holmes secretary, and Tom delighted Roosevelt, as he had the Justice, with his saucy Irish wit. Soon he and his guitar were White House habitués. Ben Cohen, gentle and modest, possessed of qualities in marked contrast to those of his ebullient associate Corcoran, was one of the most selfless and dedicated of all New Dealers.

Being a young government official was a heady experience in those days. Many of us exercised major authority years before we could normally have expected to do so in the private sector. Our work was stimulating and important. We could justifiably feel that we were making significant contributions to the nation's welfare. The young lawyers were joined by older men not only from the law, but from a variety of disciplines: economists, accountants, academics of various disciplines, journalists, and a few from the ranks of business. Indeed, part of our reward was the chance to work closely with an able group of older officials in their early middle age, people like Jerome Frank.

Frank, who later became a commissioner of the Securities and Exchange Commission and a federal judge, was a brilliant lawyer, author, and teacher. He worked vastly long hours, as did most of his fellow New Dealers, and was always imaginative and resourceful in dealing with the legal problems of the AAA. As my chief, he was generous in sending me on missions of importance to Capitol Hill and to other agencies, and, in general, he worked with his staff on completely informal, equal terms.

Among the ranks of New Dealers of middle age with whom I worked were those recruited from Columbia University. They had been Roosevelt's unofficial advisers during his later months as governor of New York, when he worked out much of his experimental approach to the problems he was to face as president.

Prominent among this group of professors, soon to be called the Brain Trust by the press, were Raymond Moley, Rexford Guy Tugwell, and Adolf Berle. Moley, who before long found Roosevelt's policies too liberal for his stomach, and Tugwell took on important administrative posts—the former as under secretary of state, the latter as under secretary of agriculture and later commissioner to Puerto Rico. Tugwell, a handsome and somewhat arrogant man, was Roosevelt's most daring and controversial lieutenant, a paradigm of the reformer in office. He took special interest in the controversies of the AAA, which brought me in frequent close touch with him. Berle, without initially assuming an official post, continued to be an adviser, especially on Latin American affairs. Later in the Roosevelt era he became an assistant secretary of state and then ambassador to Brazil.

In Albany, Governor Roosevelt had pioneered state help for the unemployed. There he had been well served by Harry Hopkins, who accompanied him to Washington and became the architect of the New Deal's innovative, imaginative, and widely successful relief program. Hopkins was witty, wry, humane, tireless, selfless, intelligent—an able administrator with a sure sense for the politically possible that never betrayed him into unnecessary compromise. Slight of build, he was the *beau idéal* of the complete New Dealer. He moved quickly from emergency direct relief to work relief with the Works Progress Administration, dotting the country with the WPA's new schools, hospitals, parks, roads, post offices—the infrastructure threatened by the disruption of the Depression. And artists, writers, musicians, and actors facing destitution were aided by imaginative programs that brought a burst of cultural activity to localities where it had never been known in the best of times.

With all his long working hours, Hopkins provided lighthearted companionship at all times, and I found myself looking forward to working sessions with him on relief projects in agricultural communities. Hopkins's goals and his compassionate, hardworking staff exemplified that element in the New Deal that causes many to look back upon the period as one of shared aspiration and comradely cooperation rather than of hard times.

Incorruptibility, dedication, and hard work were indeed the hallmarks of those who came to serve under Roosevelt in those Depression years.

There was a conscious pride in the display of these characteristics. We leaned over backward in our insistence on avoiding the slightest suggestion of personal gain. At lunch with a representative of an interested party, we scrupulously paid our own checks. I remember serious discussion of what Abe Fortas should do with a small crate of oranges sent, no doubt quite innocently, by a Florida grower who had appeared at an AAA hearing for a marketing agreement. (Ironically, Fortas's certainty of his own integrity led him, many years later, into an unfortunate appearance of a conflict of interest, which resulted in his resignation from the Supreme Court.)

Our code excluded self-interest, much less corruption, and embraced long hours at our desks. The first time that I happened to be on the streets at the official end of the working day and saw the army of homeward-bound clerical employees, I wondered what event had caused such large crowds to gather!

The New Deal had its limitations. It did not cure the Depression, though it ameliorated its distress. Only the industrial and agricultural demands created by World War II eliminated unemployment and farm surpluses. Nonetheless, I have no reservation in my enthusiasm for the New Deal and in my full-hearted commitment to its innovative programs. In that glorious Washington spring of 1933, I believed I was about to devote my full energies to the creation of a moral society. I felt, as Tugwell put it, we would "roll up our sleeves and make America over."

6

A DINNER OF SORTS
WITH H. G. WELLS

One evening in the early years of the New Deal a group of earnest young men gathered in a large house high on the Virginia bank of the Potomac, just across the river from Washington. A number of mansions in the city of Washington and its environs had become available for rent because their owners could no longer afford to keep them open for their own use. This one was home to a half dozen or so of my unmarried New Dealer friends, who had rented it at Depression rates and equipped themselves with a housekeeper. Such a ménage was not unusual in the first years of the Roosevelt administration.

We had come together to have dinner and an evening of talk with H. G. Wells, the famous liberal novelist. Wells knew the parents of one or two of the young hosts. Just arrived from his home in England for a lecture tour, he had sent word that he wanted to inspect the New Deal, which was to be one of his lecture topics. We young men represented most if not all of the variegated agencies of the fledgling regime. I had been invited to cover the farm program.

For all of us, Wells was a full-blown celebrity hero. We were pleased and flattered to have the chance not only to meet him but to be chosen

71

to brief him about the new experiment in governance that seemed to embody so much of his own liberal political philosophy. We had looked forward for days to our encounter, confident of his praise for what had already been done to alleviate the ravages of the Depression. We also felt assured of his sympathetic understanding of the obstacles we faced in achieving the basic reforms needed to guard against a recurrence of the catastrophe. We counted on counseling from a wise and friendly adviser who had long given thought to the possibilities of reform of the very kind we were carrying out.

Intending to provide Wells with a more accurate and comprehensive report on the workings and future of the New Deal than was available to any other outsider, we had prepared diligently for the meeting with our hero. And our preparations did not skimp on nourishment for the corporeal man. We prided ourselves on our knowledgeability about the good victuals that were part of the traditional culture of Maryland and Virginia. Nothing was too good for him: oysters, crabs, and other delights of the region were on the menu. We even obtained some good wine. Wells was to be served a feast that was in sharp contrast with the simplicity of our everyday fare as hard-driven civil servants in a time of economic depression.

The house where we gathered was spacious, although no longer in the pristine condition it had been accustomed to. Its new occupants, flaunting their New Deal loyalties, had christened it "Bleagle"—a contraction of the administration's familiar symbol, the Blue Eagle of the National Recovery Administration. We felt that the somewhat gloomy old mansion was momentarily being restored to its accustomed splendor by our resplendent dinner party.

We stood expectantly in a large hall, waiting as Wells came down the wide staircase from his room. He was short, rotund, and unimpressive-looking—our first disappointment of the evening. Just before the Lucullan dinner was to be served, he let us know that he would have only an orange to eat. At table he peeled his orange ceremoniously, taking great pains to keep the spiral peel unbroken. The ritual absorbed him. We watched mutely. His frugality was a bit off-putting at the very outset of the meal. But then, the real purpose of the evening was the political and intellectual feast still to come.

We were high-spirited and had healthy appetites, so we made a very good best of the situation. While poor Wells ate nothing but his orange, we tucked into our elaborate meal, though the festive mood we had counted on escaped us. From his writings, we had expected our man to be robust and full-bodied in his tastes in food and wine as well as in his manner and politics. Instead, he was fussy about his food, if not dyspeptic, and not particularly forthcoming in table talk. Still, we realized that we had little in the way of light conversation to offer a world famous literary figure. All would be set right by our reports.

After the not very gay dinner, we gathered in the large living room in a semicircle around our distinguished guest. One by one we described the responsibilities and progress of our respective agencies. Treating Wells as an insider, we were candid about shortcomings. We were painstakingly factual and comprehensive.

Having begun inauspiciously, our evening as it continued became a fiasco. There had been gross miscalculation on both sides—and on our part a self-importance that even our youthful zealotry did not excuse. No doubt Wells counted on receiving in capsule form insights into the workings of the New Deal. Instead, we took it upon ourselves to lecture our hapless guest. We had thought it our duty to give him a full accounting, but, in the event, we bored him, giving him far more than he wanted. Worse, we arrogantly resented his growing impatience.

We were most truly at cross-purposes when it came to reporting on the social and political norms that limited New Deal reforms. While we supposed we honored Wells by taking him into our confidence, as it were, we failed completely to appreciate that our recital of shortfalls was contrary to his expectations. From what he had seen in reports that had reached him in England, the New Deal had adopted the semiutopian social practices he had espoused in his writings. Instead, we had really only begun to catch up with European social legislation, while Wells's own thinking had gone well beyond it. Now, here were these young whippersnappers telling him, in effect, that his thinking had been visionary, too advanced to be politically realistic in the United States.

He was disappointed in the vaunted New Deal reforms. Moreover, he thought we were defeatist. As Wells's questions grew testy and his manner peevish, we felt let down by our hero's seeming lack of political sophistication. He clearly felt that we were magnifying the obstacles to reform. Far from sharing our pride in what had been accomplished, he appeared at times almost to believe that we were inventing obstacles. He accused us of negativism, faintheartedness, and ineptitude.

The young New Dealer who spoke for the WPA had described its imaginative projects that provided jobs for the unemployed by putting them to work creating parks, building roads and bridges, and erecting public buildings all over the country. But he had also reported that critics of the WPA had prevented a seemingly obvious project for employment. Although factories stood vacant, and simple clothing was needed for those on relief, government efforts to put idle factories to use making denim outfits and sneakers had been stopped. The project smacked too much of socialism. More concretely, it might impair the sales of private manufacturers of those items.

We went on and on. Today my sympathies are all with Wells, trapped for a long evening with a single orange as his sustenance. But, then, when it became my turn, I was as self-important as my colleagues. I spoke with pride of the Agricultural Adjustment Administration's success in raising farm prices by paying farmers to reduce production. Dutifully, however, I mentioned our vain efforts to protect those tenants and sharecroppers in the Deep South who had been made redundant by our programs.

We should, of course, in preparation for our evening of homage, have inquired about the dietary habits of our distinguished guest and asked just what it was he wanted in the way of information about the New Deal. The first lapse was attributable to our own lusty young appetites; the second, to our missionary zeal in recounting the glorious accomplishments of the New Deal.

Near the end of the evening, Wells appeared reluctantly to accept the realities we had presented—and then disclosed what must have been a central cause of his peevishness. He told us he would now have to rewrite the lectures he had prepared on the ship coming over! This disclosure hardly made us more charitable in our disappointment. There had been none of the wide-ranging, high-minded but practical discussion to which we had looked forward, and we felt cheated of Wells's wise counsel. More significantly, we had lost a hero and champion at a time when both were in short supply, especially in the world of letters and social thought. No longer could we hope to assist a revered social philosopher in becoming a prophet of the goals of the New Deal.

7

TAKING THE PROFITS
OUT OF WAR

In the late summer of 1934, I took an additional job—that of counsel to the Senate Committee to Investigate the Munitions Industry. That committee, headed by Senator Gerald P. Nye, Republican of North Dakota, had asked the Agricultural Adjustment Administration for the loan of my services. The committee received strong support from two large sectors of the public. One group, which included almost all veterans, resented the profiteering associated with arms contracts. The other, especially strong in the Midwest, cherished the long-standing American isolationist sentiments.

In the early days of the Nye Committee, as the body soon became known, its emphasis was upon "taking the profits out of war." The theme was widely popular at the time, and the committee was given major press coverage. Hitler's bellicose statements following his accession to power, in January 1933, had stirred fears of war which brought with them demands for rearmament among Germany's neighbors. Military orders from abroad were attractive to Depression-ridden American manufacturers of airplanes and other products useful for warmaking.

Much of the New Deal's ardor was prompted by resentment of the corporate greed that had preceded and in part precipitated the Depression. Consequently, many of us New Dealers were sympathetic to the Nye Committee's populist fulminations against war profiteers. Sympathy for the purposes of the committee no doubt played some part in my being lent to them, but the AAA had a more direct reason to assist the committee. Two of its members were also on the Senate Committee on Agriculture.

The presence on the Nye Committee of Senator Arthur Vandenberg of Michigan no doubt also increased the willingness of the AAA to cooperate with the committee. Vandenberg was notable for his vigor and ability as a leading Republican member of the Senate. For my part, I found the subject matter to be of national importance, and I was delighted to have the opportunity to gain more experience in the preparation of factual briefs of evidence and the examination of witnesses.

My belief in the importance of the committee's mission was not shared by Sir Willmott Lewis, the representative of *The Times* of London and the dean of the Washington press corps. As I readied my papers for the first public hearing in which I took part, Sir Willmott, who sat a short distance from my chair, spoke to me in a casual tone. He addressed me as "young man" and went on to ask if I did not know that all nations needed arms and would take pains to protect the interests of armament manufacturers. In my youthful enthusiasm for reform, I regarded his sagacity as cynicism, and with no loss of ardor I went on to examine the first witnesses, who, as I recall, were officials of the Curtiss-Wright Corporation, manufacturers of military and civilian airplanes.

Public interest in the hearings ran high. Press coverage was extensive. Selling arms to small, impoverished nations involved influence-peddling and intrigue in high places. These unsavory aspects of the arms trade provided juicy ingredients for the sensational press. A mysterious but highly successful arms salesman, Sir Basil Zaharoff, was typecast to pique popular interest. In those innocent days the international trade in instruments of destruction—so modest in their power, measured by current standards—itself was widely regarded as sinister. In reaction to the slaughter in World War I, pacifism was widespread. *What Price Glory?*, *All Quiet on the Western Front*, *Goodbye to All That*—books, plays, and films that depicted the horrors of modern warfare—were popular. In Britain, university students took the Oxford Oath not to bear arms. Veterans in large numbers shared the general revulsion against war. Peace groups, most particularly the Women's International League for Peace and Freedom, supported the Nye Committee's efforts by issuing relevant reports and arranging for lectures and debates.

My initial responsibilities were the preparation for hearings relating to the Curtiss-Wright and Pratt & Whitney companies, the latter the manufacturer of airplane engines. It was also part of my duties to interrogate officials of these companies in public hearings conducted by members of the committee. The latter injected their own questions as each hearing proceeded. With the aid of the committee's subpoena power, we of the staff obtained relevant contracts, correspondence, and other data.

In the early hearings the documentary evidence and oral testimony disclosed that it was normal practice for an aviation salesman to use actual or potential purchases of warplanes by one South American country to impress upon its neighbors their need to make matching or superior purchases so as not to be faced with an arms "gap." Use of the fear factor proved to be an effective way of bringing about spiraling military budgets. Bribery copiously supported the implanting of fear. The resulting picture was of American business stirring up tensions in an already unstable area and corrupting friendly governments in our hemisphere. One salesman's letter complained of a U.S. Foreign Service officer as "fomenting peace."

Later hearings emphasized the enormous profits made by shipbuilding firms during World War I, including the Electric Boat Company, producer of submarines. This was followed by a comparison of the costs of private manufacture of gunpowder and ammunition with those of the government's Frankfort Arsenal. To the surprise of Senator Vandenberg, the staunch Republican, the government's manufacturing costs proved considerably lower than the private ones.

One of the most important rewards from my service with the Nye

Committee was the chance it gave me to come to know Vandenberg, a relationship which lasted throughout my government career. His forthrightness and intellectual vigor impressed me from the start. These two characteristics are generally in short supply, and the combination in a politician is rare indeed. For Vandenberg, a vigorous partisan of private enterprise whose party was then very much in the minority, there was no need to comment personally on the government arsenal's superior showing. But, straightforward as was his custom, he took this occasion to emphasize it and made the fact all the more impressive by admitting that it was contrary to his expectations and prior assumptions.

The members of the committee were a diverse and interesting lot. Only Senator Warren Barbour, Republican of New Jersey, took little or no interest in the proceedings. In my few contacts with him I found him colorless. In this respect he was not only unlike his committee colleagues but also quite unlike his naturalist brother, Thomas, a personal friend of Justice Holmes. I had met Thomas Barbour during the year I served with the Justice and remembered vividly that he could always be counted on for extraordinary tales of adventure and misadventure—such as the one about the escape from its container of a large boa constrictor that he had smuggled aboard an overnight Pullman car.

The other members of the munitions committee were all men of prominence, and each was a distinct personality. Nye, the chairman, was a Midwest populist who was friendly, outgoing, and breezy in manner. For him, the committee's subject matter and its extensive public visibility were important political assets that he made the most of. He was the panel's customary spokesman and as such was usually accompanied by a reporter or two as he moved across the Capitol grounds, and a cluster of pressmen often besieged his office.

James P. Pope, Democrat of Idaho, was a large, gentle, and kindly man. Liberal in his political views, he was a staunch supporter of the New Deal and later became a member of the board of directors of the Tennessee Valley Authority. Homer Bone, Democrat of Washington, and like Pope a stalwart New Dealer, was a veteran of the political struggle for publicly owned power in the state of Washington. Like most New Deal advocates, Bone was no friend of big business. His espousal of the cause of public power had come about because, he said, large utilities were able to influence, if not control, regulating bodies set up to oversee their procedures and profits. "Who will regulate the regulators?" he was fond of asking in sessions with the committee staff when discussions turned to the possibility of wartime regulation to "take the profits out of war." Bone was intelligent, informed, and readily accessible to staff members. He later became a federal appellate judge.

The secretary of the Nye Committee was Stephen Raushenbush, an able and vigorous man with a long history of identification with liberal causes. Raushenbush was the chief intellectual force of the committee; he chose the topics to be covered and the companies and individuals to be investigated. He put together a small, hard-working staff—some, like me, borrowed from the executive departments, and some who were volunteers (especially in the summer) from academia, including graduate students; still others were hired from the private sector as full-time staff members.

One of these latter, Robert Wohlforth, was Raushenbush's chief assistant. Wohlforth exemplified the youthfulness of most of us. Able and iconoclastic, he was hardly more than thirty but was sophisticated and fearless of the prestigious lawyers who usually confronted us when we questioned their clients.

The initial concentration on the questionable practices and the profits of aviation and shipbuilding concerns was followed by investigations of the Du Pont company and its relations with its foreign counterparts and other American businesses. The resulting hearings demonstrated cartel-like arrangements among firms like Vickers of Britain, Bofors of Sweden, Schneider-Creusot of France, and I. G. Farben of Germany. But at one stage of its work the committee's main interest shifted to Du Pont's profits during World War I, particularly to the construction by the company of the Old Hickory plant for the manufacture of explosives. This factory was paid for by the government on the basis of contracts that called for the payment of the costs, plus a percentage of those costs as a fee to repay the company for its efforts. Contracts of this kind provided little incentive for keeping costs low— the higher the costs, the bigger the fee.

The urgency of wartime need adds to the mood of prodigality and greed that seems always to accompany such contracts. These twin specters haunt all military procurement, in the 1980s no less than in World War I. Cost-plus contracts may, especially, encourage waste and profiteering, but their elimination by no means reduces the opportunity for enormous profits in times of large arms outlays. The monopoly position of Du Pont played a large part in its ability to demand huge amounts either as costs or as compensations. The company was, to be sure, not alone in its insistence on being paid what it wanted. The government had no alternative. At times, the threat was clear: Pay what we demand, or we won't produce. The Nye Committee likened this to a strike by capital, noting that, in wartime, strikes by labor were forbidden. The issue of wartime profiteering was the one that most concerned labor as well as veterans, who felt their contributions to the war effort had been inadequately reimbursed when compared with corporate profits.

In preparation for the Du Pont hearings, two or three of us staff members spent some time in Wilmington, Delaware, the bastion of the Du Pont dynasty. My job was reading contracts, letters, and memoranda from the company's files and interviewing those officials familiar with the material. Our mission was taken seriously by the company, and more than once I was summoned to meet with top officials.

At the time, the three Du Pont brothers—Irénée, Lammot, and Pierre—were the senior members of the family's enormously successful corporation. Once, I was called to a conference with all three of them. Pierre, the eldest, took little part in the talk, though his very presence—gray-haired and distinguished—was impressive. And it seemed clear from the outset that the purpose of the meeting was to impress me, if not to overawe me.

It appeared that some junior officers had become disturbed at the lines of inquiry we were taking on behalf of the Nye Committee. As I recall the conversation, Irénée was the company's spokesman. His manner was authoritative and brusque. He referred proudly to the firm's service to the country in war and peace. The gist of his remarks was that the committee should praise the company for its patriotic efforts rather than single out incidents which, out of context, might put it in a bad light. I replied evenly that my instructions were to

examine certain past transactions between the company and the government and that I simply sought the facts relevant to the transactions.
Irénée was evidently not satisfied with my statement and went on to
complain that we were concentrating on matters that treated his company unfairly.

New Dealer to the core, I resented being lectured—hectored, it
seemed to me—about my official responsibilities by a tycoon who was
trying to frighten me in order to prevent the disclosure of improper
corporate acts.

As soon as the purpose of the meeting became clear, I made a point
of taking notes on what Irénée was saying. This tactic produced no
moderation in his tirades. In his summing up he went so far as to say
that, after all, I was simply a servant. At this point my tactic of note
taking may have prompted Lammot to interject that his brother meant
that I was a *public* servant. This was said in a remarkably quiet and
conciliatory tone evidently designed to soften the arrogance of his
brother's remark.

My colleagues and I continued to ask for the kind of material we
had been seeking. We received what we asked for, with no further
attempt to rein us in. After the hearings, at which I recall all three
Du Pont brothers appearing, I was informed indirectly that whatever
my government salary was, the Du Pont firm would be prepared to
hire me at somewhat more. This offer to become a servant of private
interests I took to be an intended compliment—though it was one I
did not appreciate.

No compliments were forthcoming from Bernard Baruch, however,
during the Nye Committee hearings in which I questioned him. On
the contrary, he was obviously offended and angered by the questioning. Baruch occupied an unusual place in American public life for
many years. For some, he was a venerated elder statesman, a view to
which he evidently subscribed. For my part, he was a vain and over-
rated Polonius much given to trite public pronouncements about the
nation. Many of my contemporaries shared my views about him.

As a young man, Baruch had made his fortune as a speculator,
especially in minerals and mining stocks. This gave him a reputation
for business acumen, and his independent wealth made him appear

to be above the competitive struggles of the corporate world. These attributes were emphasized during his service in World War I as chairman of the War Industries Board, to which he had been appointed by President Wilson. The board's function was to coordinate American industry to ensure maximum production for the war effort; in addition, part of its job was to minimize inflation. For general morale purposes, much was made of the board's success in eliminating excessive profits by its appeal to the patriotism of businessmen.

As I have already emphasized, one of the slogans of the Nye Committee's most vigorous supporters was that it sought to "take the profits out of war." As there was a consensus that profiteering had taken place on a huge scale in World War I, the operations of the War Industries Board were a natural area for the committee's attention. Examination of the extensive records of the board, including its voluminous minutes, led the committee to discern that the general public's impression of profiteering during World War I was correct. The presentation of much of the relevant material that the committee had uncovered was through Baruch's testimony.

It had been particularly in the years after the First World War that Baruch had achieved the status of a sacred cow. He had become known in the press as the adviser of presidents. Emphasizing his common touch, he was frequently photographed on park benches. He took an active interest in Democratic politics and was reputed to be a generous contributor to the campaign funds of various politicians. At his baronial estate Hobcaw Manor, in South Carolina, he was often host to prominent political figures. Somewhat to my surprise, even Franklin Roosevelt had been his guest there.

Baruch had a gift and a taste for publicity, and the press seemed always to regard him as good copy. Folksy in manner, wealthy, a friend to the great both at home and abroad, conservative in his public statements, he was the prototype of a popular American figure who seemed to offend no one.

In private, members of the Nye Committee expressed little genuine respect for Baruch but, as seasoned politicians, they did not wish to be critical of him in public. Our normal procedure was for the staff to present to the committee material we had obtained as part of our research and to make recommendations as to witnesses, topics, and lines of presentation of the evidence, much as trial lawyers prepare for court hearings. The committee approved or disapproved our recommendations and apportioned among the members the areas of inquiry. Part of the staff's duty was thus often to prepare proposed questions with references to supporting documentary evidence on which the questions were based. Preliminary questioning was often left to the secretary of the committee, Stephen Raushenbush, to me as the committee's counsel, or to some other staff member.

In the case of Baruch the members of the committee chose not to ask any embarrassing questions about the work of the War Industries Board. I had overseen much of the research on the board's operations, so the challenging questions were left for me to put. I had none of the reasons for reserve that led the senators to a position of caution with Baruch. On the contrary, I rather welcomed the opportunity to ask him tough questions, given my opinion of him as something of a humbug. He in his turn had expected to be treated as semiroyalty by the committee. To make that assurance doubly certain, he had Senator James Byrnes of South Carolina, to whose campaigns Baruch had contributed, appear publicly before the committee to introduce him, as it were. The purpose of this tasteless ploy seemed to be an attempt to make Baruch a privileged guest in the clublike purview of the United States Senate. The committee was not impressed.

The stenographic transcript shows, I believe, that my questioning of Baruch was fair and not hostile, but the record of the War Industries Board did not bear out its boast of having saved the government and its taxpayers large sums of money by reducing wartime industrial profits to a modest level. Baruch, who was obviously discomfited, did not acquit himself well. It was not one of his public-relations triumphs, and, as I was to learn much later, he blamed me for this rare instance of his failure to mount a scene of adulation. Baruch was not noted for his modesty. His vanity must have been damaged, though his appearance before the committee certainly caused no noticeable impairment of his public image. But later he added his voice to those who called me subversive, although as far as I am aware, he knew nothing about me except that I had once brought out facts that he wanted overlooked.

Not long after Baruch's appearance, the committee issued its report on wartime profiteering, emphasizing that the imperatives of wartime demand made control of profits impossible. In other words, Baruch's efforts were ineffective in preventing "the strike of capital." In the committee's parlance, the only way to take the profits out of war was to avoid war. This conclusion was congenial to the isolationist sentiments of Chairman Nye and—at that time—of Vandenberg, the strongest and most active member of the committee. Fear of war, fueled by Hitler's warlike policies, made isolationism widely popular throughout the nation. Not surprisingly, therefore, the Nye Committee switched its main interest to ways to stay out of war.

Pursuing this tack, the committee, after some months, devoted its hearings to the huge American loans made to the Allied Powers before our entry into the First World War. These loans by J. P. Morgan and other bankers had enabled the Allies to purchase from us armaments and other vital goods. In the committee's view the loans gave the American bankers a vested interest in seeing the Allies emerge victorious and able to pay their debts, even if this required our entry into the war. And, they reasoned further, the large, profitable trade with the Allies tilted our economy toward their side. The hearings on our economic ties to the Allies furthered the prompt passage of the Neutrality Act of 1935.

I resigned my post with the committee in the fall of 1935, for I did not share the members' views on neutrality, which seemed to encourage a passive attitude on our part toward Hitlerism.

The Nye Committee received wide public support and a good press for its disclosures of inordinate war profits and the destabilizing effects of arms traffic in peacetime. In the mid-1980s, with our enormous military expenditures and the resulting huge profits, the efforts of the Nye Committee to "take the profits out of war" seem incongruous. But in the mid-1930s the national mood of civic conscience was quite different.

8

PEARL HARBOR DAY
AT THE STATE DEPARTMENT

On the afternoon of December 7, 1941, I was in my Georgetown house listening to the regular Sunday afternoon broadcast of the New York Philharmonic Symphony Orchestra. A houseguest was resting in the balconylike alcove just above where I sat. The concert was interrupted, and an announcer's voice said that Japanese planes had attacked our docked battleships at Pearl Harbor, with resulting heavy American losses. Startled, and not believing our ears, my guest and I called out, each asking whether the other had heard the announcement. After we assured each other that we had both heard the same message, I hurriedly drove through the traffic-free streets of Washington to the old State Department building on Pennsylvania Avenue, next to the White House.

I was then assistant to Stanley K. Hornbeck, Adviser on Political Relations. Dr. Hornbeck, as he was always addressed, had for many years been the State Department's chief Far Eastern expert and as such had a major voice in administration after administration in the formulation and daily conduct of our Far Eastern policy. In a revelatory mood Stanley Hornbeck once said to me that he was often asked why he had stayed so long at his post when he could earn so much more as a consultant to some firm that did business in Japan or China. He confided to me that the answer to the question was power.

Certainly, his assessment of his influence was realistic. Important business executives, journalists, high army officials, authors, professors—all came to his modest offices on the third floor of what is now the Executive Office Building. To be a major factor in shaping the foreign policy of a great nation is indeed to wield power. And in the weeks and days immediately preceding Pearl Harbor, Dr. Hornbeck was a key participant in the small group that aided Secretary of State Cordell Hull in the crucial negotiations with Japanese diplomats that ended only with the Japanese attack.

I had come to the Department of State in the autumn of 1936 to work in the office of my former law school professor Francis B. Sayre, then Assistant Secretary of State for Economic Affairs. When Sayre went to the Philippines in late 1939 as our High Commissioner, I had become Hornbeck's assistant.

Japan's attack on Pearl Harbor caught the State Department as completely by surprise as it did the naval and military personnel at the base itself. I arrived at the Department that Sunday afternoon to find a scene of confusion and uncertainty. Like me, others had hurried from their homes on hearing the radio announcement. Knots of officials congregated in the corridors and discussed the astounding news. Succeeding reports from Hawaii were dismaying. The damage had been catastrophic. The Pacific fleet had been put out of action with heavy casualties. Eight battleships had been sunk or severely damaged, together with many other ships and planes. Initially, some suggested that the attack might have been the unauthorized action of a clique of Japanese naval officers. The other, and as it turned out the accurate, view was that this was a deliberate act of war and must be treated as such, though Japan had issued no formal declaration. In any case, our assurance that Japan—"little Japan"—would not dream of attacking us died hard.

In 1939, our Far Eastern policy was—above all other concerns— to prevent Japan from completely dominating China. My sympathies were entirely with China, then reeling under Japan's brutal invasion, and I fell to the work happily. U.S. attempts to stay Japan's hand

included such financial aid to China as we in the State Department
together with the help of officials of the Treasury Department could
devise. Japanese troops had largely isolated China so that we found
ourselves limited to loans and fiscal advice, modest aid indeed. But
the stronger portion of the policy over which Hornbeck presided was
to impose sanctions on Japan, so limited in natural resources. The
plan was to impose economic pressures gradually, thus avoiding the
appearance of confrontation. But the severity of the restrictions was to
be marked in demonstration of the firmness of our resolve.

While I was still in Sayre's office I had worked with him and Far
Eastern experts on the paperwork involved in giving notice that we
would terminate the economic treaty with Japan as soon as legally
permissible, i.e., in 1941. Once in Hornbeck's office, I found that he
and members of the Far Eastern Division were preoccupied with execution of the policy of sanctions. This meant working out the details
with colleagues from the Commerce and Treasury departments. While
still bound by the terms of the treaty we could only impose restrictions
that were necessary in the service of our own domestic needs. One
such action was the limitation of the export of high octane gasoline.
But when, in early 1941, the treaty expired, we were free to impose
full-scale embargoes and we carried out a series: scrap iron, crude oil,
and a succession of strategic metals. We took counsel with businessmen
involved to minimize the losses and found them usually supportive of
our plans. In particular, I took an active part in the consultations with
Standard Vacuum Co., which led to that company's stopping its ship-
ment to Japan of crude and refined oil from its Dutch East Indies
fields.

As we busied ourselves with this program, we remained confident
that "little Japan" would soon be brought to heel.

Japan responded by sending a special envoy, Saburo Kuruso, to
Washington in November 1941. On his arrival, he and the Japanese
Ambassador entered into intensive talks with Secretary Hull and his
advisers, led by Hornbeck. In those talks, Hull stood firm in his insistence that we would continue to aid China in its resistance to Japan's
invasion. In addition, he made it plain that we would not acquiesce
in Japan's policy of creating throughout the Far East the so-called
Greater East Asia Co-Prosperity Sphere under Japanese domination.

But though the talks were conducted in an air of tension, those Americans directly involved clearly had no concern that a breakdown in negotiations could lead to war, much less a surprise attack upon us. I do recall Under Secretary of State Sumner Welles, whose main responsibility was policies toward Latin America and to a lesser extent Europe, saying at about that time that we must avoid having to split the U.S. fleet between the Atlantic and the Pacific. He foresaw the likelihood of our soon being at war with Hitler and thought our naval forces would then have to be concentrated in the Atlantic. What he said was regarded as cautionary, but those most concerned with the conduct of Far Eastern policy thought any implication of the possibility of war with Japan was ill-informed and the caution was unjustified. To be sure, weeks earlier Ambassador Joseph Grew had said in a cable from Tokyo that if Japan's leaders were completely blocked in their expansionist program, it might mean war. But in Washington this was taken as an unwarranted conjecture, especially as it was not followed up in his later communications.

With no thought of impending catastrophe, those of us who were responsible for our Far Eastern policy had not stayed late in our offices on Saturday, December 6. I got home by midafternoon with no sense of crisis. Just before I had left work, a brief Navy message from the western reaches of the Pacific came to our office. That message is indicative, I think, of the absence of concern by American officials, diplomatic or military, that Japan might be so bereft of judgment as to attack us. The Navy reported that a Japanese fleet had been observed off the coast of Indochina headed south. The message added that if the fleet continued on its course, it would reach Malaya at Kota Bharu, but that this was likely to be merely a feint and the fleet would probably turn north into the Gulf of Siam. Since French Indochina (now the states of Vietnam, Cambodia, and Laos) had already been overrun by the Japanese after the fall of metropolitan France to Hitler in 1940, such a journey by a Japanese fleet would mean no new aggression and would therefore be of no consequence to us. The Navy message conjectured, as did we in the State Department, that the Japanese would not attack the British colony of Malaya. The message gave no indication of the size of the Japanese fleet, an omission which itself indicates how remote was military action from our concerns.

I had, then, gone home for the weekend with no foreboding of any likelihood of a change in the unpromising negotiations Secretary Hull was patiently carrying on. The Japanese demand was that we give up our support of China—a very modest support indeed. The American position seemed far from provocative. Therefore, though the talks were not likely to result in an agreement, the mood in which they were being conducted was not bellicose. There was nothing resembling a Japanese ultimatum and, from our point of view, no occasion for one. That the conversations had not been broken off added to the feeling on our side that this was just another weekend.

Surprise and shocked disarray prevailed in the Washington military establishment as well as the Department of State. That Sunday afternoon the chief of staff, General George C. Marshall, came to the State Department building to be sure of having accurate information on the latest political developments.

Symptomatic of the uncertainty among military officials was a request to General Marshall from General Douglas MacArthur, then in charge of all our military forces in the Philippines. On receiving word of the attack on Pearl Harbor, MacArthur had prudently sent aloft all of his planes stationed at our airbase at Clark Field. He had then asked for authorization to bomb the Japanese airfield on Taiwan (Formosa, as we then called it). Marshall was furious at the request. He was quoted as remarking angrily that the damned fool (MacArthur) should have realized that under the circumstances no useful reply to his request could be formulated at that time. Marshall said that MacArthur should have reacted on his own responsibility and should have carried out the bombing he had proposed.

MacArthur, later noted for his willingness to act without authorization, was evidently as unprepared for the Japanese action as anyone else. His uncertainty as to what to do shows that in our military planning such an attack was evidently not even a remote theoretical hypothesis, for apparently no responsive action had been outlined as part of contingency war-game planning.

In any event, MacArthur's uncertainty continued, for he allowed his temporarily alerted planes to return to their routine parking positions at Clark Field—for the crews to have lunch, it was cynically said later. There, as they sat wing to wing, they were destroyed by the very Japanese planes from Taiwan that MacArthur had so ineptly asked for permission to attack.

On Pearl Harbor afternoon, the sense of complete surprise was widespread. Officials throughout the government, foreign policy experts in business, academia, and the media, and the general public alike shared the sense of shock I witnessed at the Department of State. The similarity of response was generally felt, and the absence of any basis for anticipation universally accepted.

Detractors of Roosevelt in recent years have suggested that he knew in advance of the Japanese attack and had callously allowed it to occur in order to precipitate our entry into the war against Hitler. Postwar research has turned up evidence of intercepted Japanese military messages that, if properly evaluated at the time and brought to the attention of top officials, might have served as warning. But this is no adequate basis for the ugly suggestions about knowledge on Roosevelt's part.

All contemporary indications and more recent balanced historical research support what I so unmistakably witnessed on December 7 as the shock of genuine surprise by those who would have shared prior knowledge. It is therefore astounding for someone of my generation to see revisionists of later generations even contemplate the possibility that top government officials, civilian or military, had prior information which led them to anticipate the bombing on December 7.

A more justifiable criticism of officials at the time of Pearl Harbor is that of complacency. We *were* complacent, but for understandable reasons. We were certainly not irrational.

We correctly assumed—as the course of the ensuing bloody combat demonstrated—that the launching of a full-scale war against us would be suicidal. Moreover, the Japanese attack was entirely disproportionate to any existing Japanese grievances. In short, we simply could not imagine such an enormous miscalculation on the part of Japan's military leaders, a miscalculation that brought about the utter destruction of their military machine and changed the whole course of history in the Far East.

One can say that the Nazis similarly miscalculated the power of the forces they challenged. In a sense, the world was saved from global barbarism by two fateful miscalculations. But the Hitlerian misjudgment was one primarily of politics and not of industrial might. Hitler did not believe that the Western powers could make common cause with Soviet Russia. The tortuous course of East-West animosity since their joint defeat of Nazi Germany shows that Hitler's gamble was not without basis in reality.

All the benefits of hindsight, therefore, do not lead me to a feeling of chagrin that the abrupt radio announcement of that Sunday afternoon initially found me disbelieving as well as startled. It was as if a cyclone had struck without warning. We could only concentrate on steps necessary to repair the immediate damage.

This was indeed the unified national response to Pearl Harbor. It is perverse of the revisionists to argue that the public unity in support of the war effort, which they say was sought as a prerequisite to our entering the war against Hitler, is evidence of deliberate encouragement of the Japanese attack. Surely a charge of such heinous connivance requires a full array of facts. These have not been forthcoming. Moreover, the charge is quite without logic. Had the sneak attack been beaten off by our forces, it still would have been an act of war. It was the Japanese attack, not its success, that brought us into the Pacific war.

Pearl Harbor united the American people as did no other event. There was no hypocrisy in President Roosevelt's heartfelt characterization that the day of the Japanese attack was one "that will live in infamy." Our prompt declaration of war against Japan was universally and wholeheartedly supported. And Hitler's prompt declaration of war against us, in compliance with the Axis pact that joined Germany with Japan, found our country united for a global conflict.

After Pearl Harbor

With the advent of war, I wanted to join the Army. State Department officials were exempt from the draft, and the Department's policy was not to grant them leave to enlist. I spoke directly about my wish to Howland Shaw, Assistant Secretary of State in charge of personnel. He said I could better aid the war effort by remaining at my job, and he would not make an exception to the Department's policy for me. I accepted his decision.

I continued as Dr. Hornbeck's assistant during the first two of the war years. Our primary objectives were to conduct diplomatic relations with the Chiang Kai-shek regime and to advise those agencies of the government concerned with financial and economic assistance to China. We acted as earnest proponents of as much aid as could be mustered. Through the American embassy, which for most of the war years was located in the far western reaches of China, in Chungking, we were in the position to monitor the morale of the beleaguered Chinese government and to ascertain the need for loans by the Treasury and for lend-lease supplies from our military authorities. Japanese occupation of French Indochina, Malaya, and much of Burma made it appallingly difficult for our personnel to reach China, much less carry out any substantial delivery of military matériel. Contact was by air from India across the mountainous regions of Burma, a trip that was known as flying "over the Hump."

These were days of intense activity and deep concern about our ability to keep Chinese resistance alive. There were vigorous debates among those of us engaged in Far Eastern matters about the role of the Chinese Communists. They were active warriors against the Japanese invaders, but they had also long been regarded by Chiang Kai-shek as hardly to be preferred to the Japanese.

My own position in this closely contested debate was, I'm afraid, an attempt to carry water on both shoulders. It seemed to me unproductive to weaken our support of Chiang, but at the same time it was vitally important to encourage all forces that were actively resisting the Japanese invaders. I therefore hoped continually for compromise between the two contending factions—and there were certainly many moments when such compromise seemed feasible. I am convinced that we should never have ceased to seek that outcome. But this was not an area in which American diplomacy performed effectively or wisely.

The internal debate remained evenhanded until anti-Communist sentiment led to a hardening of the desire to maintain the existing Chiang government. This goal became so obsessive as to prevent the possibility of our applying pressure for compromise and led to the long subsequent years in which we refused to recognize the Communist regime after its forces had driven Chiang from the mainland in 1950.

By 1943, the scales of war had tilted more and more in our favor. The State Department increased its emphasis on preparing terms for peace and formulating our postwar policies. I was transferred to the division engaged in postwar planning, including especially plans for the United Nations. I served as secretary of the Dumbarton Oaks Conversations in the summer of 1944.

These talks were held from August to October of that year at a handsome private estate in the Georgetown section of Washington. The initial participants were the United States, Great Britain, and the Soviet Union. Later we and the British met with the Chinese, who approved what had been agreed upon in the earlier sessions. Protocol, the Russians felt, precluded their meeting with the Chinese at this conference, because the Russians were then neutral in the conflict between Japan and China.

The conference was marked by an unusual degree of goodwill and harmony. The negotiators in the first phase were Edward Stettinius, then our Under Secretary of State, Sir Alexander Cadogan tor Great Britain, and Andrei Gromyko, then the Soviet Ambassador to Washington. Stettinius, with considerable pride in their accomplishment, used to refer to the group as "the men of Dumbarton Oaks." My task was to supply documentary materials and recommendations to our delegation and, as secretary, to record the official minutes.

Agreement was reached at these sessions on major elements of the proposed United Nations. Indeed, the matters still left open after Dumbarton Oaks (and which were agreed upon at Yalta), though important, were few in number. President Roosevelt's interest in the nascent organization was indicated by his insisting on a daily report of the accomplishments of the negotiations. The outline of the charter drawn up at Dumbarton Oaks was an essential step in the creation of the United Nations.

In early 1945 I was sent to the Yalta Conference. At that time I was appointed director of the Office of Special Political Affairs, which was responsible for drawing up plans for the UN and other aspects of the peace settlement.

9

STALIN,
THE ENIGMATIC
HOST AT YALTA

As I look back on the Yalta Conference after more than forty years, what stand out strikingly are the surprising geniality as host and the conciliatory attitude as negotiator of Joseph Stalin, a man we know to have been a vicious dictator. I am also reminded that in almost all of the analyses and criticism of the Yalta accords that I have read, I have not seen adequate recognition of the fact that it was we, the Americans, who sought commitments on the part of the Russians.* Except for the Russian demand for reparations, coolly received by the United States, all the requests were ours. And, except for Poland, our requests were finally granted on our own terms. In agreeing to enter the war against Japan, Stalin asked for and was granted concessions of his own, but the initiative had been ours—we had urgently asked him to come to our aid.

The meeting, in early February 1945, came at a turning point in

---

*An exception to the general run of analyses of Yalta is the detailed study of the proposals and counterproposals in the book *Yalta* by Diane Clemens, professor at the University of California at Berkeley (Oxford University Press, 1970).

the war. A series of Allied successes had assured victory in Europe. It was time to agree upon peace terms to be demanded from Germany. But only a few weeks earlier the Battle of the Bulge had shown that the German military machine was still dangerous, and plans were needed for joint military action to finish it off. It was also important to discuss the future of liberated Europe and to complete plans for the creation of a postwar world organization, the United Nations.

The war in the Far East was then far from settled. Fanatic Japanese defense of the islands that Japan had occupied in the Pacific heralded a costly invasion of the home islands, unless Russia could be brought into the Far Eastern war in which it had remained neutral. Our Joint Chiefs of Staff thought that if Russia did not join us, we might even have to invade Manchuria, where a powerful separate Japanese army was stationed as a defense against Russia.

President Roosevelt had two main objectives in coming to Yalta, one military and one political. His military objective at the Crimea Conference (for that is what it was officially called) was to obtain from Stalin a firm commitment and a definite date for Soviet entry into the war against Japan, the subject of an informal agreement at the Teheran Conference a year earlier but there left indefinite.

Roosevelt's political objective was to outline the terms of the future peace in Europe and to complete the partial agreement with the British and the Russians for the United Nations Charter. Accord on the general structure of the UN had been reached late the preceding summer in the Dumbarton Oaks Conversations in Washington, but that accord covered only some of the essential elements of the charter.

Roosevelt gained both of his objectives, sound reason for the exuberant mood of the Americans as we left Yalta eight days after our arrival in the most trying of wartime circumstances. Soviet entry into the war against Japan had for months been a major objective of our Joint Chiefs of Staff, chaired by General George C. Marshall. The Joint Chiefs had told us diplomats that Russian participation in the war in the Far East would prevent a million American casualties. And without it, they said, the Pacific conflict would last at least until the latter part of 1946.

This, then, was a goal of utmost importance, of immeasurable value to us. As we were leaving Yalta at the end of the conference, I heard General Marshall's reply to Secretary of State Stettinius's observation that the general must be eager to return to his desk after an absence of approximately two weeks. "Ed," said Marshall, "for what we have got here I would gladly have stayed a month." And in his memoirs Averell Harriman, at the time our ambassador to Moscow, quotes crusty Admiral William Leahy, Roosevelt's personal military adviser, as saying, "This makes the whole trip worthwhile."

On our arrival at Saki airport in the Crimea on the morning of February 3, 1945, Roosevelt and Churchill were met by Molotov and other Soviet officials. An impromptu guard of honor, Russian soldiers in ill-matching field garb, had been drawn up to greet the two Western leaders. It seemed that the Russians had eyes only for Roosevelt.

I wanted, especially, to see how the sight of FDR's physical affliction would affect them. Roosevelt carried himself nobly, erect on his pile of furs. As his jeep went up and down the irregular lines, the faces of the men he was reviewing seemed to reveal quite openly a mixture of awe and admiration. To me, the incident illustrated the universal potency of the Roosevelt presence, and the warmth of the friendly attitude displayed was, I felt, a happy augury for the success of our negotiations.

We had a long, cold, uncomfortable and quite exhausting drive of seven to eight hours over war-damaged roads from the airport at Saki to our Yalta quarters. Stalin did not arrive until the next day. He then paid a courtesy call on Roosevelt, an occasion used also for a private discussion of the major American objective, Soviet entry into the war against Japan.

That afternoon the first plenary session was held. Like all the other plenary sessions, it took place at Livadia Palace, and President Roosevelt presided. This practice was based on protocol, for Roosevelt was not only head of government but also chief of state and thus technically outranked Churchill and Stalin.

My inclusion in the American delegation was a matter of chance. When Secretary of State Stettinius presented Roosevelt with a list of the State Department personnel that Stettinius proposed to take with him as aides, the President immediately vetoed Jimmy Dunn. James Clement Dunn, later our ambassador to Italy under President Truman, had at the time of the Yalta Conference been for some years the director of an office in charge of European affairs in the State Department. A small, slight, dapper man, he was by no means the only State Department or Foreign Service officer whose views were more conservative than Roosevelt's. But Dunn was perhaps outstanding in the openness of his opposition to the President's liberalism.

When FDR said he wouldn't have Dunn at Yalta, Stettinius proposed me because of my participation in the State Department's work on the projected United Nations, which included my service as secretary of the Dumbarton Oaks Conversations. As Stettinius later recounted the incident to me, the President had said he didn't care *who* was named, provided it wasn't Dunn.

This was an example of the tension that exists between a strong, liberal president on the one hand and the traditionally conservative Department of State and its Foreign Service on the other. The Department and the Foreign Service regard themselves as permanent custodians of American foreign policy, as compared with presidents, who come and go. There was a saying in Roosevelt's Washington that the writ of the New Deal ran throughout the government except for the State Department. True to its conservative bent, the State Department remained aloof from liberal elements of Roosevelt's policies. This helps to explain why, soon after FDR's death, willingness to negotiate differences with the Soviet Union, as at Yalta, changed to confrontation.

A representative expression of opposition to Roosevelt's policies, which at times almost reached disaffection, is apparent throughout the first part of George Kennan's memoirs, which deals with his early years in the Foreign Service. Almost exactly my age and with a similar background, Kennan (who was to become, briefly, United States Ambassador to Moscow in 1952) was clearly estranged from the reformist spirit of the New Deal which I found so congenial.

A good many presidents have responded to the State Department's independence by installing their own foreign policy advisers in the

White House. Roosevelt's choice for this function was Harry Hopkins, an important member of the Yalta delegation.

Of all the topics on the agenda at Yalta, completing the outline of the United Nations Charter proved to be the easiest.

Initially there was considerable difference of opinion as to which nations should be invited to the organizing conference and thus be the first members of the United Nations. All agreed that, as a creation of the victorious Allies, the UN should hold no place for countries that had sympathized with Germany or Italy—Argentina, for example. Disagreements about neutral countries were resolved with the formula that those declaring war against Germany within a fixed period after the Yalta meeting would be invited to join in drafting the UN Charter. (We did not refer to joining the war against Japan because it was militarily important to maintain secrecy about Russia's agreement to join us against Japan within three months after the surrender of Germany.)

Next, we agreed on the date, April 25, 1945, and the site, San Francisco, of the conference to draft the text of the UN Charter.

With less than three months between Yalta and the San Francisco gathering, Roosevelt and Stettinius, while still at Yalta, decided to choose the members of the American delegation. FDR accepted our proposed list of delegates: Senators Tom Connally and Arthur Vandenberg, Representatives Sol Bloom and Charles A. Eaton, and Dean Virginia Gildersleeve of Barnard College. The President seemed especially pleased with the inclusion of a woman on the list. At the same time, exercising the host country's prerogative, Stettinius and Roosevelt named me as Secretary-General of the conference.

The four congressional delegates were the chairmen and the ranking minority members of the foreign affairs committees of the two branches of Congress. These were obvious choices to further the bipartisan approach that Roosevelt was so careful to maintain not only during the war but for the peace settlement as well. The President had been an assistant secretary of the navy in Wilson's administration and now was most careful to avoid the partisan conflicts that had played so large a part in the Senate's refusal to ratify the covenant of the League of Nations after World War I.

Alger Hiss, ten months old. *Courtesy of Tony Hiss*

Before the Hiss home in Baltimore in 1916, at the age of
twelve. *Courtesy of Tony Hiss*

Alger Hiss's father,
Charles Alger Hiss.

College years.
Courtesy of Tony Hiss

Alger Hiss with Supreme Court Justice Oliver Wendell Holmes, Jr., in Beverly Farms, Massachusetts, 1930. *Photo by John Knox* ©

The young lawyer.

Members of the Hiss family. Standing, from left to right: Priscilla Hiss, Donald's wife Catherine, Alger, Donald. Seated on the right is the elder Mrs. Hiss, Alger and Donald's mother. *Courtesy of Tony Hiss*

Alger Hiss around 1935. *Courtesy of Tony Hiss*

Around the conference table at Yalta, Stalin, Roosevelt, and Churchill (in the right foreground). Alger Hiss is visible in the background to the left of Roosevelt. *UPI/Bettmann Newsphotos*

Alger Hiss, the secretary general, addressing the delegates at the United Nations Conference on International Organization in San Francisco, May 1945. V. M. Molotov is seated to the left of the speaker's podium. *UPI/Bettmann Newsphotos*

President Truman addresses the final plenary session of the U.N.C.I.O. on June 25, 1945. Seated on his left are Secretary of State Edward R. Stettinius and Alger Hiss. *United Nations U.N.C.I.O. 2906*

Alger Hiss at the State Department in 1945. *Courtesy of Tony Hiss*

Alger Hiss before the House Committee on Un-American Activities to deny the charges made by Whittaker Chambers that he had been a Communist. Hiss confers with Robert E. Stripling, chief investigator for HUAC. *UPI/Bettmann Newsphotos*

Whittaker Chambers repeating his charges before HUAC on August 25, 1948. Alger Hiss is visible on the far left of the photo. *UPI/Bettmann Newsphotos*

The confrontation between Hiss and Chambers in the public hearing on August 25, 1948. *UPI/Bettmann Newsphotos*

Testifying before HUAC on August 26, 1948. Stripling is standing. *UPI/Bettmann Newsphotos*

Alger Hiss arrives at the U.S. Courthouse in New York on December 7, 1948, to testify before the federal grand jury.
UPI/Bettmann Newsphotos

Donald accompanying Alger Hiss to the grand jury hearing.
UPI/Bettmann Newsphotos

Priscilla and Alger Hiss leaving federal court on July 8, 1949, after his first trial ends in a hung jury. *UPI/Bettmann Newsphotos*

Alger Hiss's lawyers in the second trial. From left to right are Harold Rosenwald, Robert von Mehren, Claude Cross, and Edward C. McLean. The photograph was taken shortly before the end of the trial in anticipation of a victory and Alger Hiss's acquittal.

Alger Hiss, hand-
cuffed, being led
from federal court-
house to the deten-
tion center on West
Street in New York
City, March 22, 1951.
UPI/Bettmann Newsphotos

Opposite: Alger Hiss in the early seventies.

Alger Hiss today. *Photo by Arthur W. Wang*

But when it came to our recommendation of John Foster Dulles as an adviser to the delegation, Roosevelt balked. He expressed strong distaste for Dulles, feeling that he, like Dunn, would not be in sympathy with Rooseveltian foreign policies. Stettinius and I felt that for domestic political reasons Dulles must be given an important post at the conference. We pointed out that he held the unique position of foreign affairs adviser to both of the then potential candidates for the Republican presidential nomination three years hence—Governor Thomas E. Dewey of New York and Senator Vandenberg. With the senator as one of our delegates, it was important to give a prominent position to someone who also had Dewey's confidence. Dulles was the only person who could meet this requirement. His appointment would thus further the bipartisan policy so important in assuring wide public support for the United Nations. Reluctantly, the President agreed.

There were other major agreements reached at Yalta. In what I believe was their only joint meeting during the entire war, the military chiefs of the three powers coordinated their plans for the final onslaught against Germany. In their diplomatic talks the three Allied leaders negotiated agreements on the occupation of Germany and German reparations and in regard to the liberated areas of Europe, most particularly Poland, by far the most contentious issue at the Yalta Conference. But conflicts at Yalta were submerged because of the necessity for continued military unity. This wary comity of relations, enforced by the need for military cooperation, characterized the tone of the diplomatic side of the Yalta Conference.

Additional factors bred a mood that at times approached a somewhat stiff affability. Overriding all was our hope that common interests in the ensuing peace might after the war give birth to continuing cooperation, edgy though it was bound to be. At the Yalta stage of the war, our vivid awareness of the enormity of its destruction nourished that hope, which seemed based on the same mutual calculations of national survival that had been the origin of the military unity.

I was well aware of my good fortune in being present at such a historic meeting called to settle such momentous issues. And I was fascinated by the chance to observe Stalin. Churchill and Roosevelt were exalted public figures whom I revered, and it was inspiring to be able to see them at close quarters, but they were known quantities compared to the enigmatic Stalin.

James F. Byrnes could devote a good deal of his attention to Stalin-watching since he had no assigned areas of responsibility at the Yalta Conference. It was Byrnes's claim that his political experience (as senator and congressman) enabled him to see that Stalin was not the absolute dictator he was reputed to be. When Stalin asked for time to sound out his colleagues in Moscow about the Polish issue, for example, Byrnes speculated that this was not a pretense of an excuse for delay, but a genuine need on Stalin's part to consult those with whom, Byrnes felt, the Russian leader shared power.

Our preoccupation with Stalin was understandable. From reliable intelligence sources, we knew, as the public generally did not, of many of Stalin's monstrous crimes against his people. He was like a tyrant out of antiquity. But we also knew of his adroit skill as a negotiator and of his evident success as a war leader. He had rallied the Russian people from their near rout by the Wehrmacht to sweeping victories by massive, reconstituted armies. But none of us really knew much about his personality—not even Ambassador Harriman, who had seen Stalin only at brief fixed appointments.

Now we were to see him day after day, under varying conditions. I saw him only at formal meetings and in the moments of informality as the meetings assembled or broke up. But as participants in the ceremonial dinners, Stettinius, Admiral Leahy, Byrnes, and Harriman had additional chances to observe Stalin. At Yalta and in their memoirs, their common observation was of Stalin's calm.

Sir Alexander Cadogan, British Permanent Under Secretary for Foreign Affairs (the top-ranking civil servant in the Foreign Office), in writing to his wife in letters of February 7 and 8, 1945, was more expansive: "Uncle Joe is in great form . . . and in quite genial mood. . . . I must say I think Uncle Joe much the most impressive of the three men. He is very quiet and restrained. On the first day he sat for the first hour and a half or so without saying a word—there was no call for him to do so. . . . Joe just sat taking it all in and being rather amused. When he did chip in, he never used a superfluous word, and spoke very much to the point. He's obviously got a very good sense of humour. . . ."*

And there were other personal characteristics he displayed at Yalta which I found at odds with my image of an imperious, anti-Western dictator. He was considerate and well mannered, but, more important, he appeared to be genuinely conciliatory in attitude, abandoning with seeming grace his position on a number of points.

He accepted, with reluctance, French participation in the control of occupied Germany, which he had vigorously opposed. Our drafts on the Declaration for a Liberated Europe and even on German reparations were finally agreed to largely without textual alteration, the Russians giving up changes they had strenuously argued for in lengthy debates. And the points abandoned did not—and on reexamination still do not—appear to be straw issues raised as bargaining chips to be surrendered in order to gain some more valuable points in exchange. On the contrary, they were always consistent with basic Soviet interests and policies. Cadogan, in a letter of February 11, dwelt on this mood of conciliation: "I have never known the Russians so easy and accommodating. In particular Joe has been extremely good. He *is* a great man. . . ."†

I do not take Cadogan's reference to greatness as his considered judgment, but it does indicate what an impressive figure Stalin cut at Yalta.

After insisting on detailed explanations, Stalin accepted without change our proposal for voting procedures in the Security Council of the United Nations. This provided for the veto power of the permanent members, but narrowed it to permit discussion free of the veto. Stalin did resist tenaciously and successfully the precise Anglo-American formulas designed to liberalize the future Polish regime. But the Red Army had occupied most of Poland and was soon to occupy the rest of it, so that the Americans and British had no real bargaining power on Polish issues. We thought we had done as well as could be expected

*The Diaries of Sir Alexander Cadogan, 1938–1945, ed. by David Dicks (G. P. Putnam's Sons, 1972), pp. 705, 706.
†Ibid., p. 708.

under the circumstances on the subject of Poland's new borders and
even on the final form of the provisions for free elections and the
composition of the government.

It is interesting to speculate as to the reason for Stalin's flexibility
and agreeableness at Yalta. From all accounts, this was not his mood
at the earlier Teheran Conference or the later Potsdam Conference.
Only at Yalta was there a touch of graciousness in his manner. It
seems to me unlikely that his mood at Yalta simply masked intransi-
gence. After all, it was we, not Stalin, who came bearing requests.

Stalin as well as Churchill spoke frequently and emphatically of the
importance of preserving Great Power unity after the war. Perhaps
privately each desired such unity only if it could be obtained on his
own terms without compromise. However, that was not the mood or
the practice at Yalta. It was my impression that each spoke in the spirit
of cooperation and accommodation. I like to think that it was later
events not then foreseen that damaged genuine hopes of future unity.
I like to think that at Yalta the calm dictator and his associates shared
our hopes of cooperation, difficult though it obviously would be.

The Russians were remarkable hosts at Yalta. We could not help
being impressed by their extraordinary efforts made for our comfort
under wartime conditions of enormous difficulties. Perhaps the efforts
for our comfort were due to the pride of a great power to show what
it could do even *in extremis*. In any event, the setting for the conference
and the physical arrangements and procedures played their parts in
producing the usually relaxed mood of the meeting. There came into
being for those few days a relationship among the three governments
which has never since been approached—a relationship known as the
"Spirit of Yalta."

Stalin was short and stocky, and he usually wore a freshly laundered
khaki military tunic with no medals. Looking solid under the neat
uniform, he reflected a strong pride of person and had a natural air
of authority. Churchill, in contrast, was stooped and paunchy in his
rumpled garb. Churchill's means of command was his superb eloquence, which could be sharp and wounding as the moment required.
Occasionally his eloquence betrayed him, leading him into posturing
declamation.

For me, Roosevelt had by far the greatest presence. His easy grace and charm were combined with serenity and inner assurance. His posture at the great round table where the participants sat at plenary sessions was one of regal composure. He radiated goodwill, purpose, leadership, and personal magnetism.

The tone of the diplomatic talks was informal, almost casual, and at the same time wary. I cannot speak for the mood of the important military talks, which I did not attend. But the informality of the political sessions came naturally from our surroundings and from how small we were in number. The total civilian personnel of the three delegations could not have been more than seventy-five or so. (The military, whose talks were quite separate, by contrast, numbered almost seven hundred.)

The diplomatic delegations and a few of the top military officers were crammed into three large country houses on the outskirts of Yalta, in peacetime a small seaside resort. The largest villa, Livadia, somewhat grandiloquently called a palace because it had been a summer residence of the czars, was assigned to our delegation. The presence of three young women—Kathleen Harriman, Sarah Churchill Oliver, and Anna Roosevelt Boettiger—who in unofficial roles accompanied their fathers to the conference, contributed to a mood that at times was almost like that of a country house party where the guests good-naturedly put up with overcrowding.

Each villa was supplied with a full complement of chefs, waiters, and housemaids. The Russians had commandeered the staffs of three Moscow hotels and brought them to Yalta together with the necessary bedding, linen, chinaware, glasses, silver, and kitchen equipment. We and the British were "at home" in our villas and could entertain each other at meals.

The convivial mood at Livadia Palace was enhanced by a typical Rooseveltian gesture. He had brought along "for the ride" the political boss of New York's Bronx, Ed Flynn, and his wife. They were installed in a small suite on the second floor. Flynn did not attend any of the sessions. From time to time President Roosevelt, saying Ed was "getting very bored," would direct one of us to give the Flynns a summary of what was going on in the meetings. Among the furnishings in their suite was a huge samovar for the tea always served to the bearer of such news. As there was little else for them to do, the Flynns must have drunk more tea during their stay at Yalta than even an Irish-American could wish for.

It was, however, the exigencies of war that contributed most to the "Spirit of Yalta." The vastness of the war's scope in Europe and the Far East and the enormous size of the forces involved made military considerations overriding for the participants, utterly dwarfing other issues.

I was not aware of any lack of the buoyancy and playfulness for which Roosevelt was noted. To be sure, when we finally reached Livadia, the President was weary, gray, and huddled within himself, and photographs the next day show his still-drawn face. Cold warriors used those early photographs, and his sudden death ten weeks after Yalta, to proclaim that his faculties had been impaired and in consequence Yalta was an American diplomatic defeat. In fact, however, Roosevelt in a day or two had recovered his color and vigor. All of us at Yalta had no doubt that he was in full command of his faculties, and all of us left Yalta pleased with the results of our diplomatic efforts. Today I have no reason to change my opinion on either score.

An incident that occurred the morning after our arrival showed the President's resilience. It also illustrates his constant emphasis on the political goals of the war—the proper concern of a civilian commander in chief.

Before lunch and his initial meeting with Stalin, Roosevelt asked me and another staff member to brief our military personnel on the diplomatic issues of the conference and on our positions. The briefing was in a large, bare room, perhaps Livadia's one-time storeroom or a gymnasium. Pale and tired but alert and trenchant, the President himself introduced us, thus impressing on the military staff at the very outset of their meetings the importance he ascribed to the nation's political objectives.

Ironically, it was Harry Hopkins's health, not Roosevelt's, that was a chief concern at Yalta. Hopkins had been an ill man since a major operation for stomach cancer in 1937 and had been in and out of hospitals ever since. Some months before the Yalta Conference he had become seriously ill. He spent most of our stay at Yalta in bed, getting up only to attend plenary sessions and for meetings with the President. When others of the delegation consulted Hopkins, it was in his bedroom. Nevertheless, in the Crimea he was as witty, irreverent, scornful of pomposity, and shrewdly independent of mind as ever. We of the staff congregated in his room in our rare off-hours in appreciation of his incisive comments on the proceedings and of his racy humor.

An example of the latter that has remained sharp in my memory has to do with a railroad experience which, as I recall, occurred on Hopkins's journey from Saki to Yalta. Presumably to spare him the long, jolting automobile ride, the Russians had arranged for part of his journey to be by rail from Simferopol. Later, from his sickbed at Yalta, he regaled us with a story of his discomfort at the station at Simferopol as he was waiting for his train and, in need of a lavatory but unable to speak a word of Russian, had to describe his urgent plight by agitated pantomime.

I had known Hopkins since the early days of the New Deal, when he first organized and directed with consummate executive and political skill the vast relief program of the Federal Emergency Relief Administration and the Works Progress Administration. Later, when he became Roosevelt's trusted personal aide in foreign policy, I attended informal interdepartmental meetings he called to deal with the complexities of lend-lease for China. He was able and adroit, easy in manner, very personable, and deft in never needing to rely on his ultimate authority as the President's personal representative. He was most impressive in devising solutions to ticklish bureaucratic or domestic political problems that others had given up on.

Hopkins was equally impressive in his insistence that, similarly, solutions could be found to diplomatic problems. He demonstrated that diplomacy is not esoteric, that anyone of intelligence and extensive worldly experience can, with proper use of experts, be at home there as well. At Yalta, he was fully competent to take part in decisions of policy. There, his was the primary voice of conciliation and patient negotiation. It was easy to see why he had obtained Roosevelt's complete confidence and Churchill's trust as well.

After the brief first plenary session, the schedule of the diplomatic talks was for the foreign ministers—Molotov, Eden, and Stettinius— to meet each morning. (The Americans had no complaints about the Secretary of State being called a foreign minister!) These meetings were held in rotation at each of the three villas, with the host foreign minister presiding. The procedure was informal, as at the plenary sessions. We did, however, keep minutes of these morning sessions, the host delegation supplying the minutes-taker, who at the conclusion of the meeting would check his accuracy with his opposite numbers on the other delegations. Routine matters agreed to by the foreign ministers were adopted by the three heads of government at one of the plenary sessions held each afternoon. Larger issues that the foreign ministers were seldom authorized to resolve went to the plenary sessions for the three leaders to settle. For their part, the leaders referred matters to the foreign ministers for preliminary discussion and for the drafting of proposals on topics the leaders had agreed upon in principle.

No minutes were kept of the plenary sessions; each delegation relied on its own notes. Disputes that later arose about what was agreed upon at Yalta were not over what words were spoken at the meetings but over the meaning of the actual text of the formal agreement reached and whether it had been carried out in action.

Though the plenary meetings were conducted without the slightest attempt at rules of procedure, the importance of the occasion and the personalities of the three Allied leaders ensured high drama that brought about a genuine tone of dignity and seriousness. The scene lent itself to the theatrical. The leaders and their staffs assembled around a large circular table in the great ornate ballroom, often with a blazing birch log fire in the huge fireplace. Roosevelt presided with practiced ease. All of the dispositive statements were made by the leaders, though Molotov was sometimes the spokesman for Soviet objections.

Tones of voice were temperate and earnest, usually conversational in pitch and volume. Churchill, however, was volatile and easily aroused emotionally, and he would frequently revert to his noted parliamentary style and seem to be giving a set speech. On one such occasion, Roosevelt passed a note to Stettinius, "Now we are in for one-half hour of it." Speakers would routinely pause for translation after no more than a few sentences, but Churchill was often the bane of his interpreter.

Stalin was calm and restrained, always courteous and soft-spoken. He spoke concisely and clearly, without oratorical embellishments. He was well prepared and seldom read from any text or notes. He was always alert to the discussion and reacted quickly to what he considered a weakness or inconsistency on our part. He spoke seriously and earnestly on matters he regarded as important. He was a skilled and adroit negotiator who could be decisive or delaying, as suited his point.

At times he rose from his seat at the big round table and walked slowly back and forth behind his chair as he spoke. When seated, he conferred frequently and apparently casually with his aides. Whenever the British emphasized the desirability of Soviet acceptance of democracy in Eastern Europe, he slyly teased Churchill about the absence of democracy under British control of Egypt and Hong Kong.

Stalin seemed to take special care to conciliate Roosevelt, who in turn made no secret of his enjoyment of the Russian sallies that regularly drew fire from Churchill. Reports from those who attended the ceremonial dinners, however, pictured Stalin as generous in his tributes in toasts to Churchill as the only example in history of a single individual whose personal steadfastness had rallied a great nation from the brink of disaster and led it triumphantly to victory.

During breaks in the talks, Stalin carried himself without any seeming pride of place. He stood in the lavatory line with his aides and the rest of us lesser fry while Churchill was taken to Stettinius's suite and Roosevelt went to his own. His aides spoke to him casually. His erect carriage and stolidity nonetheless gave him a touch of aloofness and reserve.

We never solved the enigma of Stalin's character. Here was a man whose paranoid nature had led him to order the imprisonment, torture, and execution of untold numbers of his fellow citizens, a rule of terror that sought to eliminate even the hint of dissent. The deep contradiction between those abominations and his rational demeanor at the conference puzzled and fascinated us. It was the subject of constant speculation in our off-duty moments.

The enigma of Stalin, however, was a question apart from the political accords reached. The scope of the agreements at Yalta led me to conclude at the end of the conference that there was a genuine possibility for what diplomats call a "correct" relationship between us and the Russians, however stiff and subject to strain. Roosevelt's death and the less conciliatory foreign policy of the Truman administration did change the historic mix at a crucial moment. But after years of brinkmanship and confrontation, Kennedy and Nixon were able to bring off their policies of peaceful coexistence and détente. Events even as I write seem also to validate the hopes with which I left Yalta.

10

MOLOTOV AT SAN FRANCISCO:
THE BEGINNING OF
THE UNITED NATIONS—AND
THE COLD WAR

Of all the high-ranking officials at San Francisco in the spring of 1945 for the conference that formed the United Nations, the most remote in human terms was V. M. Molotov, who led the Soviet delegation. At least I found him so, and I knew of no one who found him approachable. His natural stiffness and gruffness of manner were barriers enough, but in addition, he spoke only his own language, and the ever-present interpreter set him off even more from his fellow delegates and from us of the secretariat.

The cooperative spirit among the Great Powers at Yalta was largely missing at San Francisco, less than three months later. This was due to sharpening differences of policy, but Molotov's dourness did nothing to improve the situation. Had Roosevelt been present at the conference, some of the "Spirit of Yalta" might have carried over to it. The conference at San Francisco had been a long-cherished goal of his, although one he did not live to see realized. At his death he was drafting a speech to be delivered at the opening session, which took place on April 25, 1945.

The day of Roosevelt's death was one of the most vivid and shocking in my life. The news came to me in a peculiarly roundabout way. As Secretary-General-elect of the United Nations conference, I had sent to San Francisco an advance guard charged with the manifold chores of preparing for the conference—obtaining meeting sites, secretariat office space, hotel accommodations for delegates, and the like. In the early afternoon of April 12, I received a call from one of our group in San Francisco, John Peurifoy. He said that the press had just told him that there was a report that President Roosevelt had died.

My office in the old State Department building overlooked the front entrance to the White House. The flagpole was empty, as was the custom when the president was out of town. Roosevelt was resting at Warm Springs, Georgia. All was serene as I looked out the window. The rumor was preposterous, and I said so, but my colleague at the other end of the wire was insistent. Because such a rumor was in itself of interest, I put Peurifoy on hold and spoke to Mike McDermott, the State Department's press officer. He too scoffed at the report. But before I could hang up on the call from San Francisco, I saw a stream of men, about twenty or more, hurrying across the White House grounds to the front entrance. Something unusual clearly had happened. I reported this to McDermott as I watched. In a matter of moments, he learned that the report was all too true. The men I had seen were reporters, by then alerted.

How bizarre that the news should have reached San Francisco before it did the Department of State and the nation's capital. But this peculiarity struck me only in retrospect. At the moment I was overwhelmed with the loss of a hero. Soon Washington was engulfed in grief and shock. As the news spread, churches filled. People knelt on street corners or stood in agitated knots discussing the calamity. In the State Department, work was immediately suspended as we congregated in the halls and in one another's offices.

With the pulse of our foreign policy momentarily stopped, it was problematic what direction the country would follow under Truman, who had had little direct preparation for his new responsibilities. Our world would be a very different place without Franklin Roosevelt as president of the United States.

Roosevelt's intense interest in founding a new world organization to maintain peace—an interest shared by Secretary of State Cordell Hull and his successor Edward Stettinius—had caused a large staff of political scientists, economists, and international lawyers to be set up in the State Department in the early years of the war. The British and, to a lesser extent, the Russians were consulted as our studies for the scope and structure of the proposed organization proceeded. Chiang Kai-shek's China, too, was kept informed. But the exigencies of the war and the limited interest of the other countries restricted the number of people whom they could assign to this enterprise. Accordingly we became the chief architects of the United Nations.

What was put before the delegations assembled at San Francisco was the outline, begun at Dumbarton Oaks and completed at Yalta, of the powers and structure of the proposed body. This outline served as the basis of the charter that was drafted and signed as a treaty by all delegations. It specified that the United Nations was to take over the buildings in Geneva and the functions of the moribund League of Nations. A new International Court of Justice would succeed the court at The Hague associated with the League. A Trusteeship Council would administer the remaining mandates of the League as well as former colonies of the Axis Powers and any territories that members might transfer to it. An Economic and Social Council was created to carry out detailed studies and make proposals in the economic and social fields. Most important of all, there was to be a Security Council whose makeup, powers, and procedures ensured the predominant influence of the four sponsoring powers and France. Each of these five nations would be permanent members of the Security Council and would have the right to veto any of its substantive resolutions. A General Assembly, the quasi-legislative organ of the United Nations, would be composed of all member states, each with an equal vote. Its resolutions would not be binding, but they were expected to become an important element in the principles governing international relations.

The nations represented at the San Francisco conference were those that had declared war against the Axis Powers. China, for having readily accepted the Big Three's preliminary draft at the time of Yalta, had been rewarded by being made one of the sponsoring powers.

However, the United States, Great Britain, and the Soviet Union were the dispositive nations. They had been chiefly responsible for the Allied victory then plainly in sight. They had formed the alliance known as the United Nations, and they had jointly made the decision to expand the victorious if shaky partnership into an international organization to keep the peace. To be sure, in preparing their proposal they had given heed to the prerogatives and rights of the other member states. But the Big Three were as essential to a viable United Nations as their forbearance toward one another would be to future peace. Any change in the proposed UN Charter would have to be acceptable to each of the Big Three. The process of detailed drafting naturally raised some issues that they had not previously considered.

The Big Three (and China, but its role was minimal) took up such matters, together with amendments proposed by the smaller powers, at private sessions outside the procedures of the San Francisco conference itself. When the Big Three closed ranks in opposition to new proposals, which they usually did rather than jeopardize Allied unity, there was little the smaller powers could do but grumble at the arrogance of the Great Powers. Membership for the smaller countries was too important for them to opt out. Ultimate authority thus lay in the hands of the representatives of the Big Three.

As Secretary-General of the conference, I was in charge of the secretariat. Our headquarters were in the Veterans Building, a twin to the opulent San Francisco Opera House, where the conference's plenary sessions were held. We were responsible for the daily operations of the conference, for providing secretaries and interpreters for the various committee meetings (which took place in the Veterans Building), and for the housing, communications, transportation, and general comfort of the delegates and their staffs, numbering more than a thousand. In addition, my aides and I saw to the needs of more than a thousand press representatives from all over the world.

Throughout long days my duties brought me in touch with the delegates and their assistants. We saw one another on shared business from April 25 to June 25. Molotov was a key figure throughout those two months of negotiation and drafting that produced the final charter at the end of June. His severity and impassivity of manner aided him in resisting changes in the Soviet position. Whether part of a conscious tactic or, as seemed to me more likely, an integral part of his personality, those characteristics set him apart from his fellow delegates.

Jan Christian Smuts, prime minister of South Africa, a figure from another era and still addressed as Marshal Smuts, was benign and kindly, erect and spry, anything but austere. He was a statesman of stature and had been consulted by the British about the Great Power veto.

William Lyon Mackenzie-King of Canada seemed more like a chunky businessman than a prime minister. Peter Fraser, prime minister of New Zealand, Scottish as his name, had somewhat the air of a Presbyterian minister, which I believe he had been early in life. Herbert Evatt, dynamic and prickly foreign minister of Australia and later prime minister, promptly became the combative leader of the smaller nations, resentful of the arrogation of power by the Big Three. Emir Faisal, crown prince of Saudi Arabia, tall and slender, reserved and serene in manner, was gracious if formal with strangers. Jan Masaryk, son of Czechoslovakia's great World War I patriot, was gregarious, convivial, immensely popular, and expansive.

The nature of my relationships with delegates varied from informal and frequent to formal and occasional. But the festive mood of the conference almost invariably made our meetings easy and cordial. There were, to be sure, times when Evatt of Australia, for example, objected to some procedure. But he was the most outgoing and approachable of all the delegates, however vigorously partisan in moments of protest.

As I think back to the scenes of the conference, only Georges Bidault, the leader of the French delegation, came anywhere near Molotov in aloofness. The French at that time were especially prickly anyway, still smarting from their military shortcomings early in World War II. France had not been included as one of the Great Power hosts at the San Francisco conference. General Charles de Gaulle was still far from having won full Allied acceptance as the leader of a France struggling to regain its accustomed position among the nations of the world.

At the very outset of the conference, Bidault, without prior consultation or warning, abruptly asserted French prerogatives by an adroit last-minute ploy that succeeded in having French adopted as the second working language (English being the first).

Not wishing to depart from the traditional eminence of French as a diplomatic tongue, we had earnestly attempted to find adequate French interpreters. But the dislocations of the war had scattered the famous League of Nations interpreters, and our search for substitutes had been fruitless. The French protested our elimination of their language for the conference, to which we replied simply that we had no alternative.

At the initial meeting of the steering committee—composed of the heads of all the delegations to the conference—Secretary of State Stettinius began with words of welcome to our guests. He had barely finished two sentences when a man stepped forward from Stettinius's right and repeated his words in flawless French. Without acknowledging the interruption, Stettinius went on with his statement about proposed plans for the procedures to govern the conference. Again, after only a few sentences, a man spoke up from the other side of the room and somewhat farther back. He, too, translated into French the words just uttered. There was a murmur of amusement throughout the room. Stettinius turned to me and asked what was going on. I replied that we had just been outwitted by the French and that I thought we should accept their "victory" as gracefully as possible by promptly making French the second working language of the conference. It was evident that the French had been more successful than we in rounding up qualified French interpreters.

However valid Bidault's reasons for his standoffishness and for his virtual boycott of our social gatherings, Molotov's case was, we felt, quite different. This was still the Era of (Pretty) Good Feelings with our Russian allies. Other leaders from the Communist bloc, like Dmitri Manuilsky, who headed the Ukrainian delegation, were affable enough. Even Gromyko, if solemn, was perfectly accessible. But not Molotov.

The procedures adopted for the conference established that the four co-presiding officers, known as presidents, were to alternate in officiating at the plenary sessions in the Opera House. Consequently, I sat beside Molotov on the stage of that hall when he presided, with an

interpreter slightly behind us. I was responsible for communicating
the agenda to him and for carrying out the other duties of the secretary
of the meeting. I counted and announced the votes (taken by a show
of hands), identified for the presiding officer would-be speakers, and
in general saw to the mechanics of the session.

Molotov's fellow presidents of the conference were Stettinius; An-
thony Eden, then foreign secretary of Great Britain; and T. V. Soong,
the Chinese foreign minister, who had been educated in the United
States and spoke fluent, idiomatic English with hardly a trace of an
accent. My relations with them were informal and easy, uninhibited
by any need for interpretation. Stettinius kept his sessions moving
briskly, Eden was by turns bored and unsure of himself, Soong was
relaxed and casual. Molotov was all business; there were no pleasan-
tries. Communication between us was minimal. He was imperturbable, impassive in manner in his conduct of the meetings at which
he presided. He sat there like a Buddha, but was alert, decisive, and
very much in charge of the proceedings, seemingly kept fully abreast
of what was going on by his interpreter.

A few days before the formal surrender of Germany on May 5, there
was a premature report that the surrender had occurred. Molotov was
presiding when an aide came to me onstage where we sat and whispered
the information. I passed the word quietly to the interpreter. With no
change of his expression and no relaxation of his attention to the
proceedings, Molotov asked only if the report was unofficial. When I
confirmed my initial statement that it was, Molotov without hesitation
said we would ignore the report. None of the delegates in the Opera
House could have had the slightest indication that their stolid presiding
officer had just decided not to interrupt the business at hand for an
unofficial report of a long-awaited historical event.

When he was not presiding and when he thought his country's
interests were at risk or its reputation under attack, Molotov ceased to
be impassive. Small talk and affability he lacked, but anger and outspoken resentment came readily to him.

I had already had occasion to see these latter characteristics as well
as his gifts for lengthy argument and his unyielding persistence in
maintaining a diplomatic position. Just a few weeks before the begin-

ning of the conference, at Yalta Molotov had been among the most prominent participants. Even in the presence of such dominant personalities as Roosevelt, Churchill, and Stalin, he had stood out— aggressive to the point of combativeness, quick to disagree, voluble, and inflexible. By comparison, Eden and Stettinius, his equals in rank, had played inconspicuous parts in that drama.

At San Francisco, he was much less visible. He took little part in the daily debates and negotiations about the wording of the emerging charter, which he left to his subordinates. But in the private meetings, where issues of policy were settled, and where the Great Power response to serious challenges to the Yalta outline was formulated, there the inflexible, combative Molotov of Yalta reappeared. Molotov exerted himself only where the power to make vital decisions lay.

On two occasions at San Francisco there were narrow misses from what Molotov might have regarded as personal threats to his safety. I don't know whether he would have maintained his stoic calm had he known of them.

The four presidents of the conference sat together at the end of a U-shaped table for meetings of the steering committee, which was charged with overall supervision of the conference and with disposing of disputes. At the place reserved for each member of the committee were the usual pads and pencils for taking notes, and a tumbler for water. Small thermos jugs of cold water were placed at frequent intervals. When meetings of the steering committee were scheduled, the room was readied by a group of sailors who had been assigned to help with arrangements. I made a point of being on hand a few minutes early to see that everything was in order.

One morning as I waited for the committee members to arrive, I picked up the thermos between my place and Molotov's and poured myself a glass of water. To my surprise, what seemed to be pieces of ice came out with the water. I quickly realized that they were pieces of broken glass. A sailor had plunked the jug down so hard that its glass lining had shattered. As I was getting a replacement thermos and congratulating myself on a close encounter with a possible diplomatic incident, Molotov and his aides arrived. Noting my rearrangement of the items at his place, he inquired whether anything was amiss. I reassured him that nothing untoward had occurred, and he readily accepted my statement. His alertness in noticing what I cannot believe was any major indication of perturbation on my part was typical. But so was his matter-of-fact acceptance of my response to his inquiry.

The other occasion occurred when Molotov was presiding at a plenary session at the Opera House. An aide came to my side from the wings. He whispered to me that a fanatical-looking, long-haired man had climbed high in the superstructure above the stage and was pointing something at Molotov. This time it was I who was imperturbable. I realized that the long-haired man was Gjon Mili, the gifted *Life* photographer, who had been borrowed to serve as the secretariat's chief photographer. Mili was athletic and agile and given to wearing long hair well before it had become fashionable. Always eager to obtain unusual camera angles, he had climbed above the stage and had trained a telescopic lens on Molotov. My guess is that had Molotov become aware of Mili's antics, he would, relying in his businesslike manner on the adequacy of American security precautions, have remained calm.

There was a definitively dramatic moment when a plenary session voted to admit Argentina to participation in the conference and initial membership in the UN. One of the specific decisions at Yalta was that Argentina, which had aided the Axis Powers, was to be excluded. Suddenly, without warning, a motion was made and seconded that Argentina be invited to join the conference. On the ensuing vote the motion carried, amid noisy confusion and high excitement. Secretary of State Stettinius and the American delegation were taken by surprise. The move had been carefully and secretly prepared by the South American delegations with the active assistance of Nelson Rockefeller, a prominent staff member of the American delegation. Secrecy was so well maintained that no word of the stratagem had reached us of the secretariat, despite our close relations with all the delegations. The special relationship of the U.S. with Latin America made it indeed hard to believe that such an important action was carried out without top official U.S. participation. A far less suspicious person than Molotov would have been justified in assuming that there had been a deliberate violation of an important understanding reached at Yalta.

And only the most sophisticated student of American politics would believe that any American official, even a Rockefeller, could privately take part in such a maneuver. The ploy was of such a nature that it could not be undone. The conference was, after all, a functioning agency with its own independence. Argentina had been admitted, and the vote could not be reversed.

At all events, Molotov was furious and clearly believed that the United States had taken part in a piece of trickery and deception. It is not too much to say that the conference itself may have been in jeopardy. For in turn Molotov's reaction was to balk at a fundamental provision on procedure in the future Security Council—permitting discussion free from veto—that had been agreed to at Yalta. I took his reaction to be a measure of his anger over the admission of Argentina.

Fortunately for the future of the UN, Molotov did not have the power to decide the final Soviet reaction. But it was necessary for the ailing Harry Hopkins to make a special trip to Moscow to put the issue before Stalin, who promptly acknowledged the Yalta agreement on that point. The San Francisco conference went forward, Argentina and all.

In fairness to Molotov, I now recognize that his meeting with Truman in Washington en route to the West Coast must have been almost as upsetting for him as the admission of Argentina was later to be. Truman had but recently succeeded to the presidency. Molotov had called on him on his way to San Francisco, perhaps anticipating that this would be only a ceremonial visit. His last encounter with a president of the United States had been the occasion of warm farewells to Roosevelt at the conclusion of the Yalta meeting. In contrast, Truman, intent on being his own man, and annoyed at the Soviet insistence on retaining control over the new Russian-instituted Polish regime, was harsh and abrupt in speaking to Molotov at the White House. As Truman himself in his memoirs described this unpleasant meeting, Molotov complained that he had never been talked to like that in his life. To this, Truman replied that if the Soviet Union would keep its agreements, he would not be talked to in that fashion. Secretary Stettinius, who had been at that stormy meeting, told me the next morning that the tension was great and that he had expected Molotov would return to Moscow—an event he, Stettinius, thought would have aborted the San Francisco conference.

My colleagues at the secretariat and I failed to give weight to this unpleasant presidential welcome as we formed our opinion of Molotov's conduct at San Francisco. We had made every effort to provide a comfortable and efficient setting in which he, like the other delegates, could relax in the friendly and charming atmosphere of one of our most beautiful cities. After all, his country had achieved a magnificent victory and had won the respect and warm gratitude of millions. He was one of the four presidents of the conference. We could only put him down as churlish and rude.

In hindsight, I am inclined to recognize that we were witnessing the early manifestations of the cold war that has so dominated Soviet-American relations ever since Molotov was hectored by Truman. At San Francisco, Molotov tried to give as good as he got.

11

DISCORDANT VOICES IN LONDON: MRS. ROOSEVELT AND LORD KEMSLEY

In January 1946, a great lady, Eleanor Roosevelt, my favorite woman in political life, asked me to be her escort to a glamorous dinner. We were both in London attending the organizational session of the United Nations. She was a member of the United States delegation, and I had been named principal adviser. For Mrs. Roosevelt, the dinner party was but an incident in the course of the able and conscientious performance of her duties. For me, her request was one of the most welcome social invitations I have ever received. It illustrates an especially endearing characteristic of Mrs. Roosevelt: her ability to include younger people in her charmed circle. I was then forty-one, twenty years her junior.

The London conference was a difficult and trying assignment for the President's widow. This was her first trip abroad since the end of the war. She came this time not as the wife of a great and powerful leader but in her own right as an official representative of her country. But she inevitably carried with her the aura of her late husband, who had died less than a year earlier. That aura was bound to affect the attitude to her of her own delegation and of those of other member nations. And it made the British public eager to demonstrate to her their fervent admiration for President Roosevelt.

Eleanor Roosevelt met the demands on her energy and talents with seeming ease. She had the gift of being herself whatever the circumstances, which is another way of saying that she was always at her best. Her poise never left her. This self-assurance meant that she responded to each situation in a manner unfailingly appropriate to the occasion. She was an easy and interested participant in the encounters that were her major responsibilities—attending preparatory study sessions or conferences with the staff, participating in deliberative consultations with her fellow members of the U.S. delegation, and taking part in the sessions of the UN committee to which she was assigned as the U.S. representative. She was also called upon to attend countless ceremonial events and official entertainments, to receive large groups of admiring Britons paying their respects, and to grant private audiences as well.

For Mrs. Roosevelt the visit to London was a triumph, and she readily showed her pleasure. At home she had often been the target of hostile partisan attacks, especially as the butt of vulgar jibes because of her steadfast opposition to racism. The attacks stemmed also from the bitter hostility of archconservatives to her husband's New Deal policies and from male chauvinism resentful of her activism.

When as part of my State Department job I took to the Senate Foreign Relations Committee the list of those nominated by President Truman as delegates to the United Nations session in London, there were groans of "Oh, *Eleanor!*" from the committee. Tom Connally of Texas and Arthur Vandenberg of Michigan, also named as delegates with Mrs. Roosevelt, were either among the groaners or remained silent; no one countered the heavy-handed attempt at humorous denigration.

My first meeting with Mrs. Roosevelt was aboard ship en route to England. She had long been a favorite of young New Dealers. We regarded her as President Roosevelt's conscience and we followed eagerly her activities and the reports of her outspoken liberalism. Among her special New Deal interests was a little-publicized agency known as Subsistence Homesteads. That agency was a small part of the Department of the Interior's many responsibilities. It was a frankly experimental attempt to aid employed and unemployed Appalachian miners in developing subsistence garden plots. My wife had volunteered to help in the secretarial duties of that office, and there she came into frequent contact with Mrs. Roosevelt. I cherished the firsthand accounts of her vigorous encouragement of this tiny project. She visited areas where demonstration sites were established and met easily with local people and with official personnel. It seemed to me typical of Mrs. Roosevelt's self-effacing, sincere devotion to those in need that she made little of her work with the Subsistence Homestead project.

At law school I had known her son James and his future wife Betsy Cushing. My brother Donald and his wife, who were closer friends of the young couple, once dined at the White House. Their accounts of Mrs. Roosevelt's bright spirit and benign influence added to my store of anecdotes about her. But many New Deal officials thought of her as if she were a colleague and spoke constantly of her sayings and doings. Consequently, when I actually met her for the first time, on the *Queen Elizabeth* as we sailed for England, I felt as if I already knew her. Only a year earlier I had daily seen her daughter, Anna Boettiger, and President Roosevelt during the Yalta Conference, so I considered myself almost a family acquaintance.

The other members of the large American contingent destined for the first meeting of the UN were also aboard the *Queen Elizabeth*, still only partly reconverted from her wartime services as a troopship. My job in the State Department was as director of the division that helped to develop our policies with the UN and handled our relations with the world organization. Since the San Francisco conference we had been busily occupied with supplying materials and supervising the small American delegation to a Preparatory Commission entrusted with drafting bylaws and rules of procedure for the newly created UN. That commission had been provided for at San Francisco and was located in London; our delegation to it was headed by Edward Stettinius, who had resigned as secretary of state following Truman's accession to the presidency. Stettinius's deputy in London was Adlai Stevenson, later a governor of Illinois and a Democratic presidential candidate. In preparing for the first session of the new organization, my staff and I

drew up for our delegates kits of documentary materials and memoranda setting forth the positions worked out by the State Department
on the topics that were on the agenda for the London meeting, such
as the election of the secretary-general and members of the International Court of Justice, the choice of nations to be elected to the
Security Council, and the adoption of bylaws and regulations for the
operation of the UN. It was a heavy agenda. We took advantage of
the ocean voyage to conduct seminars for the delegates.

Mrs. Roosevelt was our star pupil. Eager to learn all we could teach
her, she did her homework faithfully and attended all the seminars.
She was indeed the only one of the delegates who had such an appetite
for our wares. Often she was our sole student. Her questions were
sharp and at times forced us to rethink our positions and supporting
arguments. She was alert and retentive. She fully confirmed her reputation for intelligence and quickness of mind.

Once in London, she continued to be a model delegate. Faithful
at attending delegation meetings, she took an active and helpful part
in working at policy formulations and negotiating strategy. She also
efficiently carried out her duties as the U.S. representative on the UN
working committee on social questions and human rights. She spoke
well and clearly, was persuasive and gracious in manner, and soon
endeared herself to her international colleagues on the committee. Her
early education in France permitted her on several occasions to act as
the committee's interpreter when some unforeseen contingency delayed the official French interpreter. She had to deal with technical
and legal terms, and she was able instantaneously to come up with
the appropriate translation. For a nonprofessional interpreter who had
not been continuously using her French, Mrs. Roosevelt's feat was
extraordinary. She made little of this talent, so that only those familiar
with the niceties of interpretation adequately appreciated the degree
of skill she commanded.

She was a striking figure at delegation meetings, in the conference
halls, in the public rooms of her hotel, and on the streets. Tall and
slender, with an excellent carriage and marked natural dignity, she
stood out wherever she was. Her simplicity and directness of manner
put one instantly at ease with her. Notwithstanding the constant of-

ficial, ceremonial, and personal demands on her, I never saw her show signs of fatigue or impatience.

It was a pleasure to watch Mrs. Roosevelt receive delegations of ordinary British people come to pay their respects. We were put up at Claridge's. The end of the war had relieved the shortage of manpower but not of food. The hotel's service was as full and deft as in peacetime, but the elaborately served food was lamentable. From time to time Mrs. Roosevelt's British admirers brought her the precious gift of a fresh egg or two. Once, she was presented with a great goose egg, the preparation of which stumped her and the hotel kitchen. She reported that it had tasted "pretty strong."

In the early days of the New Deal, Eleanor Roosevelt's detractors made much of her supposedly shrill voice. In London her voice was high in pitch but never strident or grating—indications, I took it, of the reported pains she had gone to to modulate her tone.

About midway through the UN session in London, a young member of the Belgian delegation whom I had come to know in San Francisco called me one morning to say that he and his colleagues were giving a birthday dinner party for the head of their delegation, Paul Henri Spaak. Spaak had been selected as the president of this first session of the United Nations General Assembly, the quasi-legislative organ of the UN in which all member states are represented. Spaak was also his country's foreign minister and later became its prime minister. When asked what he most wanted for his birthday, my Belgian friend told me, Spaak had instantly replied, "Mrs. Roosevelt."

My friend asked if I would be willing to tell Mrs. Roosevelt of Spaak's wish and of the Belgian delegation's eager hope that she would come to the party. From what I had observed of Mrs. Roosevelt, I felt that the situation would appeal to her. I knew she admired Spaak, and the quirky way in which the invitation had originated and its spontaneity and spirit of lightheartedness seemed to me would be to her taste. It was: Mrs. Roosevelt was both amused and delighted with the whole idea. And then came quickly, with no pause for reflection, an example of her graciousness and thoughtfulness that marked her stay in London. She said, evenly and pleasantly, with a disarming smile, that she had one condition: she would accept only if I were to be her escort. The fearless woman who had traveled alone all over the world, to battle-fronts and coal mines, needed an escort!

And so I had the chance to be with Mrs. Roosevelt under quite unexpected circumstances entirely different from the occasions connected with her official responsibilities. We rode together in a limousine reserved for her. Our brief ride was made easy and pleasant for me by her asking about our young Belgian host and Spaak's role at San Francisco, where he had also headed his country's delegation.

Our host had rented as his residence for the duration of the London conference a beautiful Georgian house, a noted Adam building. The service, wine, napery, and dinnerware, if not the food, were up to the handsome surroundings. Everything came together to ensure an evening of lively conversation and high spirits.

Mrs. Roosevelt was light and graceful in manner and speech, interested in and informed about a great number of subjects, and, with her quick-witted repartee, she more than held her own in the sprightly conversation. Her fluent French let the talk move easily and lightly. My own more limited familiarity with the language left me heavily taxed to keep up. She laughed readily and with a spirit of gaiety and enjoyment. These characteristics of the ideal dinner companion stimulated Spaak and the rest of the party of six or eight. Our mood reflected the hopes of the architects and founders of the United Nations for a new world of peace and international collaboration. The conversation did not dwell on the difficulties and already visible rifts in relations between the West and the Soviet Union.

I like to think that the occasion gave pleasure to Mrs. Roosevelt and was a respite from her serious and tiring official duties and taxing attendance at obligatory ceremonial functions. She certainly gave every indication of having thoroughly enjoyed herself. For me it was a golden moment.

At the final meeting of the American delegation there was an unscheduled tribute to Mrs. Roosevelt that I was in a privileged position to savor. The first session of the UN General Assembly had finished its business—the new United Nations was launched. It had adopted the bylaws and regulations by which it would conduct its operations. Elections had been held of a secretary-general and for places on the

Security Council and the other constituent organs of the UN. The Security Council had held emergency sessions on the continued Soviet presence in Iran. Our delegation had acquitted itself well, and we were in a cheerful and self-congratulatory mood.

Mrs. Roosevelt rose from her seat and said that her committee had a few last-minute matters to complete and that she felt she should join them. She expressed regrets that for this reason she must leave before the end of the delegation meeting. After she had passed out of earshot, Senator Vandenberg exemplified his remarkable willingness to correct a past error. He said in a voice we could all hear, "There goes a great lady." Senator Connally, not to be outdone by a Republican, added less audibly his concurrence.

Most of Eleanor Roosevelt's adult life was lived in a swirl of active politics, often bitterly partisan. She rose above it and did not reply in kind to hostility. Her London sojourn in early 1946 was unusual in the completeness of her triumph, an interlude from which ugly slurs were excluded. Home again, I encountered another incident of hostile prejudice toward her.

I was invited by a lawyers' group in Boston to speak about the UN session. They were forty to fifty established members of the bar who met for dinner from time to time during the winter months. At these dinners it was their custom to have a speaker on some topic of current interest to their members, followed by questioning of the speaker and general discussion. They were a rather formal lot, and the dinner was a black-tie affair.

As my audience was composed of lawyers, I described the technical procedures needed to bring the new international organization into being. I mentioned the vigorous negotiations that were an inevitable part of getting fifty nations to agree on such procedures, and I told of the lobbying our delegation had undertaken, especially when elections to various UN bodies were in process. I described the members of our delegation in some detail and commented on their performance. I thought I did pretty well and was pleased by the lively and informal interest shown during the question-and-answer period. Toward the end of my talk, when I was going into some detail about the personalities and activities of our delegates, I had noticed that several white-haired men left the room quietly. Their departure had caused no commotion and had not interrupted me. I remember thinking that they probably had to catch a late train to some suburb.

It was the chairman of the group, a senior partner of the law firm where I had worked when I began the practice of law, who had invited me for the evening. We had a friendly personal relationship, and we chatted after all the diners left. At some point in our conversation he apologized for the men who had silently walked out while I was still speaking. "Oh, Alger," he said, "I should have warned you"—and he went on to explain that each of the men had vowed never to remain in the room while any member of the Franklin Roosevelt family was being favorably mentioned.

Another London dinner party of that same period, held in an equally beautiful house, comes to mind because it illustrates forcefully the contrast between Mrs. Roosevelt's hopeful outlook on the postwar world and the continuing strength of old reactionary forces.

By the time the first meeting of the United Nations took place, the cold war was already gathering momentum and the hoped-for unity of the Great Powers had substantially faded. Mrs. Roosevelt then, and for the rest of her career in the United Nations, was one of those who sought to maintain as much of that unity as possible. She found herself frequently at odds—often sharply so—with the Soviet diplomats who were her UN counterparts. But she never favored confrontation or rupture of relations.

At London there were those who were far less willing than she was to maintain the wartime unity, tenuous as that had been. Moreover, to my surprise, there were unregenerate reactionaries in positions of influence whose early opposition to the Soviet Union had led them to a much too tolerant attitude toward Hitler. I had thought that those in Britain who had shared the views of the so-called Cliveden Set or the prewar appeasement policies of then Prime Minister Neville Chamberlain would be in disrepute. I was mistaken. In eclipse during the war, they had again come forward with the advent of the cold war and seemed as fully respectable as ever.

One such person was Lord Kemsley, then the owner and publisher of the London *Sunday Times* and of a string of papers in the north of England. Though I didn't know it at the time, he and Lady Kemsley had visited Hitler at Berchtesgaden, where, according to the German records, the publisher is said to have told the Führer that only the Communists and the Jews in Britain were prepared to fight.

Lord Kemsley's house was another Georgian gem. For all its beauty, it was cold in the winter of 1946, as British energy shortages continued. We dined in a large and lovely room in which only those seated on the side near the open fire managed to keep warm. The ladies on the other side of the table wore their fur-trimmed wraps.

The Englishmen whom Lord Kemsley had assembled were Harold Macmillan, later Britain's prime minister; the fabled Bruce Lockhart, who had been a shadowy British agent in Russia during the revolution and had long since dropped out of public notice; and an elderly, ruddy-faced peer whose name I do not remember. The Americans were Senator Vandenberg; James Byrnes, who had become President Truman's Secretary of State half a year earlier; Leo Pasvolsky; and myself.

Pasvolsky, as a special assistant to the secretary of state, had played a primary role in formulating the structure of the United Nations, and at San Francisco he had supervised the actual drafting of the charter. His (prerevolutionary) Russian origins were highly important in ensuring that Russian and English texts were in harmony.

I am at a loss to understand why Lord Kemsley invited Pasvolsky and me to the dinner party. I assume that our host regarded us as senior civil servants after the British fashion and, as such, nonpolitical but basically conservative in bent. As a White Russian, Pasvolsky no doubt seemed to Lord Kemsley to fill this role thoroughly.

I have made no mention of American women at the dinner because I do not recall whether Mrs. Vandenberg and Mrs. Byrnes had come to London to be with their husbands. I believe they had not, and neither my wife nor Mrs. Pasvolsky was in London. The ladies at the dinner were all, I think, British, and as was then still so prevalent in upper-class British practice, they played no part in the serious business of the evening. I remember about them only that they needed their wraps against the chill of the handsome old house.

It was only when the ladies had left the table, following the established custom, that we learned why our strangely assorted group had been brought together.

The men moved to the chairs at the host's end of the table for cigars and port and for what I, and certainly the other Americans, expected would be a general, and more or less inconsequential, conversation about world affairs. But Lord Kemsley wasted no time with small talk. He stated immediately the reason he had invited his American guests. He spoke quietly, without embellishment or argument, as if what he was proposing must be self-evident to all sound, respectable men. He said that, as we knew, the British government was about to ask the United States for a three-billion-dollar loan—needed to help repair the devastation of the war and alleviate widespread shortages. Receiving the loan, our host said, would ensure the continuance in power of the British "Socialists," as he called the Labour government under Clement Attlee, which had been elected six months before. Lord Kemsley urged us to oppose the loan, denial of which would, he thought, bring down the Attlee government. The British guests—including Macmillan—made no effort to dissociate themselves from the proposal.

The calmness of Lord Kemsley's delivery, the whole setting—especially Macmillan's presence—made it difficult to regard the proposal as merely an intemperate outburst at a purely private dinner of a blunt-spoken Conservative angry at the course of political events. I thought then and am still inclined to think of it as a serious probe of the attitude of Byrnes and Vandenberg to the idea of scotching the loan. If that was the gambit, the two men were seemingly well chosen. Byrnes was closely identified with conservative Democrats. Vandenberg was the most powerful Republican in the Senate and had been a staunch isolationist. They could have mounted a formidable opposition to the loan.

Neither man chose to treat Lord Kemsley's proposal lightly, as simply the personal view of our host. Byrnes fidgeted in his chair, evidently uncomfortable at the turn the evening had taken. Vandenberg met the issue head on. In an even tone he said that if, as seemed likely, the issue were to come before him as senator, he would give it thoughtful consideration. But, he went on without pause, he was inclined to favor the loan in view of the great sacrifices of the British people in the war. And what he had just heard from Lord Kemsley, he added, tended to increase his inclination.

No one else spoke. Byrnes failed to take advantage of the moment to make his position clear and left it to Vandenberg to be the American spokesman. Neither Pasvolsky nor I could match Vandenberg's impact in the matter and had enough sense to let his response be the last American word. There was no debate or discussion. Strangely, there was no noticeable tension, no sense of drama. It was like a scene from a surrealist movie. Lord Kemsley gave no sign of embarrassment at his miscalculation of his guests' response. We continued only briefly with our port and cigars and managed some general conversation until we joined the ladies.

At that time, I thought that the political orientation of Lord Kemsley was moribund, and I regarded his proposal as bizarre and unsavory. Today, however, his views would seem less outlandish. Certainly Lord Kemsley would not be isolated in today's political world, as he seemed to me to be in the early winter of 1946.

12

TRIAL BY ORDEAL

While Mrs. Roosevelt returned from the London meeting to the familiar discordant public appraisal of her, I was met soon after my return by the report that several Republican members of Congress were asserting that I was a Communist. This was told to me by Secretary of State Byrnes, who added that the rumors had come in each case from the FBI. Byrnes, who had succeeded Stettinius the preceding June, suggested that I see J. Edgar Hoover, the FBI director. Accordingly, in order to scotch the story at its source, I asked to see Hoover. I never did. Instead, his office said that the director wanted me to meet with one of his chief assistants, a man named Ladd. Ladd asked me a number of questions which seemed to me rather perfunctory, as I recall the event. He asked me whether I knew various people, some of whom I did not and some of whom had been New Deal colleagues. He seemed satisfied with my answers, and I believed I had settled the matter.

I never did discover who the congressional rumormongers were. But I was later to learn that this and all similar hostile whisperings in Washington were based solely on Whittaker Chambers's statements to the FBI, which he had begun to make as early as 1942. This instance of Hoover passing along malicious gossip is the first example of his animus toward me, an animus fed by Whittaker Chambers and that was to enlist the services of Richard Nixon two years later.

The rumor that I was a Communist led me to stay on in my State Department post longer than I had planned. I did not wish to appear to be leaving under fire. The cold war had already led me to conclude that we would make little use of the UN, and I had therefore decided that my position as coordinator of our policies toward the UN would no longer be rewarding. But I stayed on for another year, by the end of which I felt confident that the FBI story had been laid to rest. In January 1947 I became president of the Carnegie Endowment for International Peace, where I hoped to be more effective in support of the United Nations than was then possible from within the State Department. The chairman of the Endowment's Board of Trustees was John Foster Dulles, and it was he who had initially proposed my selection as president.

I have written in another book, *In the Court of Public Opinion*,* of the hearings by the House Committee on Un-American Activities and of my two trials. That book was part of my efforts to obtain a reversal of my unjust conviction, and it was therefore written primarily from a lawyer's point of view. Here I want to describe the emotional experience of the two long and heartbreaking trials, to each of which I brought such bright hopes of vindication.

I was accused of perjury because I denied, in 1948, that I had in 1938 given Whittaker Chambers documents from the files of the State Department for transmission to the Soviet Union. I made that denial before a grand jury. I could have obviated those two extensive and grueling trials by refusing to answer questions before the grand jury. John W. Davis, an eminent lawyer and vice chairman of the Carnegie Endowment, strongly urged me to take that position. Then, as in the days when I write this, witnesses summoned before congressional committees and grand juries often took the Fifth Amendment. I did not do that, in the mistaken belief that our federal judicial system was

---

*Alger Hiss, *In the Court of Public Opinion* (Alfred A. Knopf, 1957).

proof against public prejudice and was free of prosecutorial chicanery. I was certainly naive in believing that jurors would be insulated from the phobias of the cold war in 1949 and 1950, when my trials took place.

Running the gauntlet of the press was, in a sense, a more wearing ordeal than the trials themselves. Inside the courtroom, I not only had the support of my lawyers, but about half of those who daily filled the courtroom were friends or evident sympathizers. But almost every morning as my wife and I left the door of our apartment house at Eighth Street and University Place, unaccompanied by supporters, we were besieged by reporters and often photographers. New York then had several more newspapers than it does now and all the papers and the wire services covered the trials. Dutiful lawyer to the core, I answered no questions, pointing out as politely as possible that it would be inappropriate for me to comment while the case was still in progress. Likewise, I also would not stop to pose for photographers, although they were of course free to take shots as we walked along. In consequence, we were often a public spectacle, Priscilla and I walking resolutely along with photographers walking backward a few paces ahead of us.

Our route was along Eighth Street to the Astor Place subway station of the Lexington Avenue line. One morning the harassment by the press did not end at the subway entrance. Photographers followed us through the turnstiles and into our car. Startled passengers deserted our part of the car as flashbulbs popped.

There were times when we found ourselves in the same subway car with one or more members of the jury, whom we studiously avoided. We could, however, see that the jurors were ignoring the judge's injunction not to read press accounts of the case.

When we arrived at the Federal Court Building we were frequently met by other reporters or idly curious bystanders as we walked up the long flights of steps outside the building and then along the corridors. In the elevator we were accompanied by curious spectators, some headed for the show my trial afforded. Then the whole thing was repeated as we made our way home at the end of the day.

A large part of the emotional strain of the trials was due to the disruption of my family life. My nights were spent with my team of lawyers preparing for the next day's session. Since Priscilla, too, was occasionally needed, we had arranged for our son Tony, then seven, to stay with generous friends during the week. They saw to getting him to Dalton School each morning and picking him up in the afternoon. He spent only the weekends at home. His absence was a serious deprivation for Priscilla and me. In addition, we were anxious about the emotional effect on him of the publicity and consequent notoriety that even he experienced. Miraculously, Tony survived this period of difficulties psychologically intact. He became a gifted writer, author of books, and a staff member at *The New Yorker*. He is married and lives in New York City.

In court, I was the defendant "in the dock." Priscilla, who usually attended, sat beside me within the enclosure marked by a low wooden railing that separated the participants—judge, jury, witness on the stand, lawyers, and me—from the spectators. I'm not clear as to just why Priscilla was permitted to join me in the enclosure. Her presence was a great comfort.

Both trials took place in a large courtroom on the fourteenth floor. Because of the extensive press coverage, the room was usually full, with a queue waiting outside the door to take over from those who left. My friends naturally tended to sit together, and the others who were friendly to me tended to join them. I thus had the sense of a political body divided by the aisle into partisan groups. The door by which spectators entered the room was in the middle of the right wall. There were windows on the opposite side. As my supporters usually arrived early to be sure of good seats, they naturally crossed over to take seats away from the door with its rustle of murmurings and movement of those entering and leaving. And the far side with its better light was more inviting in any event. Thus it happened appropriately that my supporters were predominantly on the left side of the aisle.

The presence of friends and supporters was of major importance to my morale. They greeted me when I arrived, during the routine mid-morning and midafternoon recesses, during the luncheon adjournment, and at the end of the day's proceedings.

During the second trial, my lawyers and I and a group of close friends lunched regularly at André's, a nearby restaurant, no longer in existence. Moderate in price, with good French food and service, André's provided us with the needed place to be at ease, away from the pressures of the trial sessions. We were usually ten or a dozen at a large round table reserved for us. I remember our meals as lively in talk and spirit, even merry. We were convinced of the rightness of our cause and that we would prevail.

Throughout the first trial and most of the second, I was confident of acquittal. But as the second trial wore on, I realized that it was no ordinary one. The entire jury of public opinion, all of those from whom my juries had been selected, had been tampered with. Richard Nixon, my unofficial prosecutor, seeking to build his career on getting a conviction in my case, had from the days of the congressional committee hearings constantly issued public statements and leaks to the press against me.

There were moments when I was swept with gusts of anger at the prosecutor's bullying tactics with my witnesses and his devious insinuations in place of evidence—tactics that unfortunately are all too common in a prosecutor's bag of tricks. But at the time, my optimism prevailed over my anger. The mood at André's was my usual one. Nevertheless, I felt that I was facing trial by ordeal in the medieval sense of whether I could summon up sufficient physical strength to survive.

It was almost unbearable to hear the sneers of the prosecutor as he cross-examined my wife and other witnesses. How can one maintain an appearance of calm under such circumstances? I did, but at great cost in energy. The decorum imposed by court etiquette is an ordeal in itself. It was unnatural at such times for me to be impassive. There is no "proper" reaction. One sits naked before the inquisitive, and perhaps, as in this case, prejudiced jury. At times I despaired of justice. In court, fatigue and anger were my true enemies, though I did not usually recognize them as such. My sleeping hours were short and tension added its toll to normal fatigue. I often used the brief recesses to stretch out for a few moments on one of the tables in the room reserved for my counsel's deliberation.

When it was my turn to be cross-examined, the ordeal was of a different sort. Here, court procedures are all weighted in favor of the questioner. The witness may not argue or explain. I was able only to answer directly and briefly, however weighted or hostile the question. My lawyer could object to improper questions, but at the risk of letting the jury get the impression that we were reluctant to have the subject explored. But I was at least not forced to remain mutely impassive, and I was confident that later my lawyer could correct false impressions which bullying cross-examination might leave. It was especially in those moments of provocation triggered by false insinuations that anger and fatigue were to be guarded against. I lost my temper at least once and immediately realized I had erred. The etiquette of the bull ring did not permit the tormented to show even annoyance. I sensed that the jury thought the prosecutor must have scored a point if I reacted so sharply.

As I sat there, I recognized to what extent a jury trial is really a contest between two opposing lawyers. Only they are active throughout the entire procedure. They are the principal actors, always at the center of the stage. The more complex the issues, the more the jury is led to judge the significance of the evidence by the demeanor of counsel. As a witness, even as the defendant, I felt at times like a pawn in a game played by others. This sense of the law as the rules for a game of chance, so foreign to my previous experience as a nontrial lawyer and to my commitment to the rule of law, was unsettling. I had never before seen a jury. Often I felt like a spectator rather than a participant in my own trial. I was dismayed to feel how little I could do to help myself in the gladiatorial combat of others that was so crucial to my own life. This sense of powerlessness only increased my outrage as I had to sit by, as impassively as possible, listening to false testimony— to lies—and watching the theatrical solemnity with which factitious documents became formal exhibits.

Along with the elements of theatricality, of gamesmanship in the courtroom which made me wince at the artificiality of the proceedings, the outer world intruded. These intrusions were on balance hurtful to me. The jurors, as I had myself seen, were subjected to the tendentious accounts of the courtroom proceedings and to rumors excludable from any court of law but regularly dished out by the sensational Hearst and Scripps-Howard press. Daily during my first trial the jurors walked by the pickets protesting the trial of Communist party leaders then going on in the same courthouse. The conflicting sentiments of the spectators in the courtroom, though muted, were palpable. And a novel intrusion of outsiders, hostile to me, was a bizarre factor in the second trial. It brought the bitter hostilities to Franklin Roosevelt's policies directly into the room where I, a stalwart New Dealer, defended by many New Deal witnesses, was on trial.

Day after day, Priscilla and I were confronted within the enclosure reserved for participants in the trial by three women who in this way became participants on a level not far below that of the judge and the lawyers. Their leader was Alice Roosevelt Longworth, born in the White House, and a virulent and mordant enemy of Franklin and Eleanor Roosevelt and their political values. With Mrs. Longworth were her sister-in-law Mrs. Theodore Roosevelt, Jr., and the latter's daughter, a graphic artist who drew courtroom scenes for the press. Seats for the three had been provided in advance to the right of Judge Henry W. Goddard, a Republican of Mrs. Longworth's generation who had been appointed by President Warren G. Harding.

This was an unprecedented and really improper intervention. The judge's almost obsequious gallantry in welcoming them made it clear that it was he who had made the necessary arrangements for their extraordinary appearance. My lawyers had not been consulted in advance and were nonplussed as to how to respond to what we immediately realized was a damaging impropriety. To have objected would have affronted the judge. In addition, the jury might very likely not have sympathized with an attempt to prevent these celebrities from enlivening the court proceedings.

The three ladies normally made their entrance just after the daily sessions had begun and were greeted in a courtly manner by the judge, a deference not lost on the jury. There they sat, directly facing the jury, for all the world like *les tricoteuses* of the French Revolution, who knitted on their balconies as the tumbrels rolled beneath them on the way to the guillotine. Though ladylike in their decorum, they made no secret of which side they were on. Their expressions of approval and satisfaction when the prosecution scored a point were matched by their scornful attitude toward my witnesses.

Today, as I look back on the factors that let my trial proceedings be

overwhelmed by public passions and become more a trial by ordeal
than by rules of law, I am sometimes inclined to think that the confidence that never deserted me for long was naive and unfounded. But
I knew that we had demonstrated, in the second trial more clearly
than in the first, the failure of the documents to buttress Chambers's
flimsy and inconsistent fantasies. I couldn't help but be convinced that
despite public hysteria and prosecutorial misconduct these jurors who
had lived with the case for so many weeks would—as had those who
had voted for acquittal in the first trial—focus on the essential incred-
ibility of the charges and ignore what were truly irrelevant political
passion and prejudice.

My optimism was shared by most of my group of lawyers and friends
as we went along to André's for lunch at the conclusion of the second
trial. My soberly reflective lawyer and law school classmate Edward
McLean did say as we filed out of the courtroom, "That was a hanging
charge." He meant that Judge Goddard had emphasized factors relied
on by the prosecution. But even Ed was on balance hopeful. We were
a cheerful, even jovial group. Our spirits were heightened by a message
from a former *New York Times* reporter who had talked to many of
the pressmen attending the trial. Their verdict, he said, was "acquittal
in fifteen minutes."

In the last few days of the trial, our optimism was so great that my
lawyers posed for a group photograph to be distributed to the press
after our anticipated victory. It has remained a sad token for me, and
it is being published here for the first time.

Our mood did not change as the jury continued its deliberations all
afternoon and on into the night, until they were sent to a hotel, their
consideration of the case to be continued the following morning. As
we waited during the afternoon and evening of the first day, we played
intricate word games to pass the time in the room reserved for my
counsel and friends. Once or twice we were summoned back to the
courtroom, calls which we responded to with high hopes. But on each
occasion the jury had simply asked for further instructions or information. After one of those returns to the courtroom that evening,
Thomas Murphy, the huge chief prosecutor, put his face on his arms
on a counsel table and voiced discouragement at the jury's questions:

"The dumb sons of bitches," he said. "If there's another hung jury I'm through with this case." I did not want another hung jury either, and his discouraged growl added to my belief that instead the jury would acquit me.

I had hoped for, even expected, a quick decision. As the hours wore on during that second day, the strain of waiting, the momentousness of the outcome of these long deliberations, became enormous. I reasoned, however, that the trial had lasted for many weeks and had become complicated, so the jury could well be forced to spend much time in discussion. I imagined debates and attempts at persuasion. During the trial I had at times gotten the impression that the forewoman was skeptical of my position, even hostile to me. But I felt sure that the others were for me; they had to be, I felt. Lunchtime on the second day came and went. This time we didn't happily troop to André's; we had to be on call to return to the courtroom for possible further jury questions or for the verdict. We ate sandwiches and coleslaw brought in from a delicatessen. Our mood was quiet and restrained.

About midafternoon we were again summoned to the courtroom. This time the jury filed in and took their regular places in the box. In a matter-of-fact, cold voice, the forewoman announced the jury's verdict: "Guilty."

I was stunned.

There was a tone of surprise in the hubbub of voices that erupted as reporters dashed for the door. I couldn't believe that such a blatant miscarriage of justice was possible. Prejudices, bias, and lies had vanquished those of us who had taken the rule of law so seriously that all our procedures had been circumspect, honorable, and aboveboard. The legal world I believed in had been turned topsy-turvy. I was now facing imprisonment for a crime I had not committed.

Nevertheless, I did not despair—my mind jumped immediately to the steps that would have to be taken to overturn this incredible verdict by a prompt appeal.

My lawyers were indignant and in whispered consultations spoke immediately of plans to appeal. In the subdued murmurs that followed the verdict, Judge Goddard thanked the jury for their long service. The hard-faced forewoman responded cheerily with the statement that she would be glad to serve again. She went on to make it seem that her service in this case of grave import had been a pleasure, an outing, a spectacle. We later learned that she was a member of the church where the judge was a vestryman. Her mean-spirited remarks jarred me like a slap in the face. It later struck me as a fitting end to this chapter of a still continuing miscarriage of justice.

Later that day I was reminded of the forewoman when I was told of the appraisal of an experienced criminal lawyer. He said it was unfortunate that we had not been able to see to it that the trial had ended early in the week. Jurors do not like to give up their weekends. Consequently, strong-minded zealots—who, he assumed, would be against me—could browbeat their fellow jurors who would not wish to bear the onus of extending the deliberations over the weekend.

My friends and supporters thronged about me with expressions of consternation and shock. Together we left the courtroom, having little to say to the remaining reporters. Outside the building there were press photographers and groups of bystanders who slowed our walk down the long flight of stone steps to the sidewalk. There Priscilla and I hailed a cab and went to join our son.

Throughout the second trial the friends who had welcomed Tony as part of their own family had provided another vital supplement to my limited resources. Each Sunday they had added Priscilla, Tony, me, and my lawyers to their own family group of six at midday dinner. The hosts often also invited two or three of their friends who were supporters of my cause. The fare was uniformly excellent and our spirits robustly cheerful. It was always a splendid prelude for the afternoon's legal work that preoccupied me and my lawyers.

On the Sunday after the verdict we met once more for dinner. The tone was somber. I was intent on using this opportunity to organize efforts for the appeal we all knew had to be the next step. Ed McLean, counsel of record during both trials and foremost in carrying out the taxing preparations for them, had served at a minimal fee. I could not ask him and his firm to make the further sacrifice of taking on the appeal. For this, I was fortunate in already having a volunteer without fee, my friend Robert Benjamin, also a former Holmes secretary. It was none too soon to establish procedures for transfer of responsibilities and the release of the files, to provide staff and meet costs, and in general to outline plans for the appeal.

An appellate court would, I was confident, have none of the innate weaknesses of a jury, so vulnerable during times of aroused public passion. Once again my faith in our legal system fueled my assurance that all would be well in the next stage. And so I busied myself with consultations about future efforts. Ed McLean, long-faced and grave, came up to me and said that he found me amazing for remaining confident and even cheerful when everyone else was depressed and discouraged.

Here, too, as I look back with all the benefit of hindsight, I don't think that my confidence was unreasonable. Bob Benjamin and Harold Rosenwald, who stayed on from his position as a colleague of McLean's in the trials, shared my outlook. We set to work promptly, recruiting several law students as volunteers to help in the research. Our task was enormous, requiring familiarity with several thousand pages of the trial record and review of hundreds of reported cases in our diligent search for legal precedent. Priscilla prepared a card index of the record, based on categories formulated by Benjamin. We worked hard and harmoniously. In the autumn of 1950, we had completed what I continue to regard as one of the most persuasive, comprehensive, and elegant briefs of the hundreds I have read or worked on.

That my appeal failed brought home to me, though not for the last time, the hard lesson that not every miscarriage of justice can be set right. My trials and appeals have led me to recognize as significant the popular understanding of the gaming aspects of litigation. Without reflection as to the implications, people speak of "winning" and "losing" cases.

At the same time that I was working on my appeal, I wanted to undertake inquiry into the false testimony used against me and especially how Chambers had been able to carry out his forgery by use (as I then believed) of my wife's typewriter. Chester Lane, who had been a law school and New Deal friend, offered to do this inquiry which would be so important in the new trial we expected to get.

Chester made the unusual stipulation that if in the course of his investigation he concluded that I was not innocent, he would be free to withdraw from the case and publicly state why. I readily agreed.

It was Chester's imaginative, vigorous, resourceful investigation, impeded at every turn by the FBI, that led to our discovery that the old Woodstock typewriter, which we had located in a junkyard and brought into court, could not in fact be the one Priscilla had inherited from her father. I deal with this in a subsequent chapter on the evidence I obtained in the 1970s.

Chester Lane's inquiry was still not complete when, my appeals having been denied, I entered Lewisburg Penitentiary in March 1951. A bright hope that lightened the burden of my early months there was looking forward to Chester's success in obtaining a new trial. But again, I reckoned without the obstacles I faced. Our motion for a new trial was denied, and I had to serve out my sentence at Lewisburg.

The unjust verdict, thus left uncorrected, spawned consequences far more momentous than my continued imprisonment: It facilitated Nixon's election to the presidency and the ongoing attacks on both the New Deal and Roosevelt's foreign policies.

13

AN IMPENITENT VIEW OF
A PENITENTIARY

I spent forty-four months in prison, from Maundy Thursday in late March 1951 until just after Thanksgiving in November 1954. Except for a short stay at the zoolike detention center on West Street in New York City, I spent all that time in Lewisburg Penitentiary.

My going to prison meant a traumatic separation from my wife and nine-year-old son, Tony. I had tried as best I could to reassure and prepare Tony for this cruel separation. I managed to tell him of what I knew I would be dealing with in prison life, and he was naturally distressed. The tensions and family disruption of the trials had been difficult enough for him; my going to prison was a new disaster that he could not comprehend. Yet unpleasant knowledge, I felt certain, was better than the terrors of the unknown.

I liken the archaic prison on West Street (since replaced) to a zoo because the prisoners' quarters were barred cages. The iron bars of the cages constituted the ceiling as well as the walls.

Like a traveler to an unfamiliar land, I had tried to learn in advance as much as I could about the customs and conditions of prison life. Good fortune led me to an authoritative source for the information I sought.

161

A helpful friend arranged for me and my attorneys to meet with Austin McCormick, who had been an assistant director of the Federal Bureau of Prisons during the New Deal. In the 1950s he was the head of a small foundation, the Osborne Association, devoted to helping ex-convicts to get jobs and readjust to civilian life. McCormick was a reserved, dedicated man who had served several voluntary prison terms, the better to learn what it was like to be in prison. Later, I discovered from my fellow inmates at Lewisburg that of all the agencies engaged in aiding ex-convicts, only McCormick's modest, low-key efforts had won their universal confidence and gratitude.

McCormick forecast accurately that the particular political pressure to which the Bureau of Prisons was sensitive at the time would lead to my being sent to Lewisburg. By the standards which the bureaucrats of 1951 applied, assignment to Atlanta Penitentiary, a maximum-security prison for hardened criminals with long terms to serve, would have been too severe for me. On the other hand, the prison officials in Washington would conclude that sending me to Danbury Prison, in Danbury, Connecticut, then known as the "country club" of prisons, might seem too lenient.

Similarly, McCormick correctly foretold the prison duties to which I would be assigned. I would not be permitted, he believed, to teach in the Education Department, which plays a regular part in the daily routine of those prisoners least educated, for it might be asserted by some critic that I was teaching communism to my fellows. Nor would I be permitted to work in the library, as that might seem too soft a job. McCormick recommended against my volunteering to work as an orderly in the prison hospital, an assignment that appealed to me as offering a chance to be helpful to my fellow inmates. His practical reasoning was persuasive: In a hospital job I would have access to drugs, or others would think so, at any rate, giving me the Hobson's choice of refusing requests by prisoners for drugs or violating prison rules by complying. McCormick predicted that I would be placed in the storeroom to assist the officer in charge of issuing non-edible supplies. There I would be under continuous supervision so that I could not be presumed by anyone to be playing cards or chatting during work hours.

Austin McCormick was also clairvoyant about those convicts I would find most companionable—the "racket guys," or "regular guys," as they called themselves. Mostly Italian-Americans from New York, they were, he pointed out, affectionate family men, quick-witted, and often personable. A loyally cohesive group, their numbers, self-assurance, and natural intelligence would make them the dominant element in jail, pretty much setting the tone for the code of conduct adopted by the prison population as a whole. And McCormick thought I would find a few interesting men among the youngsters in for long-term military court-martial offenses and among those serving time for car thefts. In contrast, the tiny group of men charged with white collar crimes—chiefly businessmen guilty of tax evasions—would be, he thought, bewildered, frightened, and boring companions for me.

McCormick was also a help in providing details of the surroundings I could expect and the pattern of daily life. I would not be wearing the chain-gang prison stripes of the cartoons and comic strips. Instead, the clothing issued would be faded khaki pants and shirts. And there would be baseball diamonds for hardball and softball, a running track, and handball courts. There were radio headsets for each man and a weekly movie. Tony and Priscilla could come monthly to visit me, and we could write to each other regularly.

Though I was thus in a manner prepared for Lewisburg, I was completely surprised by the West Street center. Despite the poet, "iron bars" *did* this prison make. When we were not summoned to meals or allowed on the roof for a brief period in the afternoon, the cages were our holding pens. With only bars on all sides and above our heads, there was no privacy and, to the torment of the light sleepers, no shielding from the naked bulbs above us that burned all night.

I was put in a cage with a friendly but bewildered Cajun. He chose the top berth of our two-tier bunk. Good Friday night, my second night at West Street, I was awakened by a cry of pain from above me. Sam D., my cagemate, had been dreaming, he said, of pulling a catfish out of the bayou. He had jerked his hand into the air, only to strike the bars which were but a couple of feet above his berth. He had not really injured himself, but as we were both fully waked up, we got out of bed and sat at our small table, talking until his hand had stopped hurting and his nerves had quieted down. Sam told me that he had been charged with driving a stolen car across state lines. He said that, in fact, he had only violated the terms of a car-rental contract and that he had been done in by the local sheriff, who had tried to keep him from courting the latter's daughter. Sam, too, was sent to Lewisburg, so we continued to be on friendly terms for the several years of our joint incarceration.

Another man I saw a good deal of at West Street was Danny F. He was an Italian-American from New York who validated McCormick's forecast as to the men I would find congenial. Danny was in his forties, of medium height, personable and easy in manner. We seemed to hit it off from our first encounter on the roof. He was awaiting transfer to Atlanta, with a long sentence ahead of him. He was quiet, courteous, reserved, and, though affable with others, not gregarious. Facing a lengthy absence from friends and family, he was understandably sub-dued in mood. He had hopes of eventual parole but recognized that he was to be in prison for quite a spell. I believe he sought my company as a way of avoiding casual chatting with the numbers of confused and lonely men who approached any one of us who found himself alone. Certainly *I* valued his companionship in part for this reason. He made no demands on me, was composed and self-contained—a man of pride and courage. In large part we walked or sat together quietly, respecting the other's thoughts and privacy. Many years later I learned from former Lewisburg colleagues of mine that Danny had never left Atlanta. After years of confinement he had become ill and died in prison. At all events, it was to Danny that I owed my acceptance by those like him at Lewisburg. When he knew where I was headed, he said that there I should ask for his brother-in-law, Mike M., and say that it was Danny who had told me of him.

Julius Rosenberg was also at West Street while I was there, but I did not meet him. Rosenberg and his wife, Ethel, after a sensational trial, had just been convicted of conspiracy to commit espionage. Julius's cell was always locked. He was segregated from the rest of us except for three older men who had completed long terms elsewhere and were about to be released, having been sent to New York for that purpose. They were allowed occasional visits to Rosenberg's cage to play bridge with him. Once each day, while we others were locked in our cages, he was permitted to walk with a guard around the main floor of the building, in the corridor that separated the central block of cages from those that lined the walls. He would make a number of circuits, like a passenger on a transatlantic liner taking a "constitutional." Because we knew he was under a sentence of death, silence fell in the cages as he passed. When he was mentioned by the other prisoners, it was with respect for his composure and courage. I did meet and talk with Morton Sobell, charged with being an accomplice of the Rosenbergs. In his conversations, Sobell, who was to spend many years in confinement in Alcatraz, spoke movingly of Julius Rosenberg, whom he greatly admired and respected, as a man of intelligence and level disposition who had displayed great fortitude.

West Street was a scene of confusion and disorder, and a spirit of misery permeated this crowded and antiquated warehouse for unhappy men. The population changed constantly, for prisoners were kept there for brief periods only. There were men on trial who had not made bail; there were a few old-timers about to be discharged after serving their time; but mostly there was a coming and going of newly convicted prisoners whose momentary stay at West Street was for the compiling of dossiers before their transfer to places of regular confinement. Other than ensuring incarceration, the only routine responsibility of the West Street officers was to carry out photographing, fingerprinting, and interviewing of newly sentenced prisoners. When not undergoing registration, the inmates had no prescribed activities and little opportunity for recreation other than cards and aimless, time-killing talk.

The small visiting room was as inadequate and repellent as the rest of "the joint." (Prison terminology seemed especially apt for this house of pandemonium.) Visitors and inmates were separated by glass partitions. The prisoner sat in a box that was a cross between a telephone booth and a bank teller's compartment. The visitors, on the other side of the "tellers' " windows, carried on conversations through a speaking tube. When my wife came to see me, she looked frightened and weary. We made uneasy conversation. We had not anticipated one forbidding, symbolic act. She told me of the shock of receiving a coffin-shaped box with the clothes I had worn when I reported to the courthouse to begin my sentence. I tried to reassure her that it was simply a routine action, but I wished I had been able to warn her of this in advance. The grimness of the visiting room made my reassurance sound unconvincing even to me.

Hostility is inherent in prison procedures. Despite the trappings of "rehabilitation," there is no gainsaying that the relation between most prisoners and their warders is an adversarial one. The reciprocal hostility was palpable at West Street and taught me a lesson that stood me in good stead throughout my prison experience. The men who best maintained their sense of selfhood regarded their position much as do prisoners of war. They relied on their own psychic resources to sustain them and made use of whatever was available to build a common life. A wry, fragmented community of sorts was created by them, a community with its own rules and forms of etiquette. I was a new boy at school and behaved accordingly. The mood at West Street was too chaotic, the stay too brief for a sense of community to be felt, but I heard enough from Danny F. and others who were not new boys to make me become somewhat prison-wise, a condition that comes only with considerable experience in the ways of prison life.

My point of view had already changed. Being in the foreign country was quite different from the expectations derived from Austin McCormick's helpful substitute for a *Guide Michelin*. My feelings included anger at the injustice of my case and at the loss of freedom. But in the year that had elapsed while my case was on appeal, I had had time to merge the anger and the frustration of the trials into the confidence I felt as a result of the success already obtained by my counsel in their search for new evidence. At any rate, I had no choice but to make the best of my present lot while awaiting the outcome of my lawyers' investigations.

After a week or so at West Street, I was shipped by bus with Sam D. and about twenty others to Lewisburg. Easter was early in 1951, and as we drove across country to central Pennsylvania, I saw on a suburban lawn the first wave of male robins and bright swatches of forsythia. I told myself these were the last sights of this kind I would have for several months at least. I was wrong. During the November hunting season, pheasants startled by gunfire frequently flew over the high west wall of our exercise field. These were the longest flights I had ever seen pheasants make, and I logged them in my memory as unanticipated prison experiences.

An equally unanticipated experience the following spring gave me even greater pleasure. As I went through the yard one clear sunlit morning on my way to my storeroom job, I heard an unfamiliar bird song. In the top of the only tree within the prison confines was a rose-breasted grosbeak. I had seen only two or three before and had never heard their tumbling musical phrases. What would have been an exciting event for me at any time brought a surge of intense enjoyment. The bird's song was lengthy and repeated more than once. A small group gathered, watching and listening silently. When the grosbeak finished, no one spoke as we went on to our workplaces. I was refreshed; my senses were sharpened as if by a great aesthetic experience. I cannot think of another time when my spirits were so lifted that I was oblivious to my grim, oppressive surroundings.

I did, however, genuinely enjoy having more leisure to read books of my own choosing than I had had since childhood. I expanded the scope of my reading almost as much as in college. Then, too, inmate ingenuity in which I took part got us a large stock of classical phonograph records. What might have been a period of musical deprivation turned out to be quite the reverse. But in my sleep I always dreamed of freedom, often with elaborate details of court appearances designed to make my release from prison more credible. Today I dream of prison, almost always of the last few days before my term was up, with a heady sense of the release that can no longer be denied me.

Often while I was at Lewisburg, and since, I have remarked upon the similarities between prison and the army. Both institutions are designed to control large numbers of men. Both supply food, clothing, and shelter for large groups. Both must organize the activities of their charges and provide some recreation to balance the workload. Most important of all, both must impose strict discipline in order to ensure that these functions are carried out. An essential element in the successful implementation of discipline by each institution is the process of depersonalization. Privacy disappears; there is no individuality of dress; food and activities are as uniform as the clothing. At Lewisburg we marched in columns of twos to meals and to movies.

In federal prisons, each new arrival is placed in a separate cell,

where he is kept locked up most of the time. This semisolitary confinement is somewhat euphemistically called quarantine, ostensibly to
prevent diseases from reaching the main body of prisoners. The
forty to fifty men in quarantine at the same time march to meals
together in a separate area of the mess hall and share their segregated
exercise and library hours. After a couple of weeks some of these
newcomers are placed in temporary dormitories of their own. The
segregation simplifies the physical and psychological examinations of
the new arrivals. It also makes most of the men actually welcome their
transfer into the general prison population.

The quarantine period lasts about a month. For most of the men
in my entering batch, the limited solitary confinement was harsh
punishment. We were even forbidden to call from one cell to the
next. In addition, we were not allowed to "make commissary"—that
is, we could not purchase cigarettes or candy at the prison store. We
were told that it took several weeks for deposits to be received from
our families and for individual accounts to be set up.

This initial period of confinement at least gave me the opportunity
for uninterrupted reading. A visit to the library, which was large for
a place like Lewisburg, had been one of our first forays. Its holdings
were variegated. Many of the books would have outraged Senator
Joseph McCarthy. There had been earlier political prisoners at Lewisburg. Mr. Smith, the librarian, in order to increase his holdings
despite his limited budget, had allowed books to be sent to the prisoners
from the outside, the books to remain in the library. The collected
letters of Krupskaya, Lenin's widow, were there. So was *The Sword
and the Scalpel*, the story of Norman Bethune, the Canadian doctor
who joined the Chinese Red Army in the early days of the Chinese
Revolution.

When after a couple of weeks I was moved to a small dormitory in
the quarantine wing of the building, I discovered a fellow reader who
also had not been incommoded by our previous isolation. He was
Leiser W., a slight, young rabbinical student born in Vienna. Fleeing
Hitler, he had gone to Switzerland, where he had spent the war in an
internment camp, initially manned by guards who were hostile and
callous. Leiser said that the inmates, who were kept isolated from

world news, realized that the Allies must be winning when their guards were changed and the new guards were friendly and humorous. Leiser was devout, studious, well read, and retiring. Each morning he rose before the six-o'clock bell, stood at a window facing east, and recited his prayers quietly, the while covering his head with one hand, which served as a hat, or yarmulke. After the war he had gone to the Netherlands and worked in the diamond trade, where he had hoped to earn enough money to marry and go to Israel. His job led to his conviction for smuggling diamonds into the United States—unsuccessfully concealed within his body.

Leiser and I became the inmate clerks in the storeroom. As a result, we spent many hours together in the months before he was released. We had opportunities for long discussions of religion, the Bible, history, philosophy, German literature, and world politics. He discovered in our extensive but uneven library the Babylonian Talmud and introduced me to it. Despite the intervention of the rabbi who served the penitentiary, Leiser was unable to get kosher food. His attempts to live up to his dietary laws resulted in a most unbalanced diet. I remember his trying to fill up on one large helping of spaghetti without sauce. His digestion naturally suffered, but he was uncomplaining and even-tempered. Leiser was certainly no hypocrite. As we spent more and more time together in our months in the storeroom, I could only conclude that for him national laws governing trade in non-noxious materials were not moral precepts that he felt bound to observe.

During the month that I was in quarantine, I made my own arrangement with Mr. Smith about receiving books from the outside. He was a civilian employee, the only person in ordinary street clothes we ever saw except for those in the visiting room. He was cold and negative in dealing with us. I concluded that he preferred books to prisoners. Ken McCormick of Doubleday had most thoughtfully offered to send me his firm's books as they were published. Mr. Smith readily agreed to receive them and was even affable in doing so. I was to get first call on the books when they arrived, and I had to agree to take very few, if any, with me on leaving the prison.

While I was in quarantine, I also discovered the efficiency of the grapevine. Greetings, personal news, prison gossip, and cigarettes traveled from inmate to inmate among the general prison population, ultimately reaching the newcomers they were meant for. The last transmitter, often a stranger to the quarantined recipient, would be an inmate barber, hospital orderly, or clerk in the library. This was a welcome demonstration of friendly forces well enough organized to penetrate the isolation that seemed designed to make each man feel alone and helpless.

Prison society has devised its own customs to solace or protect its members. The effect of this routine prison etiquette on the morale of members of my group was marked—almost as much for those who merely learned of the messages (and shared the cigarettes) as for the recipients themselves. I received a packet of cigarettes, a sizable item in the impoverished economy of the prison, from someone whose name I did not know. When I later met him, he said simply that he thought I wouldn't know anyone and that cigarettes would cheer me up. And so, indeed, they did.

When I entered the general population, I was assigned to a second-floor dormitory. These were large rooms with small high windows. Around three walls and in a double row down the middle were about one hundred beds, under each of which was a footlocker for extra clothes. Each bed had its own small metal table, used for writing letters, and a metal chair. Just inside the door was a large room with five or six open showers, some toilets without seats, a common urinal, and a trough with ten to twelve spigots above which was a shelf and a long mirror.

The two-story prison building was long and made of brick. The façade had a noticeable resemblance to Hampton Court Palace. A central corridor ran its length on the first floor, with a command post midway. There were a number of large dormitories and cell blocks on both floors. At the western end of the building were unlocked separate cells that constituted honor quarters. The common entrances to these and to the dormitories were locked at night. Cells in the cell blocks were kept locked most of the time. The mess hall led off the main first-floor corridor. Behind the command post a stone stairway led to an auditorium for movies and chapel, to education and parole offices, and to an indoor-recreation room. A large exercise field, the yard, was, of course, our outdoor-recreation area.

There were about fifteen hundred men housed in Lewisburg in my time, most of whom stayed no more than a year or two, serving short terms or receiving parole. Somewhere between a third and a half of the men were black. As we were racially segregated in living and dining quarters, I had few contacts with the blacks. In consequence, I have scant knowledge of the categories of the crimes with which they were charged. Both blacks and whites used the yard at the same time, but undoubtedly because of the official living and dining segregation, a somewhat uneasy voluntary segregation prevailed during our outdoor-recreation periods.

Men nearing the end of longer sentences who were regarded as "trusties" and some "short-timers" were sent to the Farm, just beyond the walls, where vegetables for the prison larder were grown. There were, in addition, occasional transfers to and from other institutions, particularly Leavenworth, the main medical facility of the federal prison system. There was, therefore, a constant turnover, but there was always a group of about one hundred—mostly whites, as far as my knowledge went—who had terms of from five to ten years as a rule. These men gave a certain stability to prison life and were accorded something like senior status by the others of the white population. The blacks had their own leaders, who, when occasion demanded, negotiated with the white leaders about racial issues that threatened the always pre-carious stability.

The group of Army prisoners, young men whose incarceration dated from World War II, in many cases had lengthy sentences. Periodically some of these were reduced by a military board that visited the prison. This arbitrary procedure meant that for the most part the Army prison-ers' terms ultimately fell into the range that seldom exceeded ten years.

Among the other large homogeneous group, the Italian-Americans, half a dozen of the older men were the accepted "elders" of the tribe. As such, they were also accepted as informal leaders of opinion by the white population as a whole. Their sentences ran something like eight to ten years, ensuring a longer stay than that of the great majority of the other prisoners. Personal conflicts were brought to their attention, and the solutions they suggested were usually accepted.

The Italian-Americans' general attitude toward their situation re-minded me of what I knew about the attitude of prisoners of war. On release they would return to the same way of life as before. Meanwhile they made the best of it. Jail was an occupational hazard to be faced with as much equanimity as one could muster. The restraint and loss of liberty were irksome in the extreme—painful, indeed—but a man of "heart" endured them stoically. Constant complaining—"crying"— was scorned. Bocci in the yard and a card game called brist were played with zest, conversation was often spirited, prison gossip was enjoyed, news from home brought by new arrivals was eagerly pounced upon. Of these prison pleasures, news from home was by far the most prized. The presence of newcomers in quarantine was spotted from the moment of their arrival.

Later, upon their admission into the general prison population, the Italian-Americans were immediately surrounded by questioners seeking details of the familiar life of "the neighborhood." "Racket" etiquette prevented a good deal of such details from being put into incoming letters, which were, of course, censored. In consequence, the reception of the new arrivals could be likened to that of travelers from afar in times before post or telegraph.

The weekly movie was well attended as a welcome diversion from the boredom of prison life. Always attuned to potential danger, the Italian-Americans strove to sit as far as possible to one side or the other of the auditorium. We were assembled by dormitory and cell block and marched to the movies under the watchful eye of guards. As we filed in, it was difficult to choose seats, so the effort to be on the sides resulted in some jostling and changing of place in line. This was ascribed by the guards to provocation, unaware as they were of the real motivation—which was that in the event of a disturbance in the darkened theater, one could quickly reach the safest place. Against a side wall, one could stand with a good chance of avoiding the melee. This precaution also prevented one from being trapped by having his legs caught by the overturning of the long, heavy, backless wooden bench immediately in front—if one were incautious enough to remain seated after the outbreak of a fracas.

The precaution was by no means alarmist. Fights are common among prisoners. There is, too, the possibility of a riot, the all-too-natural result of the tensions that come about inevitably from the close confinement of men trapped in emotional ordeals. The Italian-Americans had an extraordinary sensitivity to even faint signs of potential danger, a characteristic no doubt acquired from a life where danger was a constant. In jail a sudden quietness from one area of the mess hall might signal the tense moments when a quarrel had deteriorated into imminent violence. James Fenimore Cooper's Indians were not more finely attuned to the danger heralded by the snapping twig.

But the analogy that seemed closer to me was the military one. It was not only that the emotional attitude or morale of the Italian-American prisoners at Lewisburg was akin to that of prisoners of war, with their sense of solidarity and their studied aloofness from their guards. It was also that their solidarity antedated prison life—it clearly existed apart from prison and was ensured by its own code of conduct and discipline. There was also a marked sense of hierarchy. Few of the top leaders of the "racket guys" turned up in our midst, and when they did they arrived on petty charges—harassments rather than condign punishments. This was because, like army generals, the top echelon of the East Side "racket guys" did not take a direct part in their front-line activities. Those posts of danger were filled by young men, who thus gained seasoning and proved their mettle. Finally, the solidarity supposedly assured assistance for the families of those imprisoned and for continued efforts to obtain their release.

I lined up for breakfast with my new roommates the morning after my release from quarantine and my assignment to a dormitory, and we marched off to the mess hall when our turn came. We walked in sullen silence, suitable for the early hour and our involuntary presence. The trip past the cafeteria-style food counters, manned by fellow inmates, was also in silence. Once we were seated on the benches at our long wooden tables, there was a little more attempt at conversation. After a bit I felt emboldened to ask if anyone at my part of the table knew Mike M. A black-haired, dark-eyed man almost directly across from me said quietly that he was Mike M. and asked the reason for my query. I told him of my coming to know Danny F. at West Street and of his telling me to seek out Mike M. Danny's name proved a password. Mike's guarded manner changed instantly. He smiled in a warm, friendly way. His prompt acceptance of me brought with it a relaxation of manner and mood at our end of the table. Mike plainly had standing among my new companions. His ready acceptance of me helped me to fit in quickly and easily with the others in my dormitory. Our relationship became a close one. We were constant companions.

Mike was then, I believe, in his late thirties. Of medium height and build, he was intelligent, quick in wit and reflexes, lithe in movement (he was an excellent handball player). He was gifted with a natural charm, quite the equal of anyone I have ever met, man or woman. He was the unquestioned, though tacit, leader of the Italian-American contingent and thus one of the two or three most important men in the prison population. His leadership came partly from his relative seniority among those of his fellows slated to serve five to ten years. Mostly, however, it was due to his calm good judgment and common sense. Problems of personal conflict were brought to him because of general confidence that he would give wise counsel.

In the yard, where we sprawled on the grass in fine weather, Mike was always the center of a small group. The conversation was lively— prison gossip and the doings of the group's friends in the outside world, but also politics, religion, and history. We spoke more than once of labor disputes in which my new associates had engaged as strikebreakers. They were surprised that I disapproved of what was "legitimate business." When we turned to the subject of religion, the most frequent topic was the trial of Jesus and the role of the Jews. They had not realized the ultimate responsibility of Pilate or the real nature of the Roman grievances against Jesus. And often I heard oral and folk history about the various foreign occupations of Sicily, of which the French occupation seemed to have left the most lasting marks. A favorite tale was that Frenchmen masquerading as Sicilians were routinely unmasked by their inability to pronounce correctly the word *gigera*, which means chick-pea.

Our conversations were sometimes interrupted by a supplicant seeking Mike's solution of a dispute. The matter might be taken up in the presence of the group, but when privacy was called for, Mike would leave us and walk around the cinder track as the case was presented to him.

My Italian-American friends treated serious matters seriously. Problems that came before Mike were explained in sober fashion and considered with gravity and decorum. Formality and courtesy were valued—as my meeting with Frank Costello demonstrated. That famous underworld figure was for a short time an inmate at Lewisburg. He had been convicted of contempt of the United States Senate. I received word that "Mr. Frank" would like to meet me and have a private talk. It was arranged that we should meet in the yard and have such a talk during recreation period. Two of my new friends accompanied me. Costello was attended by two others. The two parties came together, there were formal introductions, and Costello and I then walked around the track by ourselves. Presently we sat on a bench and carried on our talk.

Costello had brought with him his brief, which I noticed was prepared by the firm of which my appellate lawyer was a member. The law, as I had been taught it, was on Costello's side. He had at first refused to answer six or seven questions put to him by the Senate committee. Subsequently, on the advice of counsel, he had answered all but one. This, in my book, purged him of contempt as to the questions answered. His right to refuse to answer the remaining question was upheld in court. Nevertheless, he was convicted of contempt and sentenced to prison. Costello and I expressed mutual sympathy for our respective miscarriages of justice and spoke of other matters. He said that his favorite political figure was Mrs. Eleanor Roosevelt. In our brief, rather formal encounter we found nothing to disagree about. When after my release I sent word to Mrs. Roosevelt of Costello's statement, I was surprised to learn that instead of lightly accepting the compliment, she had expressed annoyance.

As I recall the roster of those I knew at Lewisburg, I find it hard to leave out of this account any of those still sharp in memory. Here is an incomplete list:

Tiny, the placid, uncommunicative, lumbering ox of a man, the only lifer in the prison, in for killing a guard.

Radar, an Army deserter, whose nickname came from large ears that were at right angles to the sides of his head. He had lived off the country in France when separated from his outfit, sharing an outcast's life with two French deserters.

JOHNNY, a black man from Washington, D.C., who stood beside me in the Protestant choir and had the unusual musical failing of sharping. With my own tendency to flat, we helped each other stay pretty well on pitch. I don't know what Johnny was in for.

LEO M., a bright youngster from the Lower East Side who was a talented professional boxer, listed in the *Ring Book*. Completely illiterate, he found the prison Education Department not equipped to teach him basic reading and writing skills. I wrote for him his letters to his young wife and helped him to learn to read, so that (as he put it) he would not have to "talk with my fists." Leo had been an early truant, and when a truant officer had roughly handled his non-English-speaking grandmother, whose protectiveness had led her to intervene on his behalf, Leo vowed never to go back to school.

"LITTLE AL" D., only moderately successful as a prizefighter, who had found other lucrative rewards in gangsterism as a bodyguard because of his ability to stun with a single punch. He came to Lewisburg in the final months of a long sentence at Atlanta, where he had studied philosophy in the prison Education Department. He arrived among us soon after Mike M. left, helping me to fill the void caused by Mike's absence. Little Al read with relish my friend A. J. Liebling's pieces on prizefighting as they appeared in *The New Yorker* and assured me that Liebling himself must have been a fighter to write as knowledgeably as he did. Joe Liebling, by the time I came to know and love him in the forties, was grossly overweight. His love of gourmet dishes and fine wines had enriched his accounts of gastronomical travels in Normandy but could not, I was sure, be consistent with a boxer's regimen. When I later told Joe of Little Al's opinion, which I regarded as proof of Joe's gift for grasping the subtleties of an alien world, my obese friend sharply rejected my intended compliment. Of course he had boxed as a young man, he snorted. During his days in Paris as a writer in the early 1920s, he had, he said, outboxed Hemingway in a gym they both frequented.

KLAUS H., my foreign-born violinist friend, who was an Army prisoner convicted of statutory rape because of his inability to gauge the age of an Austrian nymphet. Like many of the other military prisoners, Klaus was convinced that his conviction was motivated by a policy designed to appease the civilian population of the occupied country. He believed he had been a scapegoat meant to soothe the Viennese resentment at the easy conquests by American GIs, whose possession of limitless amounts of PX cigarettes and chocolates made them millionaires in an impoverished city. It was Klaus who was my associate in a joint venture that led to our acquiring for the prison a respectable library of recorded classical music. We reasoned that radio stations in our part of Pennsylvania would often have more than one recording of a given composition. We drew up a basic list of symphonies, concertos, choral works, chamber music, and instrumental pieces—a task that gave us much enjoyment. We found an officer in the Education Department who fell in with the scheme and sent the list to one after another of the local stations. Each successful request reduced the list for the next letter. The project succeeded handsomely and resulted in our being able to have occasional concerts, sparsely attended, in the auditorium and one hour a week over the prison radio system. The latter provided two wavelengths audible via the headset that came with each of our cots, tables, and footlockers. One frequency, as I recall, was preempted by country music of the most primitive kind. The other was given over to prizefights, soap operas, and serials—a favorite being "This Is Your FBI." It took a bit of politicking to get a weekly hour for our classical records. Klaus and I had to settle for Saturday afternoon, when most of the men were in the yard. In addition—and, strangely, on their own initiative—the prison authorities regularly scheduled the Sunday afternoon broadcasts of the New York Philharmonic symphony concerts.

MURPH, another Army prisoner who contended that he was a scapegoat. He had already been at Lewisburg for a number of years when I arrived. The shock of his original death sentence and of prison life and of his bitter belief in the injustice of his conviction had all aged Murph, a small man who had become almost wizened by the time I came to know him. He had been more onlooker than participant, he said, in a brief brawl in Naples between GIs and Neapolitans in which a local man had been killed. Those American soldiers present who were rounded up were charged with conspiracy, and death sentences were liberally handed out. Murph's Army counsel glibly assured him that his death sentence was simply to impress the Italians, but Murph's confidence in official assurances was minimal. Commutation to a life sentence did come, but the long period of fear was destructive. It left him mistrustful of all authority and of almost everyone, and he withdrew into himself. Each review board had reduced his sentence, but when we met he still had fifteen years more to serve, if I remember correctly, and he had already served six years or so. Murph's one outlet in prison was handball, at which he excelled. That skill and his fierce courage earned him the respect and goodwill of his fellows. But he was a loner and clearly did "hard time." Somehow he and I hit it off. He coached me in handball and told me his story. His home had been in a poor section of the Upper East Side of New York City, where he had lived for years. After Murph and I had become friends, his mother died, and he was allowed "compassionate" leave—under guard, of course—to attend her funeral. When he returned he was more desolate than ever. His mother had been the last of his small family, and his neighborhood had largely been demolished to make way for big, new, and expensive apartments. In the end Murph was paroled before my term was up. We agreed to see each other when I got out, and I gave him my telephone number. When I did get home, Murph called to ask why I had not been on the prison bus that brought to New York those who were released when I was. I explained that my wife and son had driven out to Lewisburg with my lawyer to pick me up. Murph had met the bus because, he said, there had been no one to meet him and he didn't want that to happen to me.

PIRRONE (as I shall call him), with whom I shared the relative leniency of the honor quarters after two years in a dormitory. The oldest and much the most colorful of my prisonmates, and always known only by his last name, he was a native Sicilian who had been allowed to bring with him a faded photograph of his village priest but was not allowed to keep in his cell an injured baby sparrow he had rescued in the yard. In January he would say that the almond trees would be blossoming then in Sicily. No stranger to prison life, Pirrone had no problem of adjustment. He was always cheerful, a born clown, and a font of amusing stories. He did "easy time." He was the court jester of Mike M.'s elite group and everyone's favorite. He claimed to have been the bootlegger who supplied a cheap brand of champagne for a daring bathtub scene in Earl Carroll's *Vanities*. The tale of this brush with Broadway high life might be followed by his rendition of a sentimental Italian song, "Sensa Mam'," from World War I, which told of a very young recruit leaving—without his mother—for the front. With Old World formality he greeted his close Italian-American friends as *carissim' amici*. In an attempt to provide holiday conviviality one New Year's Eve at Lewisburg, he improvised a substitute for his bootleg champagne. Wise in prison ways and sure of leniency by the guards if discovered, Pirrone produced a phial of potable alcohol he had smuggled from the hospital stores and offered his liquid merriment in the relative relaxation and security of the honor quarters.

An inmate from North Carolina whose name I don't recall and whom I seldom saw was the petard on which was hoist a misguided ruling aimed at me by the Bureau of Prisons. Some columnist given to trivia—perhaps it was Walter Winchell—reported that I was being treated with favoritism at Lewisburg by being allowed to receive great quantities of books from the outside. In true bureaucratic fashion, the resulting prohibitive ruling avoided singling me out personally, which would have been plainly discriminatory. Instead, it was ordered that no inmate could receive books—period. It was common knowledge at Lewisburg that the North Carolinian had turned to God and was engaged in serious religious study in prison, including a correspondence course. A feature of the course was a stream of books. Several of us who felt especially aggrieved by the Bureau of Prisons prohibition prevailed upon the deprived student to complain to his congressman about the godless ruling. The legislator was moved to protest to the authorities, and in consequence an initial amendment was issued—books of religion were excepted.

This was a considerable victory for those of us who had set about restoring the "freedom of the press" at Lewisburg. And it was welcomed by the librarian and the officers in the Education Department. St. Augustine, St. John of the Cross, St. Teresa—these authors and those of many other works of literary merit became admissible. Once breached, the wall of exclusion began to crumble. Now, with aid from the Education Department, works of science, history, and biography were also permitted to come in again. Then art, philosophy, geography, travel, even politics were admitted. At the end, only newly published fiction, in which I had no great interest, remained on the "Index." I had never liked arbitrary edicts, and I resent official bowing to unjustified pressure. The triumph of common sense, therefore, gave me pleasure, and I include the incident as a further example of the joint activities and associations that helped to make jail less tedious.

There were also occasions of high drama that broke the tedium of our normal routine. Unquestionably, the event of greatest drama, and one which affected the entire Lewisburg population, was the execution of the Rosenbergs. Efforts to obtain reprieve or commutation of their sentences had been eagerly followed by most of the prisoners. The June evening of the executions was calm and cloudless. We were all aware that for asserted religious reasons the executions had been scheduled for just before sunset. As the sun sank, silence spread over the recreation yard. Men stopped their games of baseball, bocci, handball, their exercises with weights, their trotting about the cinder track, their endless conversation. We sat or stood in an eerie quiet until after the sun had disappeared.

We were unmindful that the sunset at Lewisburg was some moments later than at Ossining, New York, where the executions had taken place. Our own sunset thus in fact served as symbol rather than as timepiece. But we felt we were honoring the very moments of death. Renewed activity and conversation came awkwardly and haltingly. It had been a moving and entirely spontaneous observance.

I have no way of knowing what the feelings were of most of the prisoners who took part in the moments of silence. Certainly a good deal of the attitude of anger and bitterness came from the fact that a woman was executed. I heard numerous muttered complaints on this score. But this alone would hardly account for the totality of our immobility and silence. We had all been aware of the worldwide demonstrations and protests, which at those moments were proved to be futile. In all the months I spent at Lewisburg this occasion was unique—the inmates transcending their own unhappiness and self-involvement and joining in a mood of universal sadness at an act of inhumanity.

A dramatic event that aroused excitement rather than somber emotion was the jailbreak by two Appalachian brothers imprisoned for bank robbery. They had loosened a bar in a dormitory window, climbed down the traditional rope of sheets, and somehow gotten over the high brick wall without being discovered. Their freedom was short-lived. It ended with their deaths in a shootout in New York City. And later there was an attack by two young prisoners with razor blades on an inmate clerk in revenge for his alleged report to Lewisburg officials of homosexual relations between the attackers. The multiple cuts were almost fatal.

There was only one brief period when I was conscious of a specific threat of personal danger—not counting the ever-present possibility of involuntary involvement in some fracas brought about by prison tensions. In general, I found that I was readily accepted—in considerable part, I now realize, because of my being a lawyer. A number of my fellow inmates came to me with legal questions and problems. I assured them that I was in no position to give them useful advice, but I listened sympathetically. On one occasion, however, I was warned by my Italian-American friends that I should, for a day or two, be circumspect and remain within their protective circle. I was told that two undisciplined young Italian-Americans had just joined the population and had been assigned to the early morning task of cleaning the kitchen. The guard on duty, who was particularly disliked by the prisoners because of his hostile manner, had said to the newcomers that something should be done about Hiss. He had pursued the subject by observing that the Rosenbergs were dead, so why should Hiss "continue on"? The two young men had taken this as a hint that they should do me harm.

Fortunately for me, they had consulted Mike M. and his associates, who had assured them that I was "one of them." They had also been told that the guard was inimical and that they could in no way benefit from following his implied suggestion. The only aftermath of the matter was the suicide of the guard a few weeks later, which we all took as a demonstration of his instability. We were told that he was a veteran of Guadalcanal, and we concluded that the fierce Pacific battle of World War II had left him an emotional casualty.

There was, however, an occasion when officials in Washington thought they had reason to believe that I was in danger. William Remington was killed by inmates who assaulted him with a rock in a sock. This tragedy, which occurred a few weeks before my release date, had unexpected repercussions for me. Remington had, like me, been convicted of perjury. He, too, had denied that while he was a government servant—employed as an economist—he had passed information to a Soviet courier. (To my disappointment, Remington had felt it prudent to keep his distance from me in prison.) Officials in Washington seem to have concluded that Remington's assailants had acted from political motives and that I, too, might therefore be in danger.

I was notified by the warden that for my protection I was to be taken out of my regular quarters and segregated from the rest of the population in a separate locked cell. I protested that this was unnecessary and unfair to me. I did not wish to be separated from the men I had been associated with for months and years. The move would be destructive of the relations I had developed with my fellow inmates. At my request the warden called in the head of the guard force, Captain Shaefer, who agreed with my contention that I was in no personal danger. I said that if I were segregated, I would not cooperate with the move, would have to be carried, and in every way would make it plain to the other prisoners that the change was not of my doing.

The upshot was what the officials in Washington considered a compromise, which I accepted. A veteran guard, soon to be retired, was detailed to keep me in sight whenever I left my quarters. At my insistence, he was not to come closer than twenty paces. My distant shadow aroused general amusement but did not otherwise affect my daily routine. In particular, his discreet and passive performance of his task did not impair my personal relations with those with whom I normally met in my moments of leisure.

There was one other occasion when I took issue with official directives that affected me. By statute those prisoners who have served their time without violations of prison discipline are released after serving about three-fourths of their formal sentence. The possibility of forfeiture of some or all of the statutory "good time" is an important sanction designed to encourage observance of prison rules of behavior. Like parole, however, the grant of this boon is conditioned upon the following, after release, of prescribed conduct for the remainder of the nominal sentence.

In my case, that statutory "good time" formula resulted in my serving forty-four months of a nominal sixty-month sentence. My period of "conditional release" was therefore sixteen months, during which I reported to a parole officer and could leave New York City and its environs only with his permission, even to visit my mother in Baltimore. Before I left Lewisburg, I was told of the restrictions that I would have to live with during those sixteen months. Drunkenness, a brush with the law, failure to report to one's parole officer, traveling without permission beyond the fixed residential limits—these were among the prohibited actions.

There was also a general prohibition: One was not to "associate with criminal elements." Obviously, it seemed to me, this could be construed to prevent me from seeing men I had met in prison, and I felt I could not in good conscience agree to it. I told the official who was instructing me that if such was the meaning of the rule, then there was no sense in my leaving the penitentiary, for I would not attempt to live up to the restriction. After some delay, during which the official consulted with his superiors, presumably in Washington, I was told that the requirement would not be so construed in my case.

This was one of the very few times when discretion was exercised in my favor. No discretionary time off had been allowed me, although my immediate custodian—the guard who was in charge of the storeroom to which I was assigned—had periodically recommended that I receive it for "meritorious conduct." Similarly, not even a few weeks of parole was forthcoming.

And so, having served every day of my sentence that could be exacted, I left Lewisburg just after Thanksgiving in 1954.

14

PLEASURE AND BLEAKNESS

As I walked through the prison courtyard and the gates, I was surprised and touched to hear farewells called to me by many friends crowded behind the barred windows.

The day was sunny, in keeping with my happiness at my release and reunion with my family. Chester Lane had come with Priscilla and Tony to pick me up. For this mission, he sported his new, bright-red convertible—in derision of the charges against me.

A crowd of reporters and newsreel camera crews swarmed about. I had no reason or inclination for a press conference and said little to the reporters as we made our way to Chester's car.

It had been several months since Tony had last made the trip to Lewisburg—the prison visits had been too troubling for him. Priscilla and I worried about the emotional burden on him of my prolonged absence, as well as the possible stigma on him of my imprisonment. I was overjoyed to see him looking well and cheerful. I remember his active curiosity about the bustle surrounding us and his excitedly calling my attention to the noisy press helicopter right overhead.

I was released at about noon. Our spirits soared as we drove through the Pennsylvania Dutch farm country, stopping for a big lunch at a pleasant inn to celebrate.

As the day of my release had drawn nearer, my thoughts at Lewisburg had run along two distinct lines. I looked forward hungrily to time with family and friends. I dreamed of going to museums and galleries, to concerts and plays, and simply of walking freely about the city. Yet a very different set of thoughts interrupted even those brief plans for the pursuit of happiness. I was preoccupied with money matters. Savings had long since been used up for the costs of the trials, costs which had in far larger part been met by generous contributions by family, by friends, and by strangers who wished me well. Formally barred from the practice of law and informally barred from many other forms of livelihood for which I felt qualified, I would be hard put to earn a living. I reflected wryly that I was in the opposite position Darwin was in when he recorded in his diary the entry that had so delighted Holmes. Darwin, intent on his laboratory work and resenting the distraction of social activities, wrote, "The future is bleak, pleasure every day." I saw no chance of ever returning to *my* "laboratory," public service. Indeed, it would be some time, I thought, before I could even afford much of Darwin's bleakness.

Once more at home, I found my assumptions about informal black-listing all too accurate. Friendly prep schools and college administrators, aware of the likely attitude of trustees and contributors, were politely negative. Similar refusals met me as I explored the possibility of minor executive jobs in publishing and business concerns.

While I was still at Lewisburg, I had made up my mind to write about my case, believing that most of the public was unaware of the new evidence and of the grave improprieties of the prosecution which had found no place in the daily press reports during the trials. Both Chester Lane and Robert Benjamin had wanted to write their own accounts, but it soon became clear that they were too busy to take on such a project. If the book was to be written, I must do it. Under prison rules, I could not work on the book at Lewisburg, so I planned to undertake it as soon as possible after my release.

A literary agent found publishers in America (Alfred Knopf) and Great Britain (John Calder) for my projected book. The combined advances of $10,000 would, with Priscilla's salary, just about see us through while I wrote it.

During my stay at Lewisburg, Priscilla had worked in a Doubleday bookstore. Her salary had been supplemented by help from one of her brothers and from members of my family. The rent for our Greenwich Village apartment was modest, and by careful budgeting she had been able to manage. Tony's schooling then and until he graduated from college was taken care of by scholarships.

Upon my return, Priscilla and I lived simply but certainly not in penury. We permitted ourselves the luxury of continuing our top balcony seats at the Philharmonic, then still installed at Carnegie Hall. Galleries and museums were free and it was there I spent much of what time I took off from writing. We saw an occasional play on or off Broadway and more often than that attended a chamber music concert. Never lacking friends, we saw a good deal of them.

My homecoming had many wonderful moments. On the very evening of my return, Barney Josephson, the proprietor of a nearby restaurant, brought a bottle of champagne. The next night, I was flabbergasted to have A. J. Liebling heave his heavy bulk up the three flights to my apartment and, between gasps, welcome me back. Other friends, neighbors, and even strangers who recognized me on the street and in museums and theaters greeted me warmly. One snowy morning as Tony and I were walking in Washington Square, a pretty young woman pushing a baby carriage suddenly stopped as we drew near, came up to me, kissed me on the cheek, and said kindly: "Welcome home." She then promptly disappeared without identifying herself.

Another cheerful note at about the same time was the return of my stepson, Timothy Hobson, from his medical studies in Geneva. He was on his way to San Francisco for internship at Mt. Zion Hospital. A surgeon, he now lives in California with his wife and children.

But domestic troubles began within half a year or so of my return in what I considered minor disagreements.

Priscilla had been deeply wounded by the trauma of the trials and the resulting invasion of her privacy. The notoriety of the case had led the Dalton School, where she had been teaching, to replace her. Her new employers, at the Doubleday bookstore, took pains to keep her from meeting their customers, and had her ordering books and doing other administrative duties from a basement office. And she met with various slights and acts of hostility, or thought she did. I remember her telling me upon her visits to Lewisburg that her friends seemed to be avoiding her. When I came home and inquired about this, the friends said they thought Priscilla had indicated that she wished to be left alone.

As a result of her difficult times, when I came home from Lewisburg—where I had been shielded from most of the notoriety—Priscilla wanted us to flee the scenes of her torment. She suggested we change our names and try to get posts as teachers at some remote experimental school impervious to public opinion.

My objectives, my personal needs, were directly to the contrary. As I had done nothing to flee from, I felt that public prejudice should be confronted and faced down. In my motion for a new trial, Chester Lane had uncovered new evidence helpful toward my ultimate vindication. More evidence would surely be found. In the meantime, the most effective step I could take was to write about the travesty of the HUAC hearings and the trials.

My new undertaking was profoundly distasteful to Priscilla. Here I was, intent on revisiting her worst times of nightmare, with publication of the book sure to keep the nightmare alive. No wonder she distanced herself from my writing and made no offer to take part. I dedicated the book to her, but it gave her no pleasure.

What had first seemed to me an understandable difference of outlook, of attitude, soon became a fixed gulf. Our disagreement as to our future goals became irreconcilable, and it colored all other issues. We came to disagree about Tony's education, about summer vacation plans, even about what friends to see.

In the spring of 1956, I accepted an invitation from the Whig-Clio Society of Princeton University to speak on the likely effects of the Eisenhower-Khrushchev summit meeting. (Such public appearances had been forbidden during the sixteen-month period of restricted activity.) The reaction to my talk at Princeton did nothing to still Priscilla's fears or to bridge our differences. My talk was moderate, rather dull I was told, and the meeting was restricted to the members of the club, but it had been publicly announced in advance. Indignant alumni and others demanded that the president of the university prohibit me from speaking. He upheld the rights of the students to invite me. But as I walked with two faculty friends to the building where I was to speak, we were forced to pass between lines of irate American Legion veterans and alumni. My inhospitable reception was recorded by TV and press cameramen.

Even before the Princeton talk, my wanting to have my say on matters of foreign policy had led me to write an article about Yalta, a decision which did not sit well with Priscilla. Because of the attacks on the Yalta agreements, I was pleased to have a chance to set the record straight. The article, "Yalta: Modern American Myth," appeared in *The Pocket Book Magazine* in September 1955. I have no recollection of whether I cleared this with the parole officer.

In spite of our developing marital discords and a tight budget, the early months of my homecoming were mostly happy ones. As I had no fixed daily schedule, I was able to spend a good deal of time with Tony when he came home from school. That pleasure once cost me five dollars, when a policeman gave me a summons for playing ball with Tony in Washington Square. There was no grass to be preserved at the place we had chosen, we were well away from the walkways, and there were no signs prohibiting tossing a ball, but I ended up paying a fine in Magistrate's Court. At least it was no violation of my conditional release.

With the writing of my book completed in the autumn of 1956, I was again in need of a job. The book appeared in the spring of 1957 to mixed reviews and poor sales. I had achieved my purpose of publishing in book form my account of the HUAC's shameless hearings and the unfair trials. But I could not expect to better my lot from royalties.

The task of finding a job had become no easier since 1954. A friend who owned a small business suggested that I learn typing and shorthand in hopes of becoming an executive assistant with secretarial skills in some small concern. Accordingly I applied to the Speed Writing Institute at Forty-second Street and Sixth Avenue. My reception was cordial indeed: The owner asked to see me and told me that, as a measure of his support for my cause, he would give me a scholarship. Diligently I applied myself to learning the skills. I turned out to be an utter failure. Try as I might, I could not learn touch typing. I would lie abed at night, having memorized the keyboard, and would successfully carry out in my mind the fingering I had been taught. But once at a real machine I could not replace my hands correctly on the keyboard after I had struck the space bar. I did not give up quickly. I even had special tutoring from my kind teacher. But it was no use.

For a different reason I was not much better at speed writing. That species of shorthand was not too different from the personal system I had developed at law school and used thereafter to record notes of legal or State Department conferences. Because of the similarity, I think, I invariably fell back on my primitive method whenever the pace was rapid. That might have sufficed for a job as a private secretary, but not without my also being able to type.

Most of the time as I job-hunted, my self-confidence was boundless. There was always a lead to follow up; I was sure I would find something. I was willing to settle for one hundred dollars a week as a starter, and I was prepared to take almost anything.

Almost anything, but there were limits. One acquaintance assured me he could get me a post in Haiti in the office of the company that handled green stamps overseas. I was also offered a job selling insurance for an outfit that a friend in the insurance business warned me away from on the ground that its operations were of questionable legality.

Finally, after not too many months, my optimism was rewarded. Peter Kihss of *The New York Times* was then occasionally writing a profile of someone picked more or less at random. Kihss interviewed me. His report that I was seeking a job led Andrew Smith, president of Feathercombs, Inc., to call Chester Lane offering me a job. When I saw Smith he said with disarming candor that he thought he could get me cheap and asked what I would accept as salary as his personal assistant. I told him of my willingness to work for one hundred dollars a week. He said that seemed a bit low and fixed the salary at six thousand dollars a year. (It was later raised to eight thousand and then to eleven thousand.)

Andy Smith was an iconoclastic ex-advertising man who had been brought up in Japan, where his father was a teacher in what I understood was a missionary school. Andy had devised a type of barrette to hold women's hair in place. It consisted of a backless comb made of looped piano wire, the loops serving as closely aligned teeth.

Smith had correctly believed that skilled Japanese handworkers could properly bend the resilient piano wire, which he obtained in Sweden. Rhinestones for decoration were attached in a New York loft. Smith had thus established a small but complex multinational business. He had also obtained a patent for his creation.

When I went to work for Feathercombs, the enterprise, then only a few years old, was prospering. Orders streamed in from large department stores across the country where Smith had sent attractive display materials and women to demonstrate the product's use.

Smith was bright and charming. The administrative staff of family and friends was small and congenial. A far cry from all my previous jobs, my work was nonetheless pleasant and challenging. I saw a good deal of Smith, his wife, and two sons socially, and I enjoyed their company.

For the small enterprise to expand and be able to pay dividends to the investors who had helped found it, Smith would require an entirely revamped operation. That kind of activity did not interest Smith. He began to spend less and less time in the office, and he became hard to reach on the phone. Among other things, he became preoccupied with marital difficulties.

My own had come to a head. In the fall of 1958, during an ugly scene, Priscilla had asked me to leave. I was astounded to discover that the break she proposed was a relief. But I insisted on staying until Tony returned from Putney School, where he was then in his senior year, for the Christmas holidays. The effect our separation might have on Tony concerned me greatly, and I did not want him to learn of it simply by finding out I had moved out of the family apartment. I wanted to tell him of it first, and a telephone call or letter would not do.

So, until Tony's return, Priscilla and I lived like strangers in separate rooms of the apartment and told only close friends of our estrangement. I left when Tony came back from school. I spent the next several years in rented rooms and in friends' apartments. Priscilla and I made several attempts at reconciliation, but the differences that had developed were too great and the wounds we had dealt each other were too deep.

My job at Feathercombs included seeing to corporate procedures, such as the meetings of the small board of directors, composed of Smith, his wife, and the chief investor. They were soon joined by Walter Beer, a partner of Chester Lane's, who served as general counsel to pass on contracts and other corporate problems. I had brought Beer and Smith together and was able to do much of the paperwork and drafting for Beer's approval.

Then, a major manufacturer of women's hair accessories brought out a plastic comb similar to ours, although not nearly so effective in keeping hair in place. But it was being sold cheaper than ours—its maker had long-established relationships with stores in every sizable city—and it cut into our sales. We had only the one product and could not sustain a drastic drop in our sales.

Beer and I recommended a patent attorney, who filed suit for infringement. Even as the suit progressed, we could not help being worried that the big competitor would choose to drag out the litigation in order to put us out of business, even at the risk of having to pay us damages.

Smith did take an interest in the patent suit. His confidence was such that he turned down an offer from the competitor to buy him out. He also refused an offer from the Gillette company.

We thought the lawsuit was going satisfactorily, though we could not get an injunction prohibiting sales of the competitive comb. We worked hard at maintaining the volume of our own sales, but with diminishing success. The once highly profitable little business was now limping along. The atmosphere at the office became increasingly tense. I became in effect Smith's alter ego, transmitting his decisions to the harried staff, for he continued to be almost entirely an absentee owner.

As our sales declined, our bank refused to extend credit, and we were reduced to factoring our accounts receivable. We were living from hand to mouth. I told Smith that the business could not afford our two salaries, that he should come in and take charge, and that I should leave as soon as I could find another job. Smith, pressed and high-strung, did not take my well-meant proposal kindly. Our formerly easy relations became strained, and on one of his visits to the office we had a sharp altercation in the presence of others. He charged me wrongly with having failed to inform him of some adverse event. I responded with hot anger and called him a liar. That was it. Within a day or two, he fired me.

The business did not long endure, but I am pleased that Andy Smith and I later patched things up and became friends again.

After Feathercombs, my search for a job lasted much longer. I collected unemployment insurance during most of 1959 and part of 1960. My months of unemployment were bleak in a non-Darwinian sense—except for my getting to know Jack Gilford, the gifted comic actor, as we stood alphabetically linked in the "G–H" line at the unemployment office. Our common plight let me learn that it was his wife, Madeleine, who had given me a welcome-home kiss that snowy day in Washington Square five years before.

In 1960 I met Sam Chernoble, the owner of a moderately large printing plant, who had just bought control of Davison-Bluth, an old-fashioned stationery store on the west side of Fifth Avenue between Nineteenth and Twentieth streets. Chernoble offered me a job as one of two outside salesmen for the store, with the opportunity to sell printing to be done at his plant. I would draw fifty dollars a week against my monthly commissions. I thus began a position that I held longer than any other in my life, until I retired in the late 1970s.

Printing orders suitable for presses the size of Chernoble's did not jibe with orders for office supplies. The customers I sought for stationery items might need job printing but not large runs on big presses. Sam Chernoble was always helpful in his dealings with me, and he agreed I could separately represent a smaller firm than his. For some years I thus represented Tabard Press on Varick Street as well as Davison-Bluth.

I went to work with a will. My many friends sent me to see friends or business acquaintances of theirs. Entree was easy. I sensed that the business executives who received me genially were looking forward to saying at dinner parties, "Guess who wants to sell me rubber bands and paper clips."

Getting regular customers was not so easy. A president or vice-president might see me, but it was a purchasing agent or office manager whose goodwill was essential. That officer usually had his regular sources with whom he had easy relations. Besides, his domain was being trespassed upon when one of his bosses asked him to see me. Still, enough purchasing agents gave me a fair hearing as to our prices and services so that I earned a living. Nat Sorkin of Tabard Press said he had not seen the city covered so thoroughly since the Great Depression.

After a few years, Davison-Bluth was taken over by a larger firm, S. Novick & Son, and its activities were transferred to the Puck Building on Lafayette Street. S. Novick had its own printing plant, with presses suitable for the needs of my customers. Novick employed some sixty or more people, so I now had many more co-workers, who also became my friends.

I enjoyed the work, with its technical challenges and the variety of men and women I met in the offices I visited seeking customers. I learned the rudiments of good printing. My experience as a storehouse clerk at Lewisburg stood me in good stead in coping with the great number of standard stationery items.

I also learned the seamier side of the business. There were purchasing agents who demanded kickbacks or payoffs, but I was never pressured by superiors to accede to such demands. I also departed from another common practice: I didn't take my customers to lunch or give them whiskey or flowers at Christmas. Notwithstanding my unorthodoxy in these matters, I developed a loyal list of friendly customers. Before long, I was able to achieve some success in my life as a salesman.

15

BRIGHTER TIMES, A BROADER AGENDA

My success as a salesman brought me more income than Feathercombs had and gave me more time for other things. It was at this time that I came to know the talented and beautiful Isabel, who is now my wife. Other happenings also made life more agreeable and interesting.

I continued to follow all possible leads to evidence that might help me obtain vindication. One promising development came from a young, practicing trial lawyer, Raymond Werchen. Werchen's initial interest in my case had been elicited by a television interview of Chambers that he had chanced to see. He had been struck by the close similarity of Chambers's mannerisms, strange patterns of speech, and illogical trains of thought to those of a psychopathic fellow student whom he had known at law school.

Werchen took it upon himself to read the entire records of both trials. The more he delved into the records, the more he became convinced that there had been a miscarriage of justice.

Werchen came up with independent evidence that the typed papers Chambers produced against me were not typed on Priscilla's machine, as Chambers and the prosecution had contended they were. Werchen noted that the FBI "expert," who had identified two sets of documents as having been typed on the same machine, was no scientist and had been more sweeping in his opinions in the second trial than in the first. By then he had learned that he would not be cross-examined and he could therefore be less precise. Werchen found a number of differences in the typeface characters in the two sets of documents. The similarities on which the FBI witness had relied in court were few in number and did not themselves preclude separate machines for the two sets of papers. Werchen then proceeded to the painstaking task of examining each character in the typed material. This chore convinced him beyond doubt that two different machines had been used.

However, my lawyers concluded that it was too late in the day for us to be able to present Werchen's evidence. All that came of it was an article in *The Nation* by Werchen and Fred Cook.

In 1962 the publication of Nixon's *Six Crises* added, at first blush, material help from an unexpected quarter. He wrote that the FBI had found the typewriter in my case.

My lawyers had found the typewriter that we brought into court in the belief that it was Priscilla's old machine. In 1952 Chester Lane discovered that we had made a mistake: That typewriter was not Priscilla's old machine but a look-alike, a discrepancy that is the key to overturning my conviction (see Chapter 17).

Nixon's statement meant one of two things: Either the FBI had found the look-alike typewriter but left it where they found it, or the FBI had found Priscilla's old machine. Either way, this confirmed our belief that the government had learned of the discrepancy before the first trial but had not disclosed what it knew.

When my lawyers publicly said as much, Nixon quickly disavowed his statement. He said it was a researcher's error. Attorney General Robert Kennedy looked into the files and announced that the FBI "never had possession of the disputed typewriter." That curious disclaimer is not inconsistent with Nixon's disavowed statement. But I had no way to pursue the episode further.

Later that year, Nixon lost his bid to be governor of California and told the press that they "won't have Dick Nixon to kick around anymore." ABC invited me to take part in a TV broadcast called "The Political Obituary of Richard Nixon." Several of his friends appeared on the program and my own remarks about him were measured and mild. Nevertheless, some Republicans raised a noisy fuss complaining of my having been invited to participate in the program.

I was delighted in 1962 to be asked by Atheneum to prepare a paperback abridgement of the published letters between Justice Holmes and his London-based friend Harold Laski. The abridgement appeared in two volumes in early 1963. The letters extend from 1916 to shortly before Holmes's death, in 1935, and are a rich storehouse of the Justice's daily thought and activities, written in an easy, casual style. Laski, bright, vastly well read, and in touch with European intellectual and political movements, was a stimulating gazetteer for Holmes. My task could not have been a more enjoyable one: to be back in the Justice's world and to be consulting with my friend Mark DeWolfe Howe, another former secretary to the Justice, and the original editor of the letters. Much cutting was needed to meet the publisher's requirements. It was easy to prune drastically Laski's long and often rambling letters, but for the life of me I could not convince myself that any of Holmes's spare words should be dispensed with. In the end, all the cuts came from Laski's correspondence.

I took the scholarly side of my assignment seriously. Howe had made very few omissions in the texts of the letters as he prepared them for the original edition. The original letters were kept in a safe in his office at Harvard Law School. I checked the originals for each omission, and Howe and I readily agreed that almost all the omitted passages should also be omitted in the new edition.

One series of omitted passages, however, we both thought should be restored. These passages contained Holmes's request, twice repeated, that his letters be destroyed. Laski had ignored the first request but promised to comply with the second. When Holmes raised the point a third time, Laski admitted that he had not complied, pleading his pleasure in rereading Holmes's letters and promising to make provision for their destruction at his (Laski's) death. This obviously Laski had not done—to the immense benefit of posterity. Howe and I felt that these interchanges belonged in the historical record and that it would be appropriate to publish them in the forthcoming edition. However, on reflection, he changed his mind. He told me that he had promised Felix Frankfurter to protect Mrs. Laski by letting nothing detrimental to her husband's reputation appear in the published letters.

On reflection, Howe felt that Laski's failure to carry out his promise to Holmes might be criticized by some people. Frankfurter had suffered a stroke and was in no condition to be consulted. As Mrs. Laski was still alive (she has since died), Howe felt the passages still should be omitted. He would, he said, make them public in the biography of Holmes on which he was then at work.

The second volume of Howe's biography, covering the years 1870 to 1882, appeared in 1963. Howe did not live to publish another volume, so his biography of Holmes never reached the years in question. Thus the passages demonstrating Holmes's aversion to public knowledge of his personal correspondence have yet to be published.

While I was preparing the Holmes-Laski edition, I received a letter from Dr. Meyer Zeligs, a San Francisco psychoanalyst, telling me that he planned to write about my case. I have always regarded it as an obligation to help serious authors and researchers interested in the case. What conclusions they might come to would be up to them. I was sure that objective inquiry would convince any intelligent person of the rightness of my cause. And so it proved with Dr. Zeligs, who started out with doubts of my innocence. We had a considerable correspondence (which he subsequently gave to the Harvard Law School) and numerous talks in New York and San Francisco. His book, *Friendship and Fratricide* (Viking), came out in 1967.

Not long after the publication of Dr. Zeligs's book, John Chabot Smith, a journalist who had covered both trials for the *New York Herald Tribune*, asked me for an interview and to make my legal files available to him as part of his research for a book on the case. We spent many hours together as I answered his questions, and he devoted several years to a thorough examination of the defense files. He also interviewed witnesses and other knowledgeable people. His book, *Alger Hiss: The True Story* (Holt, Rinehart and Winston), appeared in 1976. It is a comprehensive study of the case, although it antedates the Freedom of Information Act proceedings that turned up the material used in my *coram nobis* petition (see Chapter 17).

Following the same practice, I later gave many interviews and full access to my files to Allen Weinstein, then a Smith College professor. He, contrary to Meyer Zeligs and John Smith, found me guilty, and some people gratefully acclaimed his book (*Perjury: The Hiss-Chambers*

Case, Knopf, 1978) for its scholarly trappings. Other readers noted and published its scholarly shortcomings and many errors, of which I was the principal, but not the only, victim; another person was misidentified as a fugitive Communist organizer, sued Weinstein for libel, and recovered damages and a public apology.

I have also had numerous interviews and talks with other authors, journalists (including radio and TV), filmmakers, and even a playwright. A documentary, *The Trials of Alger Hiss*, produced and directed by John Lowenthal, has been shown in motion picture theaters and on television here and abroad. A television docudrama entitled *Concealed Enemies* appeared in this and other countries.

And during this period I found time for more of my own writing. I had become convinced that the New Deal was being neglected or ill-used by historians. I carried out extensive research, set up a card index file, collected books, articles, and press items, and resolved to write about it. I had something to say and I wanted to say it.

During the fall of 1967, I gave four public lectures on the Depression and the New Deal at the New School for Social Research. My subject was in tune with the times. Lyndon Johnson's Great Society program was in many ways reminiscent of the New Deal. The civil rights movement and the opposition to the war in Vietnam involved spirited public participation somehow akin to the popular spirit of the mid-1930s. My lectures were well attended, and the questions I solicited after each lecture were lively and germane. I recall no heckling. The only opposition came in a crank call to the New School before the first lecture, threatening that I would not leave the building alive. As a result, a city detective posted himself backstage, out of sight, and kept an eye on the audience.

It had been twenty years since I had so enjoyed the feeling of being the right person in the right place at the right time. The New School invited me back to conduct seminars on the New Deal. I spoke on the subject at Brandeis University and Columbia University. In the fall of 1968, while traveling in England, I gave more lectures.

But the book on my favorite subject did not go well. Lectures, talks, seminars on the New Deal were all very well, but the formality and definitiveness of a book were more difficult. I made several false starts. Angus Cameron, a book editor and friend, pointed out that I was trying to combine two irreconcilable approaches: that of the professional historian and that of the personal account of a participant.

I changed my drafts to a purely personal memoir. But that did not take care of a major problem I wanted to address. We New Dealers knew that we had not cured the Depression in the sense that our reforms would prevent its return; our efforts did not ensure a fuller life for all Americans. It was not our reforms but the coming of World War II that really cut back unemployment. I was looking for the answer to a key question: whether, without wartime demands for full productivity, we could have cured the agricultural and industrial ills that brought alternating glut and scarcity.

I wrote about the exploits of my New Deal colleagues in stopping the worst ravages of the Depression and in setting up the agencies that still endure as bulwarks of our society. But the realities of history diminished my enthusiasm as a memoirist. Even at the peak of FDR's popularity, his opponents had been able to slow down the pace of reform. It seemed clear to me that FDR's coalition had pushed ahead close to its limit when war came. I lost my zest for the book project and finally abandoned it altogether. *

Other activities soon preoccupied me. With higher income from the stable group of customers I had developed, and with my almost familial relations with my business associates, I was free to accept more invitations away from the city. In 1972, I lectured and took part in seminars at five English universities: Keele, Hull, Nottingham, Lancaster, and Reading. I was asked to speak about the Yalta Conference, and thereafter I expanded my list of lecture topics by adding Yalta, the United Nations, the beginning of the cold war, our Far Eastern policy, Justice Holmes, the McCarthy era, and the American press. I didn't include my own case as a separate topic, but it usually came up as a matter of course, and I always answered questions about it from my audiences.

My preferred practice on the lecture circuit was to spend two to four

---

*A recent historian of the New Deal, Kenneth S. Davis, shares my conclusion about the limits of the New Deal's potential for reform and has written a book, FDR, *the New Deal Years, 1933–1937* (Random House, 1986), that illuminates the question I once found so baffling.

days at a college or university, giving a public lecture on one of my proffered topics and several seminars on others. I asked to be put up on or near the campus and to have my meals with students and faculty. My schedule was arranged in advance so that I knew how many seminar students there would be, their course of study and college class, and what books were on their reading lists. This advance information allowed me to gear my presentation to the size and level of preparation of the group.

For the next ten years, I visited schools, colleges, and universities all over the country. It gave me special pleasure to return more than once to Princeton, without untoward incident. Though I did not earn very much in fees, I took part eagerly in what were learning experiences for me as much as for the students. I tremendously enjoyed the intellectual stimulation and informal contacts with students and teachers everywhere. I gave up my travels only when forced to do so by failing eyesight and energy.

The 1970s were good to me in other ways as well. The American Civil Liberties Union had brought suit on my behalf to obtain my small federal pension, which had been denied me by the "Hiss Act," enacted in 1954. (So called because plainly directed at me, it prohibited the payment of federal pensions to anyone convicted of perjury relating to the national security of the U.S.) Under the able direction of Sanford Rosen, my lawsuit resulted in the act, as applied to me, being declared unconstitutional.

Also in 1972, Harper & Row published a paperback edition of my book about my trials. It was well received, as was I in my promotional radio and television interviews.

In 1975, soon after the Watergate scandal forced President Nixon to resign, I enjoyed another court victory. I was readmitted to the bar of Massachusetts by a unanimous decision of that state's supreme court.* When I appeared to take the oath, I was delighted by the contrasting occasions of my bar admission and readmission. In 1930 we were all young men, roughly similar in age, earnest and ever so

---

*I have been told that all seven judges of that court believed me to have been innocent. It was, of course, beyond their power to upset my conviction.

dignified in our dark suits. In 1975, I was seventy, surrounded by young men *and* women in their twenties, in post-1960s attire, some bearded and others carrying their babies. My enjoyment was completed by the large portrait of Holmes in the courtroom looking benignly down on the scene.

In that same year, the Freedom of Information Act was strengthened. This enabled me, with the generous help of the National Emergency Civil Liberties Committee, to obtain the materials that constituted the basis for my petition for a writ of error *coram nobis*, filed in 1978. In the final chapter, I summarize the petition and tell of its fate in the courts, where it was doomed to face judges appointed by Nixon and Ford.

16

AN UNHOLY TRINITY

I have had forty years to reflect on the origins of my case as it was fabricated by an unholy trinity bound together by the theology of anti-communism. They joined forces against me—each at an important time in his career—in their zeal to make their theology the dominant religion of the land. They were Richard Nixon, the power-hungry politician; J. Edgar Hoover, the ultimate bureaucrat; and Whittaker Chambers, the perfect pawn.

Until now, except on rare occasions, I have not expressed my feelings publicly about these three men. I believed I should concentrate on gathering new evidence and working through the available judicial channels to clear my name. Now that all judicial procedures have been exhausted, I feel no such constraint.

Richard Nixon

My first encounter with Nixon was on August 5, 1948, when I appeared, at my request, before the House Committee on Un-American

Activities. Nixon was a freshman member of the committee, completely unknown to me. I was there to deny the statement made two
days earlier by Whittaker Chambers that I had been a member of a
Communist group in Washington in the mid-1930s. Nixon took only
a minor part in the brief hearing. I recall his tone as unfriendly,
although I did not regard it as a matter of consequence. Except for
the mild irritation I felt at his manner, I doubt whether under ordinary
circumstances I would have recalled him at all after a short lapse of
time.

It has been said that Nixon was hostile to me from the outset because
he thought I had scorned him. I did indeed have a low opinion of the
committee and probably showed it, but at that time I had no reason
for selective contempt for Nixon. He was simply a pale nonentity placed
inconspicuously on the hearing room dais among the well-known
bullies of the committee who played major roles.

At all events, whether hurt feelings on Nixon's part were a motivating
factor, he became almost immediately my unofficial prosecutor. Long
after this and other encounters with Nixon, I learned that the FBI,
with the participation of Father John Cronin (the Catholic Bishops
Conference "expert" on communism), had briefed Nixon about
Chambers's assertions concerning me. This could account for Nixon's
accusatory tone from the start. My considered view is that his basic
motives were opportunism and ambition. He chose to capitalize on
the growing tide of anti-Communist sentiment by means fair or foul.
He had been elected to his seat in Congress by falsely charging that
the incumbent whom he defeated, Jerry Voorhis, a stalwart New
Dealer, had Communist leanings. From the beginning, it was Nixon's
stock in trade to call New Dealers Communists.

In that August of 1948, the nation was in the midst of the bitter
Truman-Dewey presidential campaign. Election day was only two
months away, and the Republicans controlled Congress and therefore
HUAC. Truman and the Roosevelt tradition were the real targets, but
I was the immediate quarry, and Nixon the harrier. Long before Watergate, he demonstrated to me his willingness to descend to dirty
tricks, chicanery, and misrepresentation to advance his career.

The leopard never did change his spots. In his 1950 Senate campaign, Nixon made unscrupulous use of his persecution of me, once

again falsifying the issues and the record. He also used his hallmark tactic of attributing Communist sympathies to his opponent, who in that campaign was Helen Gahagan Douglas. Nixon called that talented and gracious actress the "pink lady," and hired noisy sound trucks to invade her political meetings and drown out her remarks. Two years later, it was the same "victory" over me that propelled him into the vice presidency, despite the discovery of his campaign slush fund that led to his famous "Checkers" speech.

In 1968, when Nixon became president, I predicted that he would leave office as our most unpopular president. But not even the insights I had so painfully gained into the flawed character of the young Nixon prepared me for the disclosures of wrongdoing that culminated in his resignation under the pressure of certain impeachment.

J. E d g a r H o o v e r

Nixon's unprincipled pursuit of me was motivated by political opportunism, his hallmark. J. Edgar Hoover's motives, I am convinced, included a large measure of personal vindictiveness against me because I had been one of the early New Dealers who had complained of his disloyalty to Roosevelt's policies, for which I believed he should have been forced out of office. Building a case against me also served powerfully in his efforts to curry favor with the Republicans, who he had every reason to believe would win the presidential election that year of 1948.

In my position as assistant general counsel of the New Deal's Agricultural Adjustment Administration, I saw that FBI agents throughout the country lent their considerable influence in local affairs to support conservative opponents of our liberal policies. Over and over again it was reported by our officials in the field that local FBI agents, in meetings of community leaders, would side with the critics of our efforts. Worse, FBI agents harassed the members of farm organizations who most actively supported our programs.

Those FBI practices seemed to us intolerable for an agency of the
federal government, which should have been assisting, not hindering,
our officials and supporters. Knowing of the tight supervision Hoover
exercised over his men, we felt sure that their actions met with his
approval. Our superiors also regarded Hoover as disloyal and were
quite ready to ask the president to fire or curb him. But when they
did so—on more than one occasion—they told us that the "boss" had
said that he, too, was aware of Hoover's disloyalty, but that he already
"had enough fights on his hands," that Hoover had established strong
Congressional support, and that Hoover was for the moment watching
his step.

But the improper FBI practices continued. The FBI under Hoover
was already an independent barony within the government. It was a
badge of honor for me and my colleagues openly to characterize Hoo-
ver's uncurbed lust for personal power as a national disgrace. Felix
Frankfurter, in a letter to a friend, once called Hoover "that swine."
We Young Turks of the New Deal shared that opinion. We were few
enough in number to be conspicuous—not least so, I feel sure, to
Hoover himself. Our views were indeed common knowledge. Senator
Vandenberg jocularly remarked to me at a social event as late as 1946,
"Alger, why don't you New Dealers stop trying to get rid of J. Edgar
Hoover. He has a dossier on every member of Congress."

Hoover's self-serving disloyalty knew no bounds. John Peurifoy—
with whom I kept in touch after I left the State Department—had
become Assistant Secretary of State in charge of security. He told me,
in that spring of 1948, that Hoover's misconduct had put him, Peurifoy, in a dilemma. It was Peurifoy's duty to report to Hoover, the
government's top security official, any lapse in security in the State
Department. But Peurifoy had noticed that when he did so, those
incidents that could be given an anti-Truman twist would be leaked
to the press. Peurifoy was indignant at Hoover's game of pleasing the
Republicans, but the FBI director's power was too great for Peurifoy
to buck.

I have never doubted that Hoover took personal charge of the FBI
preparations for my trials and made the decisions for the suppression
of evidence that turned the trials into a travesty of justice. The FBI
files in my case are replete with Hoover's own memoranda and comments, often in his handwriting. The FBI leaked Chambers's early

tales about me to members of Congress and to Father Cronin, who in turn briefed Nixon before Chambers's first HUAC appearance. Relations between the FBI and HUAC were always close, if usually without benefit of clergy, and were an example of Hoover's methods of using his files to ingratiate himself with members of Congress.

I had opportunities when I was a New Dealer in Washington, especially in the Department of Justice, to come to know Hoover's influence and repute at fairly close hand. I saw him a few times with the attorney general or the solicitor general, his official superiors, and was struck by the formality of their relations. Hoover was, and felt himself to be, an outsider.

Unimpressive in appearance, with no reputation for intellectual interests, Hoover was not a charismatic leader but a czar. From what FBI agents told me, I pictured him as assuming a Mussolini-like role to his staff, in whom he produced awe and fear, and sometimes reverence. Something of a loner and vain, he promoted elaborate propaganda machinery for his agency—favorable movies, radio programs like "This Is Your FBI," cereal box tops and souvenirs, laudatory books, friendly columnists—all of which tended to glorify him as the agency's creator and fearless director.

In my case, things came together for Hoover: settling scores with the New Deal in general and one of his outspoken critics in particular; currying favor with the Republican party and its rising star Richard Nixon; bolstering HUAC at a time when Congress seemed likely to terminate its existence; reaping the bureaucratic and personal rewards of a spectacular spy-case "victory" for the FBI and its director. And yet, as with Nixon although less dramatically, Hoover's excesses have led to a decline in his reputation.

I am confident J. Edgar Hoover will be known as one of the most evil men in American public life. For fifty years, a quarter of our history as a nation, he was constantly at work enlarging his power, which he accumulated in excess and abused with impunity. He even went as far as tapping the phone of a president of the United States and subsequently let him know about it.

Whittaker Chambers

President Reagan, in awarding him posthumously the Medal of Freedom in 1984, said that Chambers "personified the mystery of human redemption in the face of evil and suffering." Whittaker Chambers was a possessed man and a psychopath. Ever since the "Hiss Case," he has received support from a coterie of intellectuals. More important, he has become an icon of the right, another John Birch.

In the political mannequin that Chambers now is, it is impossible for me to see the unkempt, struggling, free-lance journalist I knew as George Crosley from the days of despair and hope that marked the New Deal of the mid-1930s. He was one of a number of journalists, lecturers, and students whom I met while serving as counsel to the Nye Committee, the Senate body that investigated the munitions industry. The committee staff was called on to assist all who requested information, especially journalists. We provided them with transcripts of our hearings and copies of the exhibits. We also supplied information about our future plans.

Crosley and I lunched together in the Capitol area a few times. His difficult financial situation aroused my sympathy, and I helped him out as best I could. I sublet to him an apartment for the duration of my lease, since my family and I had moved to a Georgetown house, and we put him and his family up for a few nights before their personal effects arrived. When he said he had no money to buy a car, I gave him an old Ford roadster for which I had been offered twenty-five dollars as a trade-in when I bought a new car. Little did I know that I was befriending a man without scruples or moral balance who would make use of my kindness to try to destroy me.

Crosley was good company for a while. He was well read and stereotypically the proletarian writer so much celebrated in those days. He had, he said, worked as an itinerant field hand, as had my beloved brother Bosley, moving north with the wheat harvest as grain ripened with advancing summer. His broken, neglected, teeth, startling in so young a man, I attributed to the deprivations of his life. He was apparently self-taught. To me, he appeared to be a latter-day Jack London.

I now think that I unconsciously identified Chambers with my brother Bosley, who had died eight years earlier at the age of twenty-six. They were born in the same year. Both were aspiring writers, making do temporarily as journalists. Both regarded unskilled labor as their way of seeing life in the raw. Both were bookish—indeed, thought of themselves as men of letters. Consciously, I made no connection between the two at the time; the disparities were too great. Bosley was fastidious, Crosley was sloppy; Bosley was tall, handsome, and lithe, while Crosley was short, plain-faced, and dumpy. Both had extensive vocabularies, but Bosley spoke with humor and a light touch. Crosley spoke in a low tone with little inflection and no humor and was utterly self-involved. He was a monologist.

Rather belatedly, I realized that Crosley's stories of his escapades and proletarian jobs were at best a mix of fact and fantasy. My gullibility was large indeed, and my willingness to believe astonishes me now. The light dawned when he told me that he had helped lay the tracks of the Washington trolley cars, an event I knew had taken place early in the century, when Chambers was an infant.

Crosley finally became something of a bother with his constant importuning for money. When he telephoned me one day, I told him that I was convinced he would never pay the small amounts he owed me and that I saw no reason to continue the relationship.

Years later, I learned that in the mid-1930s, when I knew him as Crosley, Chambers was a closet homosexual. I now believe that my rebuff to him wounded him in a way that I did not realize at the time. I think the rebuff, coupled with his political paranoia, inspired his later machinations against me. In 1939, in a private conversation with Assistant Secretary of State Adolf Berle, he tried out the charge that I was a Communist. In ensuing years, he enlisted the FBI in his efforts against me, efforts culminating in his HUAC and courtroom testimony.

Some people have wondered why I didn't make the connection between Chambers and Crosley sooner and have concluded that I must have had something to hide. I had not seen or heard of George Crosley in a dozen years, during which nothing had brought him to

mind. The news photographs of Chambers after his first HUAC appearance did not remind me of Crosley. Only when Nixon began
leaking to the press details he said Chambers knew of my family life
from the mid-1930s was I put in mind of Crosley. But I still could
not identify Chambers as Crosley until I saw him—when the committee finally brought us together.

He had gained forty pounds. His bad teeth had been replaced by
new dentures. His voice was strained and much higher in pitch than
the voice of the man I had known. He seemed oblivious to his surroundings, subdued, as if in a trance or under hypnosis. But when he
said he had occupied my vacant apartment (a deal, he said, between
Communists), I had no doubt that he was Crosley.*

When I next saw Chambers—at the public confrontation staged by
the committee eight days after the private meeting—he was a changed
man: a grandiloquent, self-sacrificing patriot, a man of compassion for
his "best friend," whom he had betrayed only as a matter of conscience.

As I was preparing for that public session, friendly newspaper writers
warned me that Chambers was emotionally unstable. That helped
explain the wide swing of his mood between the two hearings. That
swing, and his compounding of fact and fantasy about his relations
with me, all began to make sense: I was up against a psychopath. On
the witness stand, he could adopt a beatific yet sorrowful facial expression and tone of voice that would call to mind an early Christian
martyr. He often took on a rapt look, gazing upward as though in
search of a reply. His world was peopled by characters he created and
who were patterned after those of his literary hero, Dostoevsky. His
own life had been bizarre and disordered; his writings ran the gamut
from sacrilegious, erotic, and proletarian to apocalyptic.

---

*Nixon implied that I invented the name George Crosley. In fact, it was one of
the pseudonyms Chambers used as a writer. Samuel Roth, a publisher to whom
Chambers had in the 1930s submitted erotic poetry under the name George
Crosley, gave my lawyers an affidavit to that effect, but they did not call Roth as
a witness at my trials, because he had been convicted in the 1920s of obscenity
(for importing James Joyce's *Ulysses*), which, they feared, would not sit well with
the jurors. Cleide Catlett, my family's cook at the time, remembered Chambers
coming to the door and identifying himself as "Crosby" or "something like that."

My protection, I was confident from my respect for the law, would lie in demonstrating in court that Chambers was an irresponsible fantasist. And so I sued him for libel.*

Chambers's emotional instability raises doubts as to whether he actually was the Soviet agent he claimed to have been. Some believe he was never engaged in espionage, that his were the symptoms of the grand imposters, the successful confidence men of history. William A. Reuben, an author who has made an exhaustive study of Chambers, believes that he engaged in a charade to satisfy his own need to see himself as a man of destiny. For my part, I think that Chambers's need for self-glorifying make-believe caused him to exaggerate whatever cloak-and-dagger role he may have played.

A final word as to my last sightings of Chambers before the trials, sightings which remain vivid to this day and color my overall impression of the man. Both Chambers and I were in frequent attendance at the grand jury hearings of December 1948, but Chambers's mentors were careful to see that we never met. When I was to appear, I sat with other witnesses in a waiting room set aside for that purpose. Not so Chambers. He was whisked in and out of the Federal Building through side entrances and must have had a private room in the building where he was on call. I can only speculate why he was kept from public contacts. Nixon and the prosecutors must have been by then acutely aware of his emotional fragility and instability, and feared what he might say publicly.

Despite these precautions, I caught sight of him fleetingly as I was going to and from the grand jury room. On two or three occasions, I saw a skulking, shambling Chambers. He looked furtive and frightened. He was accompanied by a companion whom I took to be an FBI agent. The impression was of a cowed, timid creature being moved from one cage to another by its keeper. He was bent over or stooped, as if this posture might make him less visible. His guard, by contrast, was matter-of-fact, with no air of stealth, as he oversaw the movements of his charge.

---

*The outcome of my criminal trials aborted any possibility of successfully pursuing my libel case against Chambers. Accordingly, after my conviction, I withdrew it.

These sightings enhanced the opinion I had reached that Chambers was a pawn in the hands of others. By that time I was fully aware that Nixon and the FBI were manipulating him. And so he became the Witness against me.

17

WHICH THINGS
REMAIN BEFORE US . . .

In this chapter, I will deal with the final aspect of my case in the courts, a proceeding that ended in 1983. It is called a petition for a writ of error *coram nobis,* which concerns errors so egregious that they command the attention of the courts no matter how many years have gone by. The very opening words of the writ say that such cases always remain before the courts: *quae coram nobis resident*—"which things remain before us."

My *coram nobis* petition has been published,* so I will be brief with most of it. Concerning the famous typewriter, however, I have more to say.

To set the stage, I will summarize the events leading up to my petition.

During the HUAC hearings described in preceding chapters, I challenged Chambers to repeat his charge that I had been a Communist, but to do it outside of the hearings so the charge would not be libel-proof. He repeated it on the radio program "Meet the Press," and I sued him for libel.

In Re Alger Hiss (Hill and Wang, 1979).

212

In the course of testifying in the libel suit, Chambers expanded his accusation to include espionage, which he had previously denied. To back up his new story, he produced typed extracts, summaries, and copies of State Department documents dated in the first four months of 1938. He said that I had brought original documents home from my office; that my wife had typed copies of them; and that I had given him the typed copies and returned the original documents to my office. He said he had then photographed the typed copies, transmitted the photographs to a Russian agent, and destroyed the typed copies (except the ones he produced in the libel suit in 1948, which he said he saved when he quit communism in 1938).

Chambers's story hardly makes sense as an account of spy activity. The rigamarole of having a confederate laboriously type copies of original documents, thus leaving a trail back to the confederate's typewriter, and of photographing those copies instead of the originals, sounds more like a tale concocted as a frame-up. Nor do the papers themselves look like spy work. Nearly a third of the pages are copied from a nonconfidential consular report about business conditions in Manchuria. Diplomatic cables, regardless of content, are randomly excerpted, summarized, or copied verbatim. (All the papers Chambers produced were made public at the trials and are reproduced in the printed record.)

Chambers also produced four small scratchpad sheets of my penciled notes, which I used in briefing my superior, Francis Sayre, about selected cables. Those notes, too, Chambers said I had given him for espionage in 1938. I still can't fathom how any sensible person could believe a spy would do such a thing.

At my direction, the papers that Chambers produced in the libel suit were immediately turned over to the Department of Justice to find out how Chambers had really gotten hold of them.

Two weeks later, Chambers produced for HUAC some 35-millimeter film from a hollowed-out pumpkin on his Maryland farm, where he had put the film that morning. The film contained pictures of original State Department documents that Chambers said I had given him. Most of the documents turned out to have come from someone else's office, where Chambers had an admitted source of supply (Henry Julian Wadleigh), so they lost importance in my case.

Chambers's tale of espionage resulted in our both being called before a grand jury. I denied having given the papers to Chambers, whereupon I was indicted for perjury.

The perjury indictment was a technicality—to put it kindly—by the government to get around the three-year statute of limitations on espionage. The purpose of the statute of limitations is to avoid the miscarriages of justice likely to occur if a defendant is required to defend himself after the passage of so much time that potential defense witnesses will have died or disappeared, evidence will have been destroyed or lost, and memories will have dimmed. My indictment in 1948 was for perjury in denying that I had committed espionage in 1938.

I was tried twice. The first trial ended with a hung jury, whereupon Representative Nixon threatened impeachment proceedings against the judge, Samuel H. Kaufman. The jurors who had voted for my acquittal received abusive and threatening telephone calls from strangers. All these intimidating and inflammatory events were prominently reported in the New York press. The prosecutor had announced that he would try me again, so I petitioned the court to remove my second trial to a district that had encountered less publicity. The court refused to transfer my case.

My first trial lawyer was Lloyd Paul Stryker, an experienced criminal lawyer. When the jury failed to agree, Stryker told me that he could always get me another hung jury but probably not an acquittal.

That wasn't good enough for me. Besides, Stryker's rather florid style was not my style, and his hammering at Whittaker Chambers's many perjuries and disloyalties, effective as it probably was with some of the jurors, came at the expense, it seemed to me, of sufficient attention to the details of the spurious documents. So I replaced him at the second trial with a Boston civil lawyer, Claude Cross, who, while less colorful than Stryker, dealt more thoroughly with the papers.

Stryker was the soul of generosity. When I told him that he would not be conducting my defense at the second trial, he said to me, "Alger, if you ever want to come home again, you can come back." As my second trial turned out, it looks as if I paid a high price for indulging my taste in courtroom styles.

Judge Kaufman wasn't impeached, but neither was he assigned to my second trial, which ended in conviction on January 21, 1950. Some time later, Judge Kaufman said to a friend of mine, "You and I both know that young man is innocent."

The Supreme Court has never heard my case, but three times it has declined to hear it. The first time, in 1951, two justices, Hugo L. Black and William O. Douglas, voted to grant my petition for certiorari and thus hear my appeal, but four justices voted not to hear it. The remaining three justices did not vote at all: Two of them, Frankfurter and Reed, had been character witnesses for me at my first trial, and the third, Tom Clark, had been the attorney general when I was indicted.

Justice Douglas later wrote that if either Frankfurter or Reed had not appeared in my trial, the Supreme Court would doubtless have had enough votes to grant my petition and take my case. And if they had taken it, he wrote, the court could not possibly have sustained the conviction, because there was no independent evidence to corroborate the story of my sole accuser, Whittaker Chambers.* The federal rule is that a perjury conviction requires proof by two witnesses or by one witness plus independent corroborative evidence. The papers that Chambers had produced against me seemingly supported his story, but they did not corroborate it independently of his own testimony that it was I who had given them to him. However, since the Supreme Court did not take my case, that particular error of law remains uncorrected.

When the Supreme Court denied my petition for certiorari, in March 1951, I went to prison. I was also disbarred.

While I was in prison (1951–1954), my attorney Chester Lane discovered evidence impugning the authenticity of the typewriter in the case—and thus of the typed copies of State Department documents that were the crux of the prosecution's case against me.

Both of my trials had been conducted on the premise that the Woodstock typewriter I had brought into court was the old Woodstock that had been handed down to my wife from her father many years earlier. Chester Lane's new evidence indicated that the premise was wrong.

Lane's evidence entitled me to make a legal motion to vacate the

*William O. Douglas, *Go East, Young Man* (Random House, 1974).

conviction and obtain a new trial. By law, the motion had to be made within two years of my conviction and be brought before the same judge, Henry W. Goddard, who had presided over the conviction. Goddard denied the motion. I appealed Goddard's denial, and the prosecution made a special request that the appeal be heard by the same three-judge panel that had, two years earlier, denied my appeal from the conviction itself. Those same three judges again turned me down, and the Supreme Court again declined to take the case. Twenty-five years were to pass before I could document Chester Lane's point. He did not live to see it happen.

The Watergate scandal in the mid-1970s not only forced Richard Nixon to resign as president but also inspired Congress, over President Ford's veto, to put teeth into the Freedom of Information Act effective in 1975. The act directs the government to respond within ten days to requests for information, so I anticipated quick access to the government files in my case. I was confident that they would document the miscarriage of justice, and I hoped that the Department of Justice would then take action to expunge the conviction.

My hopes were, I suppose, unrealistic. The bureaucrats in the Department of Justice were so grudging in complying with my requests that I had to take them to court. But as luck would have it, my case was assigned to Judge Richard Owen.

Judge Owen, a former assistant United States attorney whom President Nixon had appointed to the bench, was not sympathetic to the Freedom of Information Act or to my requests under it. The ten-day period mandated by the act stretched into four years. Nevertheless, by 1978, my lawyer Victor Rabinowitz and his associates managed to obtain many documents showing pervasive government deceit and cover-ups throughout my case.

The Department of Justice bureaucrats were quite unwilling to admit their predecessors' malfeasance. Over their intense opposition, therefore, I initiated my next, and last, legal move for vindication, my petition for a writ of error *coram nobis*, filed in 1978.

Once again, my case was assigned to Judge Richard Owen.

The deck seemed to be stacked. I needed, and was entitled to, a scrupulously fair and unbiased judge. The matter was particularly sensitive because my petition was highly critical, to say the least, of another judge on the same court, Thomas Murphy, who had been appointed to the bench after his success as my prosecutor.

When my *coram nobis* petition landed before Judge Owen, my lawyer asked him to step aside and let some other judge handle it, but Owen refused. Four years after he got my petition, he denied it. The Court of Appeals affirmed, giving no reason except Owen's opinion; and the Supreme Court again declined to hear my case. That was in October 1983, just before my seventy-ninth birthday.

And so I have run out my string in court. I have no longer any basis for hoping to correct the false verdict "before us," at least during my lifetime. But subsequent history has adjudged many verdicts false, and I have a few words for future historians of my case.

From the start, my case has been peculiarly "political" in the sense that most people who judge it do so based on their political sentiments, fears, and desires rather than on an appreciation of the facts. The facts are indeed complex, and the case has generated some sixty thousand pages of testimony and exhibits. Not many people have the interest and patience to grapple with such volume.

Fortunately, the new material in my *coram nobis* petition supersedes much of the previous official record and eliminates a good deal of the complexity.

My *coram nobis* petition was based principally on the FBI documents I obtained under the Freedom of Information Act. They show that the government withheld evidence so damaging to the prosecution's case and so helpful to mine that the outcome would undoubtedly have been different had the evidence come out at the time of the trials. They also show government tampering with witnesses and infiltration of my legal staff. These are the main points in my *coram nobis* petition:

The informer in my camp. My lawyers hired a private investigator, Horace Schmahl, to help us find evidence and witnesses for the trial. He gave the FBI and the prosecutor, Thomas Murphy, details of our trial preparation, information that Murphy made use of at the trials.

Concealment of statements by Chambers. My trial lawyers had asked for all of Chambers's statements to the FBI, as was our legal right. But the government did not deliver all of them. For instance, the government withheld 184 pages that contain many statements by Chambers inconsistent with his testimony. Also withheld was Chambers's handwritten statement describing his homosexual activities between 1933 and 1938, which, if disclosed at the trials, would have destroyed his credibility to jurors of that time. Vincent Shaw, a juror at the first trial who voted to convict, said that the jury would have acquitted me if it had known of Chambers's homosexuality.

Tampering with witnesses. Besides Chambers, the prosecution manipulated at least two of its important witnesses, Sergeant George Roulhac and Edith Murray, to testify falsely.

Fabricating expert opinion. Before the first trial, the FBI laboratory compared the typed copies of State Department documents with letters typed by Priscilla in the 1930s and concluded that the comparison did not show that Priscilla was the typist of the former. After the first trial, a juror privately told Murphy that another juror, Vincent Shaw, had maintained in the jury room that typing errors in both the copies and the letters seemed to him similar enough to persuade him that Priscilla had typed the copies. Murphy thereupon asked the FBI laboratory to reexamine the question before the second trial. The FBI did so and again concluded that it was impossible to attribute the typing of the copies to Priscilla on the basis of the typing errors. Murphy therefore had no evidence on this question. Nevertheless, in his summation at the second trial, he specifically invited the jury to compare typing errors and reach the very conclusion that the FBI laboratory had told him was impossible.

Judge Owen simply did not come to grips with these issues. And more important, he completely missed or ignored the significance of the prosecution's concealment of what it knew about the typewriter.

The typewriter. The single piece of evidence used most dramatically against me at my trials was an old Woodstock typewriter, serial number 230,099. Ironically, it was I and my lawyers who brought it into court as a defense exhibit, believing that it was Priscilla's old typewriter.

Nixon called Woodstock number 230,099 "the key 'witness' in the case." But it was a false witness. It was not Priscilla's old typewriter. That fact was known to the prosecution but was withheld at the time of the trials. Its disclosure at that time would have destroyed the government's case.

The typewriter had become important in the case even before my indictment.

When I sued Chambers for libel in 1948, as I have already described, he produced copies of State Department documents dated in 1938, copies he said my wife had typed and I had delivered to him in 1938. Document examiners for the FBI and for my lawyers identified the typeface style on all but one of the copies as belonging to an outdated Woodstock typewriter.

We had given away Priscilla's Woodstock to our cook's children Raymond and Perry Catlett in December 1937, when we were moving from one house to another in Washington. We managed to find some letters that Priscilla had typed on the Woodstock in the mid-1930s (although none later than May 1937, which is consistent with our having given the Woodstock away in December 1937), and I turned them over to the FBI. An FBI document examiner, Ramos Feehan, compared them with the typed copies of State Department documents, found similar typeface irregularities in both sets of papers, and concluded that both sets had been typed on the same Woodstock. An "expert" document examiner hired by my lawyers reached the same conclusion, and so we accepted it at the time. It did not, of course, reach the question of *who* had typed the State Department copies or *when* they had been typed. Nevertheless, it precipitated my indictment.

And so I began to prepare for trial.

If I could find proof that we had never had the Woodstock after 1937, that would clear me and demonstrate that I was being framed, since the State Department documents were all dated in 1938. The copies could have been typed by Chambers or a confederate who had access to the original documents (or photographs of them) and to Priscilla's erstwhile Woodstock at any time from 1938 to 1948, when Chambers brought forth the typed copies in my libel suit.* So we

---

*The original documents were widely circulated to many offices in the State Department (but not always to my office) and then transferred to the archives. Chambers knew several people in the State Department, including Benjamin Mandel of the security office, who in 1924 had issued Chambers his Communist Party card and in 1948 was HUAC's director of research.

began a search for the old Woodstock and its history subsequent to Priscilla's ownership.

The FBI also set out to find Priscilla's old Woodstock. Some ninety FBI agents, thirty-five in Washington alone, combed the nation for it.

Raymond Catlett called my brother Donald to say that the FBI had come looking for our old Woodstock. The Catletts remembered that we had given it to them in 1937. From the Catletts, we followed a convoluted trail that led us finally, six weeks before the first trial began, to a junkyard and an old Woodstock typewriter bearing serial number 230,099. It looked like Priscilla's old Woodstock, and so we believed it to be. Our "expert" document examiner compared its typing with Priscilla's letters and gave us his opinion that it was her old machine.

The FBI quickly learned what we had found, but they also realized that we were wrong—the typewriter was not Priscilla's old Woodstock, because its serial number was too high. The FBI agents, in their own search for Priscilla's typewriter, had learned that Priscilla's father had bought it in 1927, and thus its serial number was in the range from 145,000 to 204,500. They knew that a Woodstock typewriter bearing the higher serial number 230,099—the typewriter we found—was manufactured in 1929 and therefore could not be the one that Priscilla's father had bought in 1927. Whether or not the copies of State Department documents had been typed on it, Priscilla's letters had not been, because it was not Priscilla's old typewriter.

When J. Edgar Hoover saw his agents' reports that Woodstock number 230,099 could not be Priscilla's old typewriter, he ordered an immediate reinvestigation by his agents. Their new investigation reaffirmed their earlier reports. A dozen years later, *Newsweek* (July 24, 1961) described Priscilla's typewriter as "an aged Woodstock, No. 200194." That number, falling nicely within the FBI's range, suggests that the FBI may actually have found Priscilla's old typewriter. I wish I knew the source of *Newsweek*'s reference.

My lawyers and I knew none of this in 1949. Having found the typewriter we believed Priscilla had owned, we introduced it as such as a defense exhibit at the trials. We and the Catletts knew, and would testify, that we had given it to the Catletts in 1937—that is, before the dates on the copied State Department documents.

When we brought Woodstock number 230,099 into court, the prosecution did not reveal that it knew the typewriter was not Priscilla's old machine. I have no doubt that the prosecutor, Thomas Murphy, knew everything that the FBI knew about Woodstock number 230,099. The FBI reports detailing how it could not be Priscilla's typewriter had been in the FBI files since before the first trial began. Murphy worked closely with the FBI in preparing for both trials.

The reader can judge what would have happened to the prosecution's case if what it knew about the typewriter had been disclosed. When Gussie Feinstein, a juror at the second trial, many years later saw the typewriter evidence withheld by the prosecution, she said: "Here's a man that might have been proven innocent and not guilty if the jury had known that the typewriter that was presented to us in the courtroom wasn't—actually wasn't the Hisses'. It was another typewriter."

My first trial lawyer, Lloyd Stryker, noted several times that Murphy acted as though he had guilty knowledge about the typewriter. Stryker said to me on one of those occasions—and I think I have his words exactly—"Alger, something's wrong with that typewriter. Murphy's afraid of it. We should worry about it, because it's being used so much against us. He dances around it as though it were a hot stove. He never touches it."

Murphy, far from disclosing what he knew about the typewriter, treated it as if it were in fact Priscilla's; in effect, he adopted it as part of his case. He called an FBI agent to type on it before the jurors "to prove that it wasn't a wreck," and therefore, Murphy told the jury in his summation at the second trial, we wouldn't have given it away to the Catletts in 1937, although we probably did so in 1938.

Since he knew the typewriter was not Priscilla's, Murphy took care not to ask his "expert" witness, FBI document examiner Ramos Feehan, a single question about it, although it was sitting right there in front of him in the courtroom. What Feehan did testify to was that the copies of State Department papers had (with one exception) been typed on "the same machine, the Woodstock machine," as Priscilla's letters. Feehan's testimony was crucial to the prosecution's case linking me to the typed copies, but his opinion was in fact quite baseless. Feenan himself demonstrated, in an erroneous report he gave between the two trials, that his opinion was just as wrong as that of my own experts.

At the end of the first trial, Murphy asked the court to impound Woodstock number 230,099. He then secretly had specimens taken of its typing for Feehan to compare with the copies of State Department documents and with Priscilla's letters. Feehan reported that the three sets of papers—the new specimens, the copies of State Department documents, and Priscilla's letters—had all been typed on Woodstock number 230,099, a manifest impossibility, since Priscilla's letters couldn't have been typed on it, as it wasn't her machine.

At least two typewriters—Woodstock number 230,099 for the new specimens, and Priscilla's lower-numbered machine for her letters— had necessarily been used to type the papers that Feehan thought had all been typed on one machine. (The copies of State Department documents could have been typed on either of those two machines or on some other Woodstock.) Feehan's erroneous report meant that he, like my own experts, could not tell which papers were typed on what machine. I don't know whether Woodstock number 230,099 was just an ordinary typewriter similar to Priscilla's older one, or whether it was fabricated deliberately to mimic Priscilla's, as my lawyer Chester Lane believed. In either case, Feehan was unable to distinguish their typing. But Murphy said nothing about this at the second trial, and Feehan's report demolishing his own expertise remained hidden in the FBI files for thirty years.

Thus did the prosecution's concealment of its knowledge bring about my conviction. As Gussie Feinstein said, "The jurors were hood-winked."

During the trials, my lawyers and I had proceeded on the widespread assumption that typing from any given machine is unique and un-duplicatable, somewhat like fingerprints. We therefore believed that Chambers, alone or with others, had committed his "forgery by type-writer" by using Priscilla's old typewriter to frame me. So indeed he may have. But it never occurred to us that there was another way, not using Priscilla's typewriter at all.

Chester Lane was skeptical and inquisitive. His discoveries led him to believe that Woodstock number 230,099 had been fabricated to forge typing.* To test whether that was possible, Lane hired a typewriter technician to construct, if he could, a typewriter that would duplicate, or "forge," the typing of Woodstock number 230,099.

The technician was so successful that Lane, in support of my motion for a new trial, gave the FBI samples of typing from both machines and challenged the FBI to tell them apart. The FBI did not accept the challenge.

We all thought Lane had made a new discovery with his demonstration that forgery by altered typewriter was possible. I later learned that military intelligence agents had done it in World War II, a decade before my trials. Their technicians included "two ruffians who could reproduce faultlessly the imprint of any typewriter on earth." The work was done at Camp X, near Lake Ontario, a site visited by J. Edgar Hoover and "chosen in part because it could be reached easily by FBI agents." The FBI claimed credit for one operation in which a "typewriter that precisely duplicated the machine in Rome had been constructed." It produced "a letter so perfectly forged by matching the imperfections of typewriter keys . . . that it caused the removal of certain key pro-Nazis in South America."†

In 1960, Hoover referred to the FBI's own capability of forging typewriting by "this technique of altering a typewriter." In the FBI's counterintelligence program against the Communist Party USA, Hoover was considering how best to frame a Party leader as an FBI informer. In that instance, Hoover preferred using handwriting forgery, but it is clear from his memorandum that typewriter forgery was an available option and not a new one to the FBI.‡ I have been told that the Hiss Case became a standard object lesson in forgery by typewriter at police conventions around the world.

When I was in prison and Chester Lane learned that Woodstock

---

*For example, he learned from the Woodstock factory manager that a machine bearing serial number 230,099 would have been manufactured in August or September 1929, whereas the kind of type on the machine we found had been discontinued by Woodstock in 1928.

†W. Stevenson, A *Man Called Intrepid* (Harcourt Brace, 1976). See also D. Stafford, *Camp* X (Dodd Mead, 1987).

‡*The Nation*, November 10, 1984.

number 230,099 was manufactured too late to have been Priscilla's machine, the FBI prevented him from obtaining the records and affidavits he needed for adequate proof in court. Therefore, when he went to court with our motion for a new trial, he asked Judge Goddard for a preliminary hearing at which his witnesses would have to give under oath the facts proving that the typewriter was not Priscilla's. Goddard denied the motion for a new trial for lack of proof. At the same time, he denied Lane's request for a preliminary hearing to get that proof.

When Lane appealed, the government lawyers argued that the proof he sought about the typewriter was irrelevant because the government's case rested only on Feehan's comparison of documents, not on the typewriter—an argument cynically contrary to Murphy's adoption of the typewriter as part of his case at the trials. The appeal was denied, thus ensuring that my proof about the typewriter did not then become a matter of court record.

Nearly thirty years later, that gap in the record provided Judge Owen with a pretext for denying my *coram nobis* petition. He said that I was trying to relitigate an issue—that Woodstock number 230,099 was manufactured too late to be Priscilla's typewriter—previously decided against me by Judge Goddard for lack of proof. It is almost unbelievable that Owen would thus ignore my demonstration from FBI documents that it was malfeasance by the government that had deprived me of that very proof.

When Owen turned to the proof itself as it appears in the FBI documents, he said the FBI reports showing that Woodstock number 230,099 was not Priscilla's typewriter were "far from conclusive," giving as an example the suggestion that Priscilla's father might have bought a *second* Woodstock—a notion not taken seriously by the FBI, never previously raised by the government, and indeed contrary to the knowledge of everyone in a position to know. Owen then retreated to the specious argument that, anyway, the typewriter was irrelevant to the government's case.

Owen's opinion runs to twenty-five pages and contains over one hundred errors of fact, ranging from significant to trivial. (The errors are noted in an edition of Owen's opinion annotated by William A. Reuben, *Footnote on an Historic Case: In Re Alger Hiss*, The Nation

Institute, 1983.) I don't attribute Owen's denial of my petition to his shoddy workmanship; indeed, the reason my lawyer had asked Owen to disqualify himself was that we were convinced he had decided against me even before he read the petition.

By the wheel of chance, my appeal from Owen's decision was assigned to Judges Van Graafieland, Meskill, and Timbers. My lawyer Victor Rabinowitz and I knew them to be among the recently appointed conservative "stiffening" of the appellate court; we would have preferred any other panel. But no amount of misgiving could have prepared us for what happened in their august courtroom.

From the outset of Rabinowitz's presentation, the judges—especially Van Graafieland and Meskill—treated him with vociferous rudeness and hostility. They soon made it plain that they would not listen to him. When Rabinowitz asserted that the typewriter at the trials was not the one that had been in my family, Van Graafieland and Meskill loudly demanded to know where that appeared in the record. They brooked no explanation, angrily repeating their demand again and again but giving Rabinowitz virtually no chance to answer. They cut his argument short and denied his request for an additional minute to rebut the government's argument. They even raised the pretext that Priscilla's father might have owned two Woodstocks.

I was more shocked by this outburst of unreasoning hostility than I had been by the verdict thirty-three years earlier. When jurors are swayed by public fears, the pillars of justice are not shaken. But those pillars are undermined when appellate judges—"all honorable men"—are so inflamed by their prejudices that they brush aside the government's concealment of exculpatory evidence, evidence that, had it been timely disclosed, would have resulted in a different verdict. It was the most depressing experience of my life.

Careers have been based on my conviction. National policies have been skewed by it. Only in the future will it be possible for my case to be seen objectively and for the verdict to be set right. I have no doubt that day will come.

Long ago, when I was a young lawyer at Choate, Hall & Stewart in Boston, I looked around at my respected seniors and knew, with absolute certainty, that I didn't want to live my life only within the confines of private spheres like theirs. Years later, after my prison term, I ran into John Hall, Esq., at an airport, and he greeted me with the kind words, "Alger, I wish you'd never left us." I replied, "Sometimes I wish so myself." The "sometimes" of my reply meant that I was satisfied with the bargain I had made with my life. And so I am today.

My private life has been rich in love and friendships, and it still is. My public life has been deeply rewarding. In the New Deal, in the wartime State Department, for the nascent United Nations, I did what I could toward the common goal of a better world. Since the war, in my adverse circumstances, the fact that I fought for my beliefs has been more than just a private good for me alone—I continue to meet people who take heart from what I stood for. I count as successful my efforts to live according to my goals and principles, and so I have no cause for bitterness or regret, nor have I ever felt any.

My goals still seem to me bright and attainable. In any event, I subscribe to the view that the way the journey is traveled counts for more than the goals reached. In the words of Job, I have pursued my goals "in mine own ways." In that I am content.

CHRONOLOGY

November 11, 1904   Birth of Alger Hiss (Baltimore, Maryland)

June 1926   Graduation from Johns Hopkins University

June 1929   Graduation from Harvard Law School

October 1929 to
October 1930   Law clerk to Justice Oliver Wendell Holmes

October 1930   Employed at Boston law firm of Choate, Hall & Stewart

Spring 1932   Employed at New York law firm of Cotton, Franklin, Wright & Gordon

March 1933   Went to Washington to join Agricultural Adjustment Administration (AAA), then in process of creation

July 1934   Lent by AAA to Nye Committee

August 1935   Joined Solicitor General's office

September 1936   Joined Department of State. Employed in office of Francis B. Sayre, Assistant Secretary of State

September 1939 to
1944   Assistant to Stanley K. Hornbeck, Adviser on Political Relations

Spring 1944   Joined State Department Office of Special Political Affairs

August–October
1944   Secretary of Dumbarton Oaks Conversations

February 1945   Member of American delegation at Yalta Conference

April 25–June 26, 1945	Secretary-General of United Nations Conference on International Organization (which drafted the UN Charter)
January 1946	Attended first meeting of UN, in London, as principal adviser to American delegation
February 1, 1947	Took office as president of Carnegie Endowment for International Peace
August 3, 1948	Accused by Whittaker Chambers before the House Committee on Un-American Activities in public session
September 27, 1948	Sued Chambers for libel in Baltimore, Maryland
December 15, 1948	Indicted for perjury by New York grand jury
May 31–July 8, 1949	First trial
November 17, 1949–January 21, 1950	Second trial
December 7, 1950	Appeal denied by U.S. Court of Appeals
March 12, 1951	Writ of certiorari denied by U.S. Supreme Court
March 22, 1951	Began prison term
July 22, 1952	Motion for a new trial denied
November 27, 1954	Released from prison
March 1972	"Hiss Act" declared unconstitutional with respect to Hiss
March 25, 1975	Initial requests for documents under Freedom of Information Act

August 5, 1975   Readmission to bar in Massachusetts by de-
                        cision of state supreme court

July 27, 1978   Petition filed for writ of error *coram nobis*

July 15, 1982   Petition denied

February 16, 1983   Appeal denied

October 11, 1983   Writ of certiorari denied by U.S. Supreme
                        Court

INDEX